THE BLACK PENCIL
WOMAN

THE BLACK PENCIL
WOMAN

A Portrait of My Mother

Ros Holland

Book Guild Publishing
Sussex, England

First published in Great Britain in 2012 by
The Book Guild Ltd
Pavilion View
19 New Road
Brighton, BN1 1UF

Extract from 'In This Time' by Elizabeth Jennings (from *Collected Poems*,
Caracanet Press) reproduced by kind permission of David Higham Associates Ltd.

Extract from 'Burnt Norton' by T S Eliot (from *Collected Poems 1909–1962*)
reproduced by kind permission of Faber and Faber Ltd.

Typesetting in Garamond and Helvetica by
Keyboard Services, Luton, Bedfordshire

Printed in Great Britain by
CPI Group (UK) Ltd, Croydon, CR0 4YY

A catalogue record for this book is available from
The British Library

ISBN 978 1 84624 691 3

This book is dedicated to my brother,
David William Holland

Contents

Foreword by Peter Kelly

In my work as a psychotherapist I come across many adults and children who struggle in relationships as a direct result of early traumatic experiences. When a child has an opportunity to talk about and make sense of what is happening – and has happened – in their lives, the potential for life-long distress is greatly reduced.

When a child has little or no opportunity to share their thoughts and feelings with adults who are strong enough and secure enough, then they often carry too much pain and responsibility into their adult life. There is a trans-generational passing on of pain and emotional trauma until someone decides to do something about it. This book tells such a story.

Unresolved feelings and trauma can result in deep anxiety, fear, insecurity and anger; these feelings will be acted out in all of our relationships – they will affect our view of ourselves, others, and the world in general. They can result in a wide range of emotional difficulties, such as low self-esteem, depression, eating disorders, behavioural disorders, self-harm, or ongoing and repetitive relationship problems.

I see this in many of my adult clients – unresolved issues from the parents being passed down through the generations. I clearly remember working with a client whose grandmother's grief at the loss of a young child during the traumatic events of the First World War had been passed down through her daughter to my client, who was acting it out with his own son in not letting him out of his sight, despite his son being an adult himself.

One of the most powerful aspects in the development of a secure attachment is that when a baby is small she is constantly giving out signals to her mother, or other primary carers. All babies are born with a strong urge to seek out the best possible attachment relationship the parent can manage. How satisfactorily or unsatisfactorily the mother responds to these signals will affect the way the baby's brain develops, and the sense of OK-ness that the baby develops. If the mother is emotionally unavailable, through grief, depression, or for other reasons, the baby will often develop pathological ways of understanding the world and her place in it, and will go on to live her life based on these early decisions – for good or ill.

In this moving, alive, engaging and very witty account of her early experiences and the effects they had, the author gives us the chance to witness the effects of love, loss, separation and neglect – not the selfish neglect of the parent wrapped up in their own wants and desires, but the tragic neglect caused by deep maternal pain and unresolved grief.

We can learn much from this sensitive recounting: how we might better help children in families that have experienced loss and separation and how to give those children a voice at the time they most need it. Too easily, we still leave families to their private grief without ensuring they have support and appropriate intervention. The locked-away pain may lead someone to seek help later in life, when the stress and energy of holding on becomes just too much – too often, however, this just doesn't happen, and the pain is passed on from generation to generation.

This unresolved pain and grief takes immense levels of energy to contain – energy that is diverted from healthy, autonomous living.

When reading this story, I am mindful of so many clients I have worked with – adult and child – who either lost, or were never given, the opportunity to express their grief and confusion. Imagine the author as a small child, witnessing the long, gradual decline of her father, followed by his tragically early death. And imagine this happening in a family where external appearances were highly important, and the internal distress, pain and confusion of children needed to be neither seen nor heard. Keep a stiff upper lip; hold it together; don't be a bother or a burden; don't talk about it – or even think about it. Be strong.

That little girl needed to be very strong and brave. She held it together, didn't become a burden for her quiet grieving mother, was a rock and a pillar. So she locked away her pain, like a good little girl. To do this she needed to build a wall around her heart, to stop it from bursting; this was very important when she had learned that to show how she really felt was not OK. The brick wall, of course, once built, has the long-term effect of stopping us from really knowing what we want, and keeping people out. If only there had been someone there when she was little, to tell her it was fine to cry...

As you read this story you will recognise the need to say, 'There, there, you cry' to the distressed, grieving child, rather than, 'There, there, don't cry'. Then the child can give up the guilt, and free up the energy that would otherwise be used in denial.

At the heart and root of our self-esteem and our general sense of OK-ness is the history of our attachment. As described earlier, our attachment style, and how we create and develop relationships is the result of the bonding process that takes place between ourselves as infants and our main carers – usually, but not always, our biological mother. Many things influence our attachment styles and security, but key is the emotional availability of our primary carers. When this is lacking, for whatever reason, it is up to society to find some way of supporting that child to seek to prevent future mental health problems.

Peter Kelly
Psychotherapist, United Kingdom Council of Counselling and Psychotherapy

1

The Grandfather Clock

I am feeling particularly reflective, enjoying my coffee in my kitchen, listening to Katherine Jenkins on my iPod, nobody to bother me for a few hours. I'm in a haven of self-created peace except for the tick-tock of the grandfather clock. If it weren't for those sounds and hourly chimes I wouldn't have a clue what time it is – neither do I care. My whole life has been dominated by the effective and proper use of time, rules, doing well, what the neighbours think, as well as family, study and work. I've had very little fun, and never known what carefree meant, never mind felt like. Now I am beginning to understand what carefree feels like for the first time: I'm fifty-three.

Recently I've been self-absorbed and while not actually enjoying it, I'm not too bothered about it either. I know I am spending too much time thinking, and for the first time in my life I am allowing myself to do so: to be gloriously, selfishly, self-centred. My mother's recent death followed too quickly that of my stepfather, hot on the heels of my maternal and paternal aunts, uncles and two friends a few years before: twenty-one people in all including my father. It seems so much of my childhood and much of my adulthood has been littered with death – and not put to rest.

I know, and can voice the thought – though none particularly want to hear it – that recent deaths have touched and tugged at those that have gone before. Deaths that caused pain and grief which I'd buried somewhere deep inside myself, then carried like an overstuffed suitcase all my life to date. My suitcase has weighed me down and is bursting at its seams, threatening to overwhelm me by spilling its contents onto the kitchen floor when I least want to know what I have hurriedly, urgently, rammed inside it bit by bit over the years.

The grandfather clock caught me out when I least expected it: I'd been making some curtains, sewing peacefully, minding my own business, when the clock and its secret mechanism decided it was time to remind me. As I stitched away, the clock suddenly struck three. I looked up at the time. I was overcome by emotion. The clock was showing one minute past three on a Wednesday, four weeks after my mother's sudden death, the exact time on that Wednesday when my mother died – and I wasn't there. It was so poignant and disturbing: my tears fell in torrents onto the newly stitched curtain. They continued to fall for what felt like hours. The guilt lurking in my tears was squeezing the breath out of me, I felt my sobs as an acutely painful spasm in my chest and abdomen, and I had a hard job to find the rhythm of my breath in between my heaving sobs. I too was dying, that's what it felt like; I was going to die, here in my chair with a cream curtain on my knee.

What secret force was at work that day, in that clock, that it took upon itself the task of reminding me of the last lonely minutes of my mother's life and death, at the exact time it happened, four weeks on? I quickly put the curtain aside and got up to check the cooker clock to see if the grandfather clock had gone wrong, got itself mixed up: it hadn't. The tears issued from my wracked body, dropping like glittering icicles onto the kitchen floor. Something I couldn't see, hear, or touch was working a spell on me. It was another hour before my sobs subsided and I could begin to take hold of myself, get on with the curtain. I was washed out and drained, felt I'd been in the spin drier for hours. I was cotton wool, wispy and frail; too soft and fluffy to be real.

I remember my mother's dying day, and the day before too. I was unable to leave the university because it was master's degree marking and examination board week. My mother had been taken to hospital from her care home because she was bleeding profusely from her anus. My brother and my cousin were keeping me informed, and agreed that before I came home I had to finish the work in hand, for the sake of the students whose careers depended on their results. I had spoken with the doctors who'd been confident that my mother wasn't dying and that they could make her comfortable, although of course it was likely that the problem was life limiting. I felt comforted by this knowledge and happy that I could go north at the end of the week. I spoke to the doctor each day, got on with the tasks in hand.

The day before my mother's death the doctor telephoned me. At the time I was checking the references for the book I was writing on loss and bereavement, a book that summed up my recent academic work but would also fulfil one of my 'active research objectives' for my department. The doctor said they needed my permission to carry out a colonoscopy so that they could better diagnose our mother's illness. She had dementia and so could not give permission herself. I was very loath to give permission for the procedure, and expressed my point of view to the doctor: our mother was frail, she didn't know where she was or what was happening to her, what purpose could this colonoscopy serve? The doctor suggested that it would help to make decisions about her future care needs, and would help all concerned to make her as comfortable as possible. There was a general sense that this illness, whatever it was, was life threatening then? The doctor thought so, but said that death was not imminent. I did not wish my mother to be tampered with, she had suffered much during her lifetime and I desperately wanted her to have a peaceful, kind death, when death came. I hummed and hah-ed, still reluctant to say yes. I asked the doctor what my brother was saying. I was told he was in favour of the test so that he could have a diagnosis. So, reluctantly, I gave my permission and reiterated that I would be in Newcastle at the end of the week, Friday evening to be precise, and would be able to stay until September if necessary, as I could work wherever I was once the examination boards were over.

At my desk a day later, Wednesday morning, struggling with a task I hate – checking each reference for my book – I heard the phone ring and rushed downstairs. It was the doctor, her voice low and quiet. She was saying she was sorry, sorry; my mother had become very ill during the colonoscopy. She had suffered toxic shock and had had a heart attack – she was dying. Could I get there quickly? I found myself saying to the phone, which suddenly seemed disembodied from the caller at the other end, '*I told you she wasn't up to it, I told you; why couldn't you leave her in peace?*' I dropped the phone. It took Herculean effort not to scream at this doctor. Instead I spoke quietly, repeated that I lived in Wiltshire, I would need to get to Heathrow for a flight, and I would get there as soon as I could.

I telephoned my secretary to ask her to book the first flight from Heathrow, then rang my daughter at the bank to tell her what was happening and asked her to request compassionate leave to come to Newcastle with me: I'd booked her seat and would pick her up in Marlborough on my way through to the M4. Minutes later my daughter rang to say that the bank didn't give compassionate leave for grandparents. Incensed, I telephoned the bank and told them in no uncertain terms that trouble would ensue if they didn't allow my daughter to have compassionate leave to say goodbye to her grandmother. The bank capitulated unwillingly, ungracefully. In my view they were hardhearted and cruel: I made a note to change my bank.

My husband didn't want to come to Newcastle – he had his own reasons for disliking my mother – but he drove us at breakneck speed to Marlborough where my daughter was waiting, and then at frightening speed we hurtled to Hungerford and up the M4 to Heathrow. I hadn't thought him capable of such speed, as he was a slowish driver, often asking us to look, see a particular species of bird on the side of the road, on a fence, in a field: unnerving in its own way. He made Heathrow with fifteen minutes to spare before the plane left – ample time, as my secretary had apprised the airport staff of the urgency of this trip so we were rushed straight through.

We fell into our seats, thoughts tumbling around our heads: my brother had said he was with my mother but he would drive the short journey from the hospital to collect us at Newcastle airport. Controlling my anger and tears I turned to my quietly distraught daughter, who loved her grandmother so much, and said, '*If Uncle David is there to meet us, Granma will have died. If he is not there, we know we will have to get a taxi and she will still be alive.*' My daughter looked blankly at me, turned her head to the window and sobbed uncontrollably, quietly, her body rising and falling to the crying song we all know.

My secretary had made an arrangement for us to be the first to disembark from the aircraft because of the urgency, and so we ran through the arrivals lounge as fast as we could, only to see Uncle David, head down, shoulders slumped, propping up the arrivals desk. Mother, Granma, was dead – she had been dead for the last hour. David had left her dead side to come and pick us up at the airport. We cuddled and cried in full view of everyone in the airport. I felt lonelier, guiltier, sadder than anyone could imagine.

David took us to a pub on the riverside in the Tyneside Country Park, his solution for grief: a pint or two, maybe three. We sat disconsolately at a wooden table wrapped in a veil of impossible silence – it was hard to see through our individual veils, or hear, and it seemed there was nothing left to say either. Eventually someone we'd known for years jauntily came to our table full of life and drink, eager to see me and remind me of my past, to laugh and joke with David. He was bemused at our silence. He didn't notice our reluctance to join in his conversation at first, then after a few minutes he asked if anything was wrong. We had to speak those unspeakable words. '*Aye, there is, our Mam's just died,*' said my brother. '*She's dead. Just over an hour ago she died.*' Stricken, our acquaintance said he was sorry and wandered off. Our silence continued; we were paralysed by a shock that prevented any of us saying anything. I remember we couldn't act to help ourselves in those first hours.

After two pints of ale David finally found it possible to put some words together. He told us he had been at the hospital and had seen our mother before she went into surgery. He told her he would be there when she returned. He was there, only to be told she'd suffered toxic shock and had a massive heart attack under anaesthetic, she was deeply unconscious: this had been triggered by the colonoscopy as the ulceration in her bowel was so infected. He sat with her, talked to her, decided to take a walk for a few minutes because he was so upset. When he returned she was dead; she'd not recovered consciousness. He was desolate, guilty, hurt, bereft. He had gone home before he came to the airport, and while there had taken an axe to the things he stored in his garage: his anger knew no bounds as he smashed everything in his sight to pieces. He was still angry – at her for leaving, at her for being the difficult woman she sometimes was, for being the woman he loved, for being his mother, now gone.

Meanwhile, as we listened to him tell his story I remember how shocked I was and how guilty I felt. I wasn't there, and neither was David in those last moments. We were not there to comfort her, to say we loved her, we were not there when she died. She died alone. I felt then, and still do, that this is a burden no daughter should ever have to carry; the burden of guilt caused by putting work before family, before the ill patient, my dying mother. I couldn't see that I would ever be able to get over such guilt. I should have been there. My mother died alone and I would never come to terms with that. I was deranged and that trite popular saying, *What goes around comes around,* kept coming into my mind. I too would die alone, and I was afraid. For a long time I was afraid. I still fear that I may die alone, and my knowing and rational mind cannot shift this thought from the darker recesses of my mind: it will be my punishment for my selfishness, I accept it. It has also made me terrified of colonoscopies.

We left the riverside in bereft silence, a silence so personal and wretched it is almost impossible to describe even now, ten years later: the silence was cold, still, angry; it shivered, pined. I pined, especially for a few moments more with my mother alive, just a few moments. My silence was black and dark, impenetrable; it shrouded my shocked self. Suffocated the 'me' I once knew, before this happened, and the 'me' I would have to get to know without my mother: 'me', now the abandoned child. In a few hours my life changed and I could not reverse this change; I could never again be the woman I was. I was certainly not the woman I'd been that morning before the phone rang: neither was David the same man or my daughter the same young woman.

I remember those difficult days: my daughter and I stayed with my cousin and from there arranged the funeral, and also the removal of all my mother's personal possessions from the care home. We had to share a double bed and so there was no personal or emotional space for either of us. There was no room in my cousin's house for any kind of personal space, people called and jabbered constantly, their way of trying to avoid talking about Emily, my mother – avoid talking about death as they always had done, in case it upset anyone. It was a word they tried never to utter, as though by magic the whole act of dying and death could be cancelled out, yet they were trying their best to give us sympathy and love. I still think about my first motherless night, the words I wanted to speak at the funeral ran around my head like rats. I couldn't stop this rat pack of words, couldn't answer the questions pressing against my skull. How on earth do I do justice to my mother's life, and then to her sudden death? I hadn't seen her for four weeks.

I'd taken my mother out four weeks before her death, to buy her some new underwear and shoes. She was as particular as she'd always been about feminine underwear and the design of her shoes. I remember I noticed then how the sweat was running off her, little rivers running between her breasts. Her skin was hot and her cheeks flushed. I should have done something then, but

I thought she was just stressed by being in John Lewis and the assistants fussing around her. She'd never liked trying things on, always preferring to take them home to try them there, in front of her own dressing table mirror. If they didn't fit, she'd take them back. She'd always been very particular about her clothes and how she looked.

I was consumed by questions and procedures. How can I let her go? How do I write a eulogy I can be proud of, one she would be proud of? How can I ensure that her funeral is not the last time anyone will remember her, speak of her, think of her. How can I make her eulogy honest and realistic, not fall into the trap of fantasising, playing make believe? Her life was what it was, and it needed to remain so: she was what she was; have I to honour that? These questions ran, scratched and skittered around my head, and I couldn't find answers; neither could I sleep.

The next morning we had to go to the hospital to speak with the doctors: they seemed nervous on the phone, terrified that I was going to make a fuss, perhaps even try to take them to court. I had no intention of either. I hadn't slept and was now sleep walking. My daughter wanted to see her grandmother and so I had no choice but to go into the morgue with her. All my life I'd avoided funerals, I'd only been to a few: my aunt's, my mother's eldest sister's and the funeral for the mother of the friend who'd spoken to us in the park. I'd gone to her funeral because I wanted to support my friend. I'd taught him in Sunday school and then in school. I'd been to my stepfather's and my aunt's because I had to. I found funerals too painful, and I'd avoided visiting the dead for a last look too.

Now I had no choice, and I felt sick at heart. My daughter had a courage I didn't have and so I must have courage too. We were taken into the morgue, where thin curtains separated yesterday's dead from today's dead, in case they disturbed each other. My daughter sat by her grandmother's side and held her hand wordlessly. I stood at my mother's feet, frightened to look, aware of a man's feet at the other side of the curtain. Then I too sat by my mother, stroked her face and talked to her, told her I loved her. I cannot believe to this day that I actually did this: it was the only time my mother didn't answer back or try to argue. She was alabaster white, she'd not had many wrinkles anyway, being blessed with a beautiful skin, but now she was wrinkle free, her hair the strangest colour it had ever been. She still liked to cover over her few grey hairs. Recently someone at the care home had coloured her hair with a reddish dye: it was horrible, most unlike my mother.

We were just leaving the hospital when a very young female doctor followed us. When she caught up she said she was sorry, she had not thought that the procedure, the colonoscopy, would have killed our mother: she was very, very sorry. I had never challenged doctors, I'd always seen them as demigods, but I looked this young, thin, doctor straight in the eye and said, '*I did try to tell you, our mother was frail, and maybe you have learned that relatives know their loved ones better than doctors; they intuitively know; all of us have to learn. I said yesterday that she was too frail to undergo these tests and asked if we could leave her in peace. That is what I wanted; we wanted.*'

There were many complications following my mother's death. I pondered a great deal on her young widowhood. During my childhood she'd told me that she'd made arrangements for when she died: '*I will be buried in the same grave as my Bill,*' she would say. Her Bill, my father, had died young, aged forty-four, in Dunston Hill Military Pensions Hospital after a very long illness. I knew where these arrangements had been kept, and my first task was to find them, since the house had been cleared when my mother needed to go into full-time care. The documents confirming my belief were amongst her personal possessions, she had listed the hymns she wanted, and the prayers. The certificate giving permission for her to be buried in the same grave as my father was with her papers, as was a photograph of him with a torn, ragged love letter she'd once written him, inserted in the frame.

I'll walk beside you through the passing years
Through days of cloud and sunshine, joys and tears
And when the great call comes and sunset gleams
I'll walk beside you to the land of dreams.

All was complicated by the fact that she'd been married to her second husband Bob for over twenty-eight years. Bob had died three years previously after a very short but shocking illness: cancer of the liver that reduced him from a six-foot, seventeen-stone giant to a wreck of his former self in less than six weeks. By some cruel twist of fate we had also sat through his illness and witnessed the same things as we had as children, because he died of the same cancer as our father: terrible for our mother. At the time it didn't seem credible. Bob had asked to be cremated and had insisted before he died that our mother should be buried with her first husband, our father Bill, in their previously agreed shared grave, which she'd paid for when my father died. Bob and she had talked about it and he accepted it, just as he'd accepted that she continued to wear my father's wedding ring, with his sitting on top of it, throughout their marriage – the most magnanimous gesture and his greatest gift to her and to us.

My brother had pored over these arrangements: he could not face opening his father's grave to put his mother in. He was demented at this thought. We had not been at our father's funeral; children were not allowed at funerals in 1959. Opening his grave would be the hardest thing we would do. I knew I could do it, because I had to do it, that was what our mother wanted and I had no choice. I agreed with my brother that he would go to the church and not come to the cemetery. During this time I also had to look after my daughter and help her with her grief, help her plan what she wanted to say at her grandmother's funeral. She and I walked a great deal, walking the paths her Granma and her Granda Bob walked every day: they walked miles after their retirement, most days. We knew their paths and we followed them, walked in their footsteps, and it helped; we felt close to them both on Heddon Bank Top and along the river path to Wylam. My daughter had walked these paths since being a baby on her Granda Bob's shoulders; for years afterwards when she got tired of walking he would carry her on his shoulders until she was too heavy for such a treat.

My mother wanted the same hymns as she had had at our father's funeral: *Lord and Father of Mankind* and *Lamb of God I Come*. Unfortunately the organist played a more modern version of Lamb of God, so no one could sing except the vicar and a friend. This didn't help us as we hadn't been able to sing it at our father's funeral, and singing it now might have helped us bridge the gap. Instead we were trying to sing a tune we didn't know, no one else knew it either, and it was one of our darkest moments. We were distraught because we had let her down. Now, I think it was appropriate because I don't think I could have borne the tune my mother had expected. I have never been able to sing this hymn without breaking down. The other hymn she requested was her wedding hymn, *Love Divine all Loves Excelling*. I got through that and felt better. I asked my childhood friend to say the prayers, I gave the eulogy, and my daughter read a poem, all without tears.

We carried my mother into the church to *All in An April Evening*, which she used to sing beautifully accompanied by my terrible piano playing, and we carried her out to *I could have danced all night*: she was a great dancer. My brother had drawn the line at having her silver dancing shoes sitting on top of her coffin. I wish we had had them, they were her symbol; she was a natural expert dancer, light as a feather on her feet. If only her life had been as light.

We left for the cemetery, and to my surprise I found my brother was in the car: I hadn't noticed him climb in at the last minute which just shows what grief did to my mind. I'd bought white lilies, her favourite, and distributed one to each member of our family to place on top of her coffin once it was in the grave. I cannot tell you how I felt when I saw the gaping slash of the open grave, knowing my father's bones and spirit lay at its bottom; all I could see was his face, his smile and all I could think about were his rotten flesh and bones. I desperately hoped the gravediggers had dug far enough down that there would be no trace of him. I was simply terrified of seeing anything that looked like a bone or skull. Just a glimpse and I would have dropped in beside the traces and clung to them screaming; I just couldn't allow myself to look, nor to think about any of it. It was grim. My brother couldn't face it either, and so stood away from us all, breaking his heart. He was under a tree crying his eyes out, not just for his mother, but also for the father he'd known for such a short time. All I could see was his black suit and a white handkerchief. I managed, despite the tussle of my visual images and thoughts, to remain tearless and calm. After the funeral tea my daughter and I walked once again in the footsteps of her Granma and Granda. We bought dozens of packets of poppy seeds and scattered these as we walked, knowing that they would flower year after year, and many would enjoy Emily and Bob's poppies along their path.

My tears came when I sat on my mother's bed in the care home, days later, touching her clothes, still smelling her in their fibres, and in her room. Two days later my daughter and I were on the train to Wiltshire, our lives forever changed. It was cold, I remember, for the end of June and we were so sad. She had to catch a different train from me and so we said our goodbyes at Kings Cross. It was one of the hardest goodbyes. The powerful invisible tie that had always bound us, through thick and thin, was strained to snapping point, I knew. She was so deeply distressed and angry with me, very angry with me and the world in general, and at that moment I was conscious of a loss even greater than my mother's: my daughter's anguish was palpable and she wasn't able to share it with me. I knew, too, and she couldn't fully comprehend my knowing, that my life to date and my unresolved losses sustained over many years, those I had not come to terms with, had had a powerful effect on me and therefore on her too.

I was still struggling with unresolved grief, and this had impacted on her throughout her life.

My suitcase of old and recent junk, my clobber from the past, was open, and it was not going to be easy to close. It had been gaping at the seams for a long time and the grandfather clock, when it struck one minute past three that day, reminded me I had work to do on my packed and worn-out life. I have been working on the spilt contents ever since. I looked askance at the mess around me, inside and outside of me. My life was lying on the floor in the piles of muddled clothes; cloth memories. Each pile was demanding something from me – to save them, re-fashion them, discard them. These last were the most persistent; they did not want to be discarded. These were the most frightening muddles. It was hard for me to imagine some of these muddles having any place in my life from now on and yet it was even harder to imagine my life without them: they'd always been part of me. If I couldn't cope with one muddle or another, I just locked it in my suitcase until I could face dealing with it. Many had been locked there for almost fifty years, not forgotten, just out of sight. Following the grandfather clock's urgent chimes, hiding my muddles was no longer possible. I was facing the most difficult challenge of my life: re-designing myself because nothing in that suitcase suited me or fitted any more. I didn't even fit my skin: I was bursting out of my skin, like a snake sloughing it off. I needed to have a new skin. There was now no lock strong or large enough to keep my suitcase shut even if I did have the energy to try to pack the muddles more neatly inside it – which I didn't.

Many people have asked me why I retired early, long before my time. Many of my closest friends begged me not to give up my career. Why did I end such a good career seven years before I needed to and only sixteen months after I had been lucky enough to get a job I could previously not have imagined applying for, never mind being appointed to? I was travelling all over the world as part of the research community. The simple answer is that I became ill and was diagnosed with a mood disorder, manic depression. I knew somewhere in my muddled, raddled, mind that it wasn't quite the right diagnosis; I was having a hard time explaining how I felt, or understanding what was wrong with me so it wasn't the doctor's fault either. It was impossible to tell a fifty-year story in the few minutes of snatched time in my appointments. And anyway, I was too ill to know and didn't really care. The blackness had come suddenly, imperceptibly: I didn't know what was happening to me. And yes, I had been running around filling my life with activity, usually positive activity but had covered up the real reasons for my busy challenging lifestyle. The more the bulging suitcase resisted any more junk, the harder I worked to keep it firmly closed, zipped up and locked. I talked openly about my issues but I hadn't exorcised them.

With my mother's death something snapped and I could no longer keep up the increasingly desperate pretence of being strong and coping. I didn't care a hang what label I was given, or how my feelings were interpreted. I couldn't think. I simply became incapable of thinking a rational thought. Half the time I couldn't find my thoughts or explain them. I spent ages trying to find the words I needed just to get by in my job. I was reading research papers and not understanding a word they said, reading and reading the same words over and over again. Once a colleague noticed and I had to dissemble, which wasn't difficult because my life had become a paradoxical pretence. I didn't know what day it was – when I woke in a morning I had to fight with my brain to work it out. I was as muddled up as a ball of wool in a tangle when you cannot find the end to rewind it again. Cloaked in a soft, dark, blackness and emptiness, I thought I had gone mad. In a sense I had. Five months later it was found that I was physically ill and I was admitted to hospital as an emergency from the doctor's surgery, with chronic pain and jaundice. I was in a state of collapse with my blood pressure so low they elevated the foot of my bed. After x-rays and other tests they found a group of gallstones, as round and chubby as the doctor's thumb and two forefingers, blocking my digestive system. He said he didn't know how I had kept going: I'd had no proper nutrition for probably two years. I'd had a lot of pain and sickness but just kept going because I was in a new job. I'd noticed I seemed an odd colour, that I looked strange, yellow. It hurt a great deal when I swam. I ignored it all, even the pain in my right side that often stopped me in my tracks. I was often, mostly on stairs, doubled in two with the pain. I just continued to ignore it.

Afterwards, and as part of my recovery, there came a time when I knew I had to go home for a while: to Northumberland and Newcastle to sort my old muddles, my myths and legends, and make some sense of what had been a difficult life to date.

I'd become very depressed, suffering debilitating blackness on a daily basis. I couldn't read, not even a newspaper, and couldn't think. My mind was a cavern of black sticky mud, where thoughts couldn't move, they were incoherent, slipped easily from my grasp. I couldn't sleep and if I did so for an hour or so my brain teased me with horrible images, so I didn't want to risk sleeping. I wandered the house all night. I became exhausted, completely and absolutely exhausted – an exhaustion that I'd not experienced before; it paralysed me and I started to make chronic mistakes at work. Or I at least believed they were chronic: I became terrified of being found out. My confidence, having previously leaked slowly away, was now completely absent. It took me all my time to crawl out of bed by lunchtime. I will never forget the burden I became to myself and others. My confidence eroded, people chased me with demands, and my fear of making mistakes meant I chose to leave work and no one tried to talk me out of it: that was the strange thing, no one seemed to want me to stay or to understand what had caused my depression. I was scared I would lose my job, so it was better for me to give it up. And I didn't try to tell them. It wasn't their fault either and I don't blame them. I didn't have a shred of self-perception or self-image left.

2

Walking My Past

During my long recovery I continued to muse about the past: homes, families and landscapes. Simon Schama's *Landscape and Memory* kept me company, along with George Eliot's *Middlemarch* and my library of books and poetry. I was moved by Elizabeth Jennings' poem *In This Time* which suggests that we reach a stage in our lives where, in her words:

If the myth's outworn, the legend broken,
Useless even within the child's story
Since he sees well they now bring light no longer
Into our eyes: and if our past retreats
And blows away like dust along a desert,
Not leading to our moment now at all,
Setting us in this place and saying, 'Here
In you I will continue' – then what kind
Of lives have we? Can we make myths revive
By breathing on them? Is there any taper
That will return the glitter to our eyes.
We have retreated inward to our minds
Too much, have made rooms there with all the doors closed,
All windows shuttered. There we sit and mope
The myth away, set by the lovely legends;
Hardly we hear the children shout outside.
We only know a way to love ourselves,
Have lost the power that made us lose ourselves.

O let the wind outside blow again
And the dust come and all the children's voices.
Let anything that is not us return.
Myths are the memories we have rejected
And legends need the freedom of our minds.

As I read this poem over and over, I felt Elizabeth spoke my mind and would have understood my mood. I too needed to let the wind blow again, to lose myself in my history. I needed to travel backwards to be able to go forward. Jennings certainly knew what depression was like, she lived with it. She also knew loss. She is piercingly, poignantly clear about our need to integrate our past and at the same time reach a point where we can let it go, in the sense of not allowing it to surreptitiously disrupt our lives. She exposes the long-term effects and affects of attachments, families, filial and romantic love, as well as our inheritance: the stories of our infant-hood, our childhood experiences, and of our unknown absorption of the stories we are told about ourselves and others. She speaks of the facts of our inheritance more beautifully than I ever could. I love her poem and it acted as a trigger for me to look outside of myself for healing and growth.

When I felt strong enough I made my first trip to Northumberland, to Haltwhistle where I was born. I stayed in Haltwhistle itself – the first time since I was six when I had stayed with my cousins, because my mother was in hospital having an operation – and I was homesick. I'd always loved going to my maternal grandma's in Melkridge, a mile along the river from Haltwhistle. Of course, I had made regular trips north to see my family over thirty years but not to Haltwhistle. My family lived in Throckley and the surrounding area. This visit was not about duty or visiting relatives. This was different, I wanted to explore my history, ecology and geology: I wanted to learn to embrace my culture, the one I'd lost to become the professional, socially mobile woman my mother wanted. This was my trip, to re-acquaint myself with my Geordie heritage. I had never completely rejected it, having always been proud to be a Northumbrian Geordie: I left the north east to go on to further education. There was now so much I needed to understand for me to make the best of the rest of my life: and to heal. Too many of these old-fashioned clothes in my suitcase were fashioned from my life in the north.

Homes and families, like landscapes, have feelings and moods; they are affected by particular internal or external catalysts, sometimes changing gently and calmly but at other times violently and catastrophically, responding to weather fronts, global warming, extreme events, history, economics, people's needs, desires, health and wealth. Individuals, families and communities become psychological and physical barometers registering the emotional and physical changes around them.

The landscape of my birth is moody, sitting as it does near the border to Scotland and the west coast, trapped between east and west coasts, a prisoner of both weather fronts. It is not a temperate zone. As the weather suddenly changes the landscape darkens or brightens within minutes. It can be eerie: black angry skies boasting a bright yellow sun one minute, confusing the eye, and tipping down with rain the next. You can never walk in Northumberland without carrying a raincoat and umbrella, a warm sweater, because of sudden rain or drop in temperature, even in high summer. Suddenly from soft balmy sunshine warming your back you stand a-feared in black stormy depressions: heaven descends to earth creating hell on the moors. The Roman Wall, only a quarter of a mile from Melkridge, the village where I was born, can be warm, mellow, willing you to sit upon it one minute and looking every bit the dark, protective military edifice it was intended to be the next: threatening. At other times the weather fronts from east, west and the North Sea settle, and the sunlight and warm breezes make it the most beautiful, tranquil, verdant place to be, watched over by huge skies.

I understood why there came a point in my life when I needed to return physically and emotionally to Northumberland's beautiful landscape to re-kindle my spirit. Over the years I realised I had closed my mind to understanding my past, and therefore twice in twenty years failed to grasp change – change I really needed to make. I had accepted my mother's stories, myths and legends as the absolute truth: I trusted my mother. Now change had been forced on me and I needed to understand why.

Around the Millennium I was only just beginning to understand that I had come to the end of the life I had quarried, just as my grandfathers who'd putted for coal, I had putted to keep my life going; putting and quarrying is gruelling hard work. That's how I felt as 2000 dawned. I knew I was now at the beginning of the life I wished to create, but hadn't a clue how I might achieve it. It was a very real struggle: I couldn't find the appropriate words, my story was too painful to acknowledge, and my desperate quarrying and visionary creation amid the shallow chalk of the Wiltshire Downs, where I'd lived for the past 20 years, had proved to have little permanence or point. My will and strength had failed. I was facing a major mental breakdown. My visions and goals had not been born of burning desire but of a very real need to avoid poverty and assure my independence. I really did walk as a ghost in my grandmother's and mother's footsteps; the fit was perfect. If I was ever to make my own footprints I needed to understand the landscape and songs of my inheritance, the arias of the Whin Sill, the main Northumberland rock formations, the moors, those of my birth, once rejected because fleeing the past and its effect on me was easier than confronting it, even if I'd known that I should confront it. I'd had a piercingly acute longing to return to my roots for more years than I cared to remember: now it had become an urgent need, one I could not ignore.

After leaving school, during my years of absence from my family and friends, I lived for three years in what felt to me like the flat, drab, damp lands of Keele and Madeley in Staffordshire, where the skies seemed to hang low almost all year. Yet, I learned over those years there was much beauty here too. I felt lost, lonely and frightened. I had chosen teacher training because my teachers had advised me that was what I should do; nursing and teaching were the two main careers for young women then, even in the enlightened grammar school I attended during my sixth form education. I wasn't clever enough for university, they'd said. My dream had been to study English literature at university, but they believed I would not get the grades to be able to fulfil my dream. I trusted my teachers knew better than me, so did as I was told and applied for teacher training college to study home economics with a science option, the weakest of my three A level subjects. I could cook, my mother was an excellent cook and I learned from her. I had been trained in silver service waitressing at Fenwick's French Cafe in their Northumberland Street store in Newcastle. What more did I want? I had vocational as well as academic qualifications: the perfect package. So, I was able to get into my first choice college. I'd always wanted to teach so I now had what I wanted. Or so I thought.

When my A level results came in they were far better than my teachers had predicted and so they wanted me to drop my teacher training place and apply to do English literature at university. The headmaster asked to speak to me on the morning I went to collect my results. I had no confidence in myself by then, believing that my teachers were right: we had excellent teachers and support and I didn't question their decision. I didn't try to apply through the clearing house because I believed in their point of view: they were the experts.

I had a regular customer in the cafe on Saturday mornings who always took an interest in what I was doing. He was a retired university lecturer and when he saw my results he begged me to apply through the clearing house for a place, even said he would be my referee. I still said no, for the simple reason that I believed that my teachers were right and that I would find university a bit beyond me, too hard. My self-image was not damaged by these events, I'd got my A levels and I was pleased. My mother was proud of me and that was what mattered to me then. Literature has remained the love of my life; maybe it wouldn't have been so if I'd studied it. That's what I've always assured myself. I'd always been good at home economics and so I talked myself into accepting my place.

My 'better than expected' results were a present to me for more than one reason. The weekend before my A level mock examinations my cousin Monica was murdered in her own home on an army camp in Germany. Everyone in our family was shattered. Monica's mother, my aunt, my mother's eldest sister, had been a widow since she was in her early 30s and had raised her two daughters herself. Monica and my mother were like sisters.

I was expected to go to school as normal the next day, having read about my cousin's murder in the *Evening Chronicle* and having to tell my mother who hadn't yet read it. Obviously I didn't do as well in my mock examinations which started that same Monday morning. I didn't achieve my predicted grades in the mock examinations: hence the lowered expectations for my future. Neither did the school or my teachers know what was going on in my life. We didn't tell teachers much in those days, only notes for absence ever said why we were absent, nothing more. I was never absent: all through school I had a very high attendance record. There weren't school counsellors or pastoral care programmes either. We had excellent teachers, supportive teachers, but we wouldn't have dreamt of telling them about our private life.

Going to Madeley Teacher Training College attached to Keele University to do home economics was a very big mistake indeed: I hated my course and the college, and I was not as good at home economics as I had thought I might be. I was bored out of my mind. Yet I completed the course and applied for teaching posts in Worthing where my long-term boyfriend was studying and working, supported by Beecham Pharmaceuticals. Even then, my lecturers were telling me I was more suited to mass catering than home economics where each dish had to be a perfect ten out of ten, and at the very least, nine out of ten, otherwise one was a failure. Perfectionism is not something I have ever aimed at, nor do I do it well. I do the best I can and live by the mantra that it will do, it will be good enough. Good enough was all right, it beat working in the Inland Revenue, a shop, or an insurance company. I knew I would be bored out of my mind in any of those occupations. Office work was not for me so home economics and being a teacher were absolutely fine. How we can kid ourselves. The other major career choice for girls was nursing, and I knew without a shred of a doubt that I could never be a nurse. I had had my fill of hospitals by the time I was ten years old.

My long-term boyfriend, whom I'd sat next to at junior school and with whom I was best friends at Sunday school and church, was held back for a year as he didn't pass the 11-plus with expected grades either. He was almost a year younger than the rest of the class so had to repeat the year. He duly passed the following year and was in the top class of the grammar school. We started going out, we met every week at the church youth club when I was sixteen and a half. I ended the relationship when I was almost 18, after Monica's death: significant only because the two events occurred together by chance. He was very distressed and followed me everywhere, turning up in places to meet me unannounced. He begged me to return to him. I kept saying no. My mother then put pressure on me as he was a nice lad and he loved me. This was disingenuous of her because she'd constantly told me he wasn't good enough for me, and would go on doing so for all the years of our courtship and marriage: an inauspicious start. He was very clever, a natural scholar, but from an even poorer family than mine. Social mobility depended on girls marrying above their station not below it! Between him and my mother, tricked by my own lack of courage and belief, I eventually gave in and returned to my forlorn boyfriend. At the end of my three years in college I went to join him in Sussex having got engaged on my twenty-first birthday in The Lanes in Brighton. We bought a beautiful opal ring in an antique shop and then went off to see Brighton and Hove Albion play football.

There was a great deal of pressure in the third year of college to get engaged. We were in competition with each other; no one wanted to be the one left on the shelf; and I was too emotionally immature not to be seen as part of the crowd. I had not enjoyed my time in college or indeed in Staffordshire. It took all my time and energy to finish my course, even though I was always graded as an excellent teacher on teaching practice. I was going to go on and do a B.Ed but knew I couldn't spend another year in Madeley so turned the opportunity down.

I had fun during my third year in college and understood another aspect of me was developing: a more confident person was emerging. I had three relationships during the period my boyfriend was engaged to another woman in Sussex – he'd broken off our engagement and unknown to me at the time, become engaged to someone else in Brighton.

One of my new relationships was very tempting indeed but I didn't have the courage to give it a real try. The man in question was completing his MA(Ed) at Keele University having gained his degree from Oxford University. He was going on to teach physics and chemistry. We had so much fun. He owned a car and we drove all over the place, had a trip on a horsedrawn barge down the canals. He was an Oxford Blue in rowing, a great walker and mountain climber. We walked and danced all the time.

When I ended the relationship with him, for reasons that seemed so silly later, already pointing to my lack of confidence with men, I regretted it bitterly. It hadn't helped our relationship when he'd met my family. He'd driven me to Lancashire for my cousin's wedding, an opportunity to meet my parents. He had a rather snazzy way of dressing which I liked, but my parents most definitely did not. When we walked into my uncle's house I introduced my boyfriend, only for my stepfather to blurt out loudly, '*What's she brought in now? A poofter!*' Everyone laughed. I have never felt so hurt or embarrassed since; for him and for myself. This was in front of a crowded room of relatives. My boyfriend wasn't going to the wedding and left saying he would pick me up later. He was not the least bit bothered. When I look at the one photograph I have of this man, in his climbing gear facing a great mountain he is about to climb, I feel I hurt him, and I feel sad. We hadn't been together long enough to know whether we were in love. I ended the relationship because I knew my parents would never accept him. Months later, after I did end it, he tried to find me and turned up at my parents' home. How he found the address I have no idea. They told me he'd been, and that they'd said I was engaged and living in Sussex. You see, in working class communities like mine, in northern England, you had to be a *man*! In other words you had to earn your living by hard graft otherwise you were a bit of a poofter. If you dressed as my young suitor did, in jeans, floppy shirts and a silk neck-scarf, you very definitely were not a man. He was also a pen pusher! No one had much respect for pen pushers in the village I'd lived in. If you hadn't worked down the pits, or in the factories, been to war, you were most definitely not a man.

I'd regretted my naivety once before this particular romance, yet learned nothing from my feelings and emotions. I'd met a boy on holiday in Scarborough when I was fifteen – he was seventeen, my first romantic relationship. My mother was horrified, made such a fuss, cried and cried and told me I'd ruined her holiday. My aunt who was with us stepped in and encouraged my mother to leave me be. She arranged that we had a chaperone, my new boyfriend's older brother-in-law. My mother made such scenes on this holiday about me going out with a boy but Aunty Vi, her very strict elder sister, stood up for me and told her to let me go. We also had to take my younger brother with us, which I didn't mind and neither did the boy, they became friends. We had a wonderful week's fun. Yet when we met later when he came to Newcastle for the weekend I was so self-conscious about being seen with him that I didn't invite him again.

He sent me wonderful love letters, marked with SWALK on the back of the envelope, for months afterwards. I was so shaken by these initials in capital letters; I hadn't a clue what they meant and was too embarrassed to ask anyone. I thought it was some sort of swear word and he thought I was a tart. I didn't have the courage to ask anyone else so I didn't write back. He kept writing and I threw his letters away – SWALK and all on every one. I have one photograph of him with my brother: blond, laughing and good-looking. I was too shy and innocent to acknowledge these assets as a more confident young woman might have done. It is interesting too, looking at both photographs, that these suitors were tall, slender, yet strongly built.

I'd also had a short but very close relationship with a guy at Keele who turned out to be a drug addict. He turned up at my twenty-first birthday party uninvited because he was interested in what was going on. Keele University, because of it position right next to the M6 motorway, gave all of us easy access to travel: we'd nip out the back gates of the university and be straight onto the bank-side; or across the bridge if we were going north. We were never there for more than minutes before we had a lift to wherever we wanted to go. We girls always hitched in twos for safety but I can honestly say we never ever felt unsafe. It was mostly lorry drivers who gave us lifts. I loved sitting up in those cabs where I could see so much of the journey. The motorway unfortunately also gave easy access to drug dealers. The university's position meant that drugs became a problem during our second year in college and in the university itself. Drugs did not tempt me at all, but they had tempted this guy. He died not long afterwards having swallowed a massive quantity of drugs to avoid detection from the police. He telephoned me from the motorway to tell me he was ill; I never heard from him again.

There was no penetrative sex in any of these relationships because I was a good girl, brought up by the Church of England, and believed there should be no sex before marriage. I was terrified of sex, as my mother always said that if I got pregnant before I was married she would drown herself in the river. I didn't need telling twice: I didn't want to be responsible for my mother's suicide.

And there was another short-lived fling. An Indian guy I met at a concert asked me out and I went to my first Indian concert. I had no idea what to make of the music but I enjoyed it. Unfortunately we didn't fully understand the rules about mixed-race relationships then. He was so persistent I had to hide in my room and ask the other girls to tell him I was out. It became a bit unnerving to say the least, nice as he was.

Eventually, after months of being apart but no definite split, I asked my ex-fiancé to choose between me and his new girlfriend. Unbeknown to me they were engaged, and I believe they were engaged even when he and I became engaged. Eventually he broke it off and chose me, out of guilt more than for any other reason I think. His heart remained with her for many years and it was never mine after his relationship with her. As my aunt said at the time, '*Better the devil you know than the devil you don't know.*' Such positive advice!

Despite all these hiccups in our relationship I went to live in the beautiful South Downs to join my fiancé when college came to an end. Historically, there is another reason why 'getting engaged' became a pressure: the pill was only just available and as a young woman you either had to have a letter from your parents saying they agreed to you having the pill or you had to be engaged and twenty-one years old. I – we – chose the latter. It would have been impossible to discuss this with my mother: we were brought up in a community that still saw shotgun marriages, as they were called, as a disgrace to family and community. No one had any sympathy for those involved and always blamed the female for having 'given in.' Divorce was not easy for a woman even then and no one cared much what sort of life a woman that had got herself into this position had: she'd made her bed and had to lie on it.

As a newly engaged couple we had so much fun in Sussex, it still stands out as one of the happiest times of my life. We married the Christmas after I left college in 1970. By then I knew that I'd been an absolute fool not to remain to do the B.Ed. at Keele.

I was only just beginning to understand at some subliminal level that recent and past events in my life had affected me seriously. Once or twice in my third year in college I had really lost my temper and got very, very angry, to the great shock and chagrin of my close friends, who witnessed my reincarnation as a demon. I'd had the most awful temper tantrum, only the second of my life; the first had been with my mother when I was sixteen. This outburst shocked me and shocked my friends. I knew I had been irrationally emotional and this was unusual. I had always been seen as a strong and reliable coping person; and a very conscientious hard worker. I couldn't fathom this other side of me. I didn't understand this at the time, nor did I understand my friends' reactions. I felt lost, hurt, and very, very alone. So leaving college was my chosen escape, one I thought was both rational and right.

So, having finished college, in a kind of make-the-best-of-it mood, we started our life together in Sussex where I had a teaching post in a girls' school – a new experience for me as I was educated in mixed secondary and grammar schools and had chosen a mixed teacher training college. I knew instinctively, even then, that being in mixed environments was important to me, and remembered being totally and worryingly out of my depth with the posh southern ladies who were my colleagues and absolutely hating the strict rules and regulations in the girls' school. I had been lucky to be in state schools that had encouraged self-regulation and discipline with very few rules, so this new environment was a shock, a very real one, and I had no idea how to cope with it. I didn't know what was expected of me and on top of that I found I was bored stiff and disliking the repetitive teaching of home economics. I wasn't very good at it either. Despite my inner feelings, I was popular and made friends easily, so it was all a puzzle. Keeping up this confident front was such very hard work.

Yet I knew that, even though I didn't like my job, I loved Sussex. We made many friends, and we had the time of our life, thanks to Worthing Rugby Club. Our daughter was born in Worthing so it remains a special place. I remember the decision we took to move, because of the expense of Sussex: we always had money problems and houses were so expensive, and now we had a baby we had to be grown up. I knew I had always been grown up, I'd had to be, but being responsible for my own child was almost too much responsibility on top of a lifetime of responsibilities. I was in no way mature enough to be a mother, although I did everything conscientiously and wanted the best for my child. I wanted a nice house and garden and a nice life for our family. My husband left his first job and joined the police force. I wanted things he didn't want and wasn't bothered about: I was more materialistic. I learned to drive in Sussex and we had great fun in our ancient Morris Minor and then our Triumph Herald: both had leather seats and the Morris had the old yellow signal that popped out of the side of the window. I also, much to my regret later, was pressuring him to be a career man, to earn more money to improve our lifestyle. He wasn't interested in this, and I respect him for this now – I didn't then. Whenever we travelled home to Newcastle my Mam and Bob (my stepfather) constantly compared us with our school friends, their houses, their cars, their jobs; and we were not doing as well, at least in their eyes we weren't. It was horrible and upset both of us every time we visited. His parents couldn't have cared less.

So, when an opportunity to move north again came via my husband's job we ran away from our problems, back to our homeland; to Newcastle, to our parents and old friends where we were for almost four years. We didn't realise at the time that we were also running away from each other. In a sense we were two children wanting their mummy and in his case daddy too, even though we had a child of our own we loved very much: we needed and wanted support. We settled very quickly, picking up with old school friends and new ones too, and continued our good time. As with Sussex, the Rugby Club was the centre of our social life and friendships, as well as work of course: this time Hexham Rugby Club where there were very quickly rumours about another woman.

And now, aged sixty-one, I really struggle to understand my feelings about our next move, to the soft chalky Wiltshire Downs, a landscape I loved within three months of being in it, and still do; but yet another alien culture. I had by then learned a good deal about de-camping and setting up new camps, how to adjust and learn, and I came to love both the land and the culture. I remember the moment when the struggle of the decamping faded. It was a warm spring evening, we were out cycling, and I knew once and for all that I liked it here in Wiltshire, even though by now my daughter and I were alone in the most difficult of circumstances. No friends, no support systems and a new house partly refurbished. My marriage had finally broken down and my husband had left us to return north to a woman he loved. I had known: I'd opened the divorce papers from his suitor. He was in Syria working, and when abroad he always asked me to read him his mail. We had, that day, just sold the house ready to buy the one in Wiltshire, and I had the decision of my life to make within minutes.

We were just about to de-camp to Wiltshire for my husband's job and I was about to embark on a fully funded psychotherapy diploma at Newcastle University paid for by my employers. My marriage was on the rocks. I had also fallen passionately in love with another man who was divorced but also in another relationship. I walked away from this relationship but it took years for me to get over it even though it never really got started – though he did compose a wonderful piano melody for me. Standing by my bay window, with the letter from my husband's lover's solicitor in my hand detailing his affair and breakdown of his lover's marriage, with my husband cited as the co-respondent, at the same time as talking to my husband on the phone in Syria – this was bizarre. I knew our lives were now impossible. Yet I still, despite all advice, decided to accompany him to Wiltshire. I look back and wonder if I was totally and utterly mad. Neither of us could ever have told our parents and we knew it, and that was one reason I decided to go. I was terrified of others' reactions as well as of my parents' reaction. He was terrified of his parents' reaction too. Later, when I finally told my mother, she was devastated and wouldn't allow me to visit the house because I was divorced. She hadn't told our relatives or our neighbours I was divorced.

My husband and I had been parted briefly during this time in Newcastle – he was drinking heavily and there were rumours about another woman, which I did my best to ignore. We had a child and we had to try and make a go of our marriage. Of course I knew we had married too young and had been together too long, growing up together, and in psychological terms were only now mature enough to know that we were childhood friends who loved each other as friends but were having a hard time trying to love each other as adults: we just didn't have the passion, commitment and love, those three essential elements necessary for a long-term successful adult relationship. We had love and affection, but the other two requisites for long-term successful relationships were absent. We'd metamorphosed into adults who needed to explore the world and other relationships, and our daughter was trapped in the middle. There had only been one divorce in our extended family; none in his. Both families looked on divorce as a sin.

So, as two chaotic adults who couldn't part but couldn't live together, we came to Wiltshire with the sincere hope, in my case anyway, that we could revive our relationship and all would be well. I desperately wanted to make it work for the sake of our daughter and I know he did too. I changed my course to London University, against all professional advice, and settled to making a new life near Marlborough. Sadly my husband needed to stretch his wings, and within five weeks he had returned to be with his new partner. My daughter and I were left to make a go of living in Wiltshire alone: as my aunt would have said, '*What an unholy mess.*'

I still think sadly about the circumstances of this last move. I followed dutifully, finding a job once we were settled; my budding career had been constantly disrupted in favour of his. I was being counselled by my head teacher to be careful about this move because I was in a job I loved, doing well and had just won a scholarship to train as a psychotherapist at Newcastle University. It was a lot to give up. After long agonising reflection I decided that I would follow, as I had a child to think about, not just myself. Our marriage was already falling apart but I kept this fact successfully hidden from everyone, especially from our daughter and our parents. I feel, and still do, I was right to try to save my marriage for the sake of our daughter, if for no other reason. Neither of us behaved well and we failed to protect our little girl.

Wiltshire lacks the harsh weather fronts of Northumberland and I settled quickly into its balmy warmth. I love change, so I am always positive about moving house and area: it is exciting and challenging. I believed at the time that this was all part of growing up. It may seem hard to understand now – with Newcastle being one of the top ten European Cities and Geordie voices on our radio and television – but then, to cope in another subculture meant denying one's Geordie heritage and trying to soften one's accent. In true feisty style, my style, I have always refused to change my voice – it's softened, but it is still mine. My head teacher in Worthing had once called me into her office to tell me I must learn to speak properly. When I asked what she meant she said I must learn to say *parth* and *barth*. I looked at her in astonishment and told her I couldn't. I haven't. I'm proud of my Geordie accent and I was then too.

By this time I – we – knew our marriage was failing, breaking down; already broken down. We had been separated briefly during the previous year but, because of pressure from both sets of parents, we tried to repair our marriage, though our heart was not in it. After five weeks in Wiltshire we separated for the second time: I remember the fights, the tears, the struggles and the pain. It was traumatic.

Among the muddle of my clothes tipped out of my metaphorical suitcase there was a dress: maroon jersey, long and tight as the seventies demanded. I find it hard to believe I ever got into it, though I know I did. This dress was an icon to those days of tension, the knowing that it was all over: my marriage was over but I couldn't tell anyone, not even my young child. And it was not anyone's fault: the fact was that we had outgrown each other, we had sucked the life-blood from each other, and our search for financial and personal security had worn out our marriage, as well as us.

I remember my distress and my trips to the standing stones at Avebury. I went most days, except for those when I was in London doing my diploma. I'd transferred to London University, thanks to the generosity of my headmaster and MIND, who'd funded my scholarship to complete my Advanced Diploma in Psychology; travelling twice a week to London to study, having found a lovely Wiltshire lady to collect my daughter from school and look after her until I came home. I remember the physical warmth of those Avebury stones warming my back; it was a beautiful autumn. They were so ancient, strong and permanent and they filled me, my very being, with strength – strength I very badly needed for me to make the difficult decision to stay or leave, to stay in a strange land, alone, with my child. It was, and remains still, the hardest decision I've ever made and I've not regretted it either. When I'm distressed, even now, I go to lean against the Avebury Stones, where I gain strength, wisdom and comfort. A year later I met my present husband, and here I am still.

My daughter and I frequently travelled back to Newcastle to our family and they visited us, although my parents were not at all happy or supportive of my decision: in fact they were sure I was quite mad, as my stepfather said at the time, '*You've gone out of your mind, you're mad!*' My daughter grew up knowing my land and culture, as well as developing a love of Wiltshire. My mother and stepfather travelled the long journey to Wiltshire from Newcastle for every one of my daughter's concerts and ballet concerts, over almost twenty years, as well as for holidays, and my graduation ceremonies. They gave unstintingly to their granddaughter.

Yet, over the years, I became more restless and unsettled than I'd ever been in this land I loved. I gradually realised my growing spiritual and emotional poverty: for over twenty years I have been ghost walking, I know what it is like to be 'dust to dust, ashes to ashes', in the midst of life. My soul died slowly, imperceptibly, just managing to retain a dying candle flicker of light in the hope that the vessel in which it resided might cherish it just a little, allow it to burn. By 2000 it was just about burned out.

3

Accepting My Past

My New Year's resolution in 2001 was to travel north. I was recovering very slowly from my breakdown, and learning about my land was my way of trying to put the past and the present into some understandable perspective. I found that the Whin Sill, those rocky foundations beneath the land of my birth, is very resistant to erosion and dates back to the Carboniferous age. It is composed of limestone, millstone grit and coal measures: limestone is predominant and complemented by sandstone, shale and coal.

The penultimate town in Northumberland where I was born, Haltwhistle near the Cumberland border in the South Tyne Valley, sits on ridges of glacial boulder clay above a floodplain. Man colonised this habitat centuries ago: Gauls, Celts, Angles, Saxons, Vikings, Romans, Normans and Scots all invaded and played their part in the development of an heterogeneous Northumbrian people. Like the rocks around them they are tough, feisty, ready to fight for, and protect what is theirs, warm, friendly and fun loving with a darker, grittier shadow personality when crossed: an ebullient people. Geordies have a self-deprecating, defensive sense of humour designed to prevent anyone getting above himself: to outsiders this can seem acerbic and hurtful, although it is rarely intended to be.

The county towns and villages proudly display their history as fortified towns. Castles, bastles and pele towers are still a major feature of the area. Many belonged to the Scottish kings for years and were constantly under attack. The town in which I was born

35

is still a market town. Originally markets were held on Tuesdays and Thursdays, sheep and cattle fairs were held twice a year. It was proud to be industrially modern with Pigot's Directory listing sixty major traders. In 1860 the Quakers set up a baise factory for weaving, fulling, dying and spinning; there were four collieries.

In the seventeenth and eighteenth centuries the area was alive with 'reivers' and 'borderers' at war with Scotland. These wars railed for over a hundred years forging an anarchic, tough, defensive fighting people. The inhabitants had to defend themselves, their families and their lands, as well as having to survive this moody, turbulent, wild landscape, and scratch a living from it. Poverty was never far from their door. They made their own laws outside the state and it was only James I who managed to persuade them to accept his laws in return for protection. On both sides of the border these reivers and borderers were violent men warring with each other as well as the Scots: quarrelling and making up has a long history in these border-lands. New words came to the English language from their activities: bereavement (to lose all you had) and blackmail, because these men ran complicated large-scale protection rackets. There was always uncertainty as to who was on whose side: sides could change within the hour.

Like their lands the people are proud and defensive, characterised as well as sometimes caricatured by their dialect; Northumbrian up the Tyne valleys and Geordie within and around the city of Newcastle: Northumbrians, as my mother said, do not call themselves, nor do they see themselves as, Geordies. It is no surprise that the mining of rocks or minerals has been the basis of the Northumbrian economy for centuries; the land was ransacked to provide the local economy. Hewing rock, both men and women become strong, resilient, careful and courageous: rock can kill in a flash as it falls without warning. The Aborigines and Native Americans believe you have your spirit in the land in which you have your being: you are your land, your memory and spirit is irrevocably bound together with those in tune with the land, enabling the development of an active and powerful intuition.

I know Northumberland and Newcastle shaped me. I was an integrative part of this rich, diverse, tapestry of life in both; they shaped my identity. And for years I have tried to deny it. I understand the part played by religion insidiously woven into the land and my own story from the early saints onward. This land and its stories helped form the elemental psyche of its people, including me. Like many ancient tapestries, including the Bayeux, there is no planned original design; more happenchance: a unique design for survival and surviving, developed from people's life stories, and their interpretation of their experiences in this rugged wild county fringed by the North and Irish Seas. Much of this culture is heard and felt in our folk songs, as well as our poetry and literature. Over a number of visits, and alone, I wandered the countryside, exploring my maternal and paternal habitats, sitting on my bedrocks for hours at a time. The rocks hummed to me, singing and chorusing their stories of history and culture, scoring a dramatic opera as they did so: *musique naturelle* in romantic style.

They sang me the prelude, my mother's birth. Emily, born into this Northumberland landscape on 19 December 1919, a dark-haired, pretty, Gallic-looking baby. Her home a dark mining cottage, two up two down, a hive for Grandma's industrious production and Granda's forced silence and inertia. The pastoral melody denoted the parlour, looking out onto soft, steeply rising, green, velvet-dressed fields. The Saxon village, with its houses of original wattle and daub, led on to common grazing land called 'inbys', creating agricultural capital for the various generations of marauding absentee landlords. Majestically they trumpeted the Norman manorial inheritance scattered along the high sides of the valley with castles and manor houses, they warbled about men finding Jerusalem in this green and pleasant land as they greedily grabbed these residences in the nineteenth century: industrial barons took them as their prize for diligently creating the twin gods of *industrialisation* and *mammon*. They regally praised the 'Halts', small, select train stations, built at their feet for royal trains to discharge their elegant passengers on a Friday evening for their weekend entertainment in a land of poverty.

The intermezzo, winged by soprano rocks in sonorous voice, made the hairs on my neck stand on end, I remember, with their rendering of the clear cold waters of the South Tyne, sparkling, wriggling and skipping its way over boulders; white water in the densely wooded valley, immense spaciousness afforded by its breadth, and lack of habitation. Abruptly the altos joined in with their counterpoint hymnal, praising the religious icons rising on the skyline proudly displaying Puritanism: chapel and church like petrified bride and groom standing side by side at a scruffy street wedding. All joined in the dirge for the marring, black, gritty colliery (and three others in the town) at the end of my grandma's street: a bucolic blisteringly disfiguring industrial infection feeding the community, making muck and money, mocking nature; at its demise, miserably ingesting the life-blood of a community, four times over.

The base and tenors delved low in their repertoire as they sang of their turbulent history including the war cries of the various invaders over the centuries: the plain chant of the monks and saints, the rallying violent songs of the border reivers, the puritanical songs of the industrial revolution, alongside the folksongs of the miners and farming folk, the scarlet-clothed hunt included.

The altos joined them, developing vivid scenes of travelling people bringing their produce to Hexham market where there was a good trade in cattle, sheep, horses and the produce of many farmsteads and kitchens. It was also the place to sell people, brisk trading in farmhands, servants, cooks and laundry girls, veritable but honourable slavery for those who were not miners, artisans or gentlemen.

As a quartet they each took a separate part, depicting scenes from the different social strata living and working side by side in this system, composing a largo of values and mores for those who may otherwise wander from the path of the Lord and his appointed earthly masters: the *untermenchen* were needed to preserve the wealth of the few, but also needed to be controlled by being overworked, ill treated, underpaid and taught, by cruelty if necessary, due respect and ambition. And this was expected in redundancy or unemployment too. Their voices cried in palpable fear of this system breaking down, turning the tables: peasants posing a threat to ordered community life. In crescendo the rocks sang their respect for a decent, God-fearing, strong, generous, witty, hard-working people.

In andante they provided me with some understanding of my grandma's life, her imagined feelings especially about eight pregnancies in twelve and a half years in her poverty fuelled days: cynically I wondered whether she was only a sperm receptacle, a comfortable relief for Granda's itches and urges, or was their union passionate and loving? How can I ever know? Like many of my grandma's generation these pregnancies and sexual relations were part and parcel of marriage. It would be arrogant of me to judge, using my feminist perspective, the quality of my grandparents' intimate relationship.

But, I know my grandma was known to have feelings about pregnancy. Her street was often cynically referred to as 'Kittle Belly Row' a harsh reference suggesting constantly breeding rabbits. This gentle stoical woman, my grandma, was on the bus from the market one day when she heard a man refer to Kittle Belly Row as she got up to alight: she clouted him violently with her handbag. Grandma guarded and protected her self-respect, inculcated this in all her children, but perhaps also knew anger and felt shame.

Whatever they felt, my Grandma and Granda nurtured their family, and very strong bonds held throughout their children's long lives, and between them all. Despite the 13-year age gap between my mother and her eldest sister Vi, they were very attached to each other and Vi became my mother's confidant and guide, as well as mine. They only quarrelled badly once; it was dreadful, painful, and their split from each other lasted for two years, neither willing to forgive. Aunty Vi had objected to my mother's second marriage because she didn't believe you should take two children into another marriage. She survived as a widow and my mother should survive as a widow too. As far as she was concerned it was simple. My mother didn't listen to her sister and for almost 28 years she regretted not listening. Although she had financial security in her second marriage it remained an extremely volatile relationship.

But it was with her brothers George and Bill, closest to her in age, that my mother had the strongest bond, it too lasted a lifetime. With Ella there was a natural empathy and attachment, although Ella stayed close to her brothers and sisters, she was always her own person, unlike the others she didn't and wouldn't abide by the rules. It was Bill and George who protected my mother as they walked to school with her, went to dances in Bardon Mill as teenagers with her, protected her from her father's wrath, as she did them too, especially when they were late or they were round the corner canoodling with a girlfriend. All three were often threatened with Granda's leather belt.

I talked to my grandma's neighbours: I advertised in the local paper for anyone who'd known my grandparents. Many replied and when I talked to them they gave me a vivid picture of my grandparents, their life and work, as well as my mother and my aunts and uncles. These neighbours remembered my mother as an attractive, laughing girl and teenager, although after her best friend died from TB aged 17 she seems to have become more serious and prone to sadness. One man, who'd known her as a happy young woman, was able to give me a vivid picture of the change to a sadder quieter Emily. She loved clothes and was fashionable, although how she afforded to be so remains a mystery. She adored dancing and would do anything to get to a dance: she was an elegant dancer, light and nimble on her feet, as was George.

They told me that my mother worked in the shop alongside grandma and she always managed to have lots attention from the salesmen and customers. She knew early in life what it was to be noticed and flattered and as a consequence she learned to like attention. She made up the lack of attention from grandma with lots from her brothers and their friends as well as those coming into the shop. Aunty Vi always said that my mother learned early in her life what it was to be spoilt. '*She could always cock a feather to the salesmen,*' Vi remarked sardonically one day: Emily, my mother, had already developed the canny knack of being huffy when she chose.

From this country landscape I moved down the Tyne Valley to a pit village, Throckley, five miles west of Newcastle to explore the early life of my father and his family as well as retracing my own childhood and adolescent history. The Whin Sill ran beneath the collieries in this area too, and this time the rocks sang dark, dank, dirges of dirt and grit, lightening to arias of community spirit, the bass line transposed from Methodism. The altos and bases sang of our family myths, tantalising me; my mother hated moving to the outskirts of Newcastle and hated every day of her forty years in the pit village, no matter that she admired, adored and loved my father with a passion I have longed for in my own life, and only found once, and then for a very short time. She hated the area and my father's family: her word was hate; she used it animatedly. Her hate solo in my personal opera would be best sung by Jesse Norman or Maria Callas because they would imbibe it with the passion she felt so strongly. Once my mother had the opportunity, she kept us children away from my father's family, and hence the tantalising myths and legends – those I so need to understand, Elizabeth Jennings would say.

Like many northern pit villages the one I lived in was political and the Durham Miner's hymn filled my ears as I walked on my long-lost land with its imprints of my father's family and of my own. I thought at the time that this aria would have to be sung by a male voice choir. I could hear their voices as I walked the familiar paths of my childhood: I knew I was proud to have been raised with both a social and political conscience. This hasn't made my life easy, but I would not have wanted it otherwise.

4

New Year's Eve 1999: Looking Back to 1959

I am thinking about you, my mother, as I sit among the many New Year revellers in Salisbury Cathedral. Is this what remembering the dead means, I wonder? Thinking of someone, still knowing you have an ethereal bond? Memories roaming around my mind: your spirit living on in my memory. It helps that I have, as you once had, a good visual and aural memory: you were always a good storyteller in the wonderful oral tradition of northern communities. You are always in my mind and especially when I am here, where my spirit moves with ease: my memory, the spirit of my past, is very active today.

You didn't know I'd moved from Devizes to Salisbury because you'd lost your mind by that time: you were long gone into your own past, though in your world I was once again a little girl living in Throckley with you, Dad and David, even though Dad had not been with us since his untimely death in 1959. Last time I saw you, you were absorbed in your preferred past as we walked from your nursing home along the River Tyne path to Wylam. It always amazed me, when I was younger, how far you could walk and made us walk, but when you were frail, it amazed me even more. You had such tenacity, a very real love of the countryside, flowers, trees and birds: and you encouraged David and me to develop these loves too. We walked ten miles that day and you knew the names of all the birds and trees even though you didn't always know where you were; or who I was.

That day in your mind you were still married to Bill, my Dad, and talked of him all the time we walked, your second husband Bob wiped out of your mind by the ravages of life, in favour of your past love. You kept our Dad alive for us, even wearing his wedding ring; your first, with Bob's on top. It was courageous of you to keep your marriage pictures and Dad's photographs around too. You were so strong, then. Others found this strange and unfair to Bob, even though he didn't: it was a credit to him that he accepted it, a rare glimpse of Bob's emotional possibilities even though in everyday terms we saw little of them until Louise, your grand-daughter, was born. She released his emotion and love in ways none of us could ever have dreamed of doing. She adored her Granda, and he her. We so often made him powerfully angry and you managed to anger him despite his very real love for you, especially if he had had a few beers: then he became bullish.

I wonder if you could have imagined this change, to the twenty-first century. I wish you had lived long enough to see it, you tried hard and only missed it by eighteen months. Your parents experienced a similar, though I expect a more low key, transition in their early life, which had cataclysmic consequences. Your life and that of your brothers and sisters was turned upside down as two world wars as well as economic decline wore your parents and the community down. They all survived but could not have known how much would change, as 1800 became 1900 and the twentieth century. How can we know what this year's end will bring either? What will we experience as 1900 becomes 2000: the twenty-first century? It will remain a well-kept secret; reality will unfold month by month and year by year just as it did for you too, there will be joys and sorrows, hardship and wealth, ups and downs – and like your parents and your siblings, like you, we will survive somehow and love life just the same.

It is lunchtime on Millennium Eve; I am waiting for a very special concert to begin. I know you were never fond of books, always referring to them as dust collectors, but Dad and I were book lovers, as his Dad was too, and I have gone on loving books and poetry. Today's concert combines poetry and music; I got my love of music from you, Dad and the BBC Home Service. You sang in the Co-op women's choir: do you remember how we used to dance and sing around the dining room to our Bakelite radio standing in the corner? I have never forgotten. We loved our radio; you and Dad loved dancing. My love of music was a gift from you both, one I treasure. You had a beautiful soprano voice and you were both wonderfully skilled dancers, light as air on your feet. Louise inherited your voice, love of music and dance; and your great-grandson is musical too.

Do you remember teaching Bob to dance when he had more than two left feet? He was a giant trying to coordinate his wayward body and feet: yet you persevered and he became a credible dancer – all down to you and your need to dance. Although he never quite replaced Dad's nimble movement, did he? Yet Bob too, such a very large, shy, yet somehow burly man – his height unusual in our family as even your brothers were only five foot four or so – sang in a male choir. Do you remember when he was part of the huge joint choirs' concert in Newcastle for that wonderful performance of Aida? Music was in our soul and New Year was always the time for singing and dancing: emotional renditions, and finally Auld Lang Syne.

I'm not sure how much I am going to like Messiaen's 'End of Time' today, an apt title as it is the end of *this* time: I find him rather difficult to understand but I will follow your dancing example and try to make something of him. I have a friend who loves his music, though I find it a strain because it is atonal. Screeching comes to mind, and I am sure if I understood more about it I might actually enjoy it. I really came to hear my favourite actor, Simon Russell Beale, read the work of one of my favourite poets: T.S. Eliot. He is reading 'The Four Quartets'. Beale is a man who can sing beautifully as well as being able to read any text, empathetically communicating the writer's intended emotion or passion. His reading will act as the narrative to Messiaen's music.

That is something else that reminds me of you. If there were

45

too many people around, too much noise or stress, you would walk away shaking your head, your hands pressed to your scalp, saying, '*Ah, there's just too much narration around here.*' This was the sign that you needed space and peace. Louise and I still use the term narration, especially when we need to withdraw from a crowd or there is too much going on around us, we also say, '*There's too much narration in here, let's go.*' And no one ever knows what we mean, though we do. We give the impression of being natural extroverts but we are serious introverts who love their own company as well as being able to enjoy the crowd for a time: both of us enjoy narrating, telling stories, as well as narrative – the pleasure of reading others' stories: we are insatiable readers. Dad would have loved that about us, especially his unknown grand-daughter, Louise. Will, your and his great-grandson, has an umbilical thread to books and is an expert six-year-old storyteller who can make people laugh by his throwaway comments; he is a great raconteur just as you and Louise always were. You would be doing something quite inconsequential and suddenly come out with the wittiest, funniest comment, and we would down tools and laugh until our sides split. Louise and Will are just the same: David is good at it too.

Those who remembered you as a teenager in Haltwhistle and Melkridge said you were always laughing and full of fun. You knew how to 'cock a feather' at the salesmen who came into grandma's shop too, so they said. You were good at narrating as were the rest of the family: family and community stories past and present were our manna, always dressed with much humour so that we would find ourselves rolling around with laughter, often dashing for the loo, fighting our way up the stairs before there was an accident in the sitting room. On one occasion when you were doubled up with laughter, you made it to the loo first; overcome with hysterical laughter you shouted to us that the lid was down. Oh dear! The rest of us were hogging different positions on the stairs shouting at you to hurry up. When you emerged we were past ourselves with mirth, and so were you, despite your embarrassing wet look. Funny that you married Bob, who only had a shred of a sense of humour.

So, I am really here to celebrate New Year's Eve, something I have not been able to do since New Year's Eve 1959–60. Do you remember that ghastly New Year's Eve, your first without Bill and ours without our father? Do you? Was it wiped out of your mind? I don't think so, rather you put it somewhere in your mind, buried it deep enough that it couldn't trouble you. You had to do that. I couldn't. Actually you didn't manage to banish it; it constantly trapped you, catching you unawares every few years. I never did manage to keep it buried although I was able to give a very good impression that I could. I am hoping that after today I will be able to integrate my past so I can get on with my future, New Year's Eves included, and enjoy all New Year's Eves yet to come.

Did you realise how much I was troubled by the events of that New Year's Eve? We didn't understand, then, how some life events disrupted something fundamental to living: we didn't know how trauma worked on a human being, in a human being, and why it needed to be released, exorcised. We had the beginnings of that knowledge in relation to soldiers, so we should have understood that civilians of any age, class or role could be affected by trauma too; they too may need help. W.D. Rivers at Craiglockhart in Edinburgh was working with soldiers who were worn out by fear and by war, including some of our most famous poets, Siegfried Sassoon and Wilfred Owen. As a result we knew by the time of the Second World War how our mind could be affected by stressful and tragic events that pushed it beyond what it was designed to cope with. Probably because it was thought only war could cause trauma, we didn't use this carefully recorded knowledge, as it was seen to be only of use for shell-shocked soldiers – or were we unconvinced by the evidence because it was politically inconvenient? Much later, during the 1970s, we came to understand the effect of negative life events on human beings, the long-term effects of such experiences, and knew that Dr Rivers had been right; trauma could be eased and prevented by rest, counselling and psychotherapy, talking and writing therapies. It was really debilitating and required treatment. It is particularly poignant that neither Dad, who was almost a permanent patient in a military hospital, nor you, were offered any counselling: you were prescribed barbiturates, even though we knew enough about their long-term consequences even then.

What a beautiful rendition of 'The Four Quartets', an evocation for Messiaen's 'End of Time', which in the context of the poem said more to me than I ever thought it could or would. We are ending one time and beginning another with no idea of how the next century will play itself out. I don't know where I will be, or what will happen to me as we enter this new time. Eliot was inspired by the idea that past, present and future, triadic time, was ever interactive in one's life:

> Time past and time future
> What might have been and what has been
> Point to one end, which is time present.

Every New Year's Eve so far I have relived, with differing intensity, that New Year's Eve when you cried all day, your heart-wrenching sobs violently shaking your thin, worn body; nothing could console the black pencil woman you had become in six months. Gaunt, sad and lonely, your soul dripped from your body in your tears, they ran in torrents down your jumper and onto our dining room floor. You'd sent our uncle away without answering the door, when he'd come to take us to his New Year's Eve party as he'd always done in the past. You put your thin back against the door, refusing to move, your convulsing body still exuding rivers of tears that ran over your shrunken breasts. He tried to talk to you through the letterbox, and begged you to open the door but you wouldn't. His pleas, my crying, David's crying, couldn't persuade you to open that door. There was no rescue for our grief-sodden triangle.

I was distraught as I stood in the hall, and couldn't understand why you would not let uncle in, and why you wouldn't take us to the party. I begged you and begged you, we were so alone, but you were in another world, unable to think or act: you were drowning in your own deep misery. I have only experienced this once since, long afterwards: when I worked with children in care. A mother didn't turn up as promised and her child was grief stricken in a similar way to you that New Year's Eve. I had to sit with her and listen to those desperate sounds all over again; she howled like a wolf for almost two hours, poor child. No one I worked with knew that I had heard it all before.

Eventually you dragged your stricken frame back to the dining room and we followed you. You opened the sideboard doors and got out a range of bottles, poured the dregs, that's all they were, into your glass and drank it down in one go. Years later someone offered me a gin and tonic, I accepted the glass and then gagged – it smelled of your drink on New Year's Eve 1959. I couldn't touch it, and to this day I cannot stand the smell of gin.

The tears still poured and we could not console you. Eventually you said it was bed time and as you crawled slowly upstairs in a pathetic all-fours crouch, desperately grasping each stair as it presented itself to you, a handle by which you could heave yourself to the next one, we followed behind. You ushered us into my bedroom, not yours, and told us to get into bed with all our clothes on. We did just as we were told – funny, as I rarely did *exactly* as I was told. And then you uttered those words that I can never, and will never, forget: I have tried, but they are indelible and very real even now. You said, '*I'm going to turn on the gas fire and end it all. End all our suffering, you'll know nothing.*' You got into bed in your tear- and snot-soaked clothes and cuddled David in tightly. He had pride of place under your left arm. I was next to your right hip; your tears were now running over our hair and face. We were very silent, hardly daring to breathe. I don't know where all those tears came from: it was as though you had a reservoir of tears ready for such an evening. And perhaps you did, you had had such a long ordeal.

Mam, can you understand how terrified I was? David can only say that he remembers something horrible but has no memory of what, thank goodness, but it affected him too. I was absolutely terrified, and oh so alone in my fear. I couldn't shout, there was no one to hear me. All I could do was stay awake to ensure you didn't act on your threat. I forced myself to stay awake and very alert, the gas fire in my sight all night. I am sure now that it probably wasn't all night but it seemed like it. I knew I wanted to live, suffering or not. I understood your sadness as only a child can, knowing there was something very wrong with you. This was not my mother, not the one I knew anyway. I was very, very sad too, but I was most certainly not ready to die even if it did mean, as I was constantly told, that I would meet my dad again. I wanted to live, and death terrified me. Fortunately you soon fell asleep as did David; your gin cocktail had worked like a sleeping draft, its job made very easy by your total exhaustion and broken heart. Consequently for most of my life I have been a light sleeper, hypervigilant and so often exhausted in the morning. I tried over the years to make friends with darkness and night but I have never truly been able to feel safe. I have never known the bliss of 'zonking' out, knowing nothing.

Next morning you said you didn't remember what had happened the night before. I was so cross because I remembered every minute of it and couldn't believe that you didn't. And we never spoke of these events again, never. I was left as the cargo vessel holding its heavy burdens tight, heaving under their weight as it traversed the ever-changing tides. You instructed me not to tell anyone what 'I had said had happened'; it was to be a secret. We were good at secrets in our family. Do you remember your rules about secrets Mam? We were never ever to tell anyone anything about our private business otherwise we would get a good hiding, and you had very, very strong hands. I was an inveterate chatterbox and you threatened me with hidings to stop me spreading our secrets. I learned to still my tongue about our private business, learning early in my life to keep things locked inside, especially my feelings and fears, but continued to chatter about everything else. And I had many hidings from your tough work-ravaged hands.

After that New Year's Eve you stopped us going to see Nana and Granda, Aunty and Uncle: Dad's family. We were not allowed to visit and we lost touch. Even then I knew this was not right, that it was irrational, although I did not have such a word in my vocabulary then. You hated the fact, you said so often enough, that Granda, Dad's father, was still alive while your husband and our dad was dead. You said it wasn't fair. You blamed Aunty, Dad's sister, for passing our door and not coming in, and I believed you. I went on believing it was their fault until I was 47 years old. Only when you were very ill yourself did the truth come out. Then I was sad, and very, very angry with you.

I didn't tell you how I felt after that New Year's Eve and you never asked, parents didn't ask their children how they felt in 1959/60. You were no different. But had you asked me, Mam, I would have said I was very frightened, that I hurt all over, it was like my body was aching, stinging and bleeding: my energy felt as though it was pouring out of me but I couldn't see it lying on the floor in front of me: I was bleeding energy not blood. I would have been able to see blood and so know that something was very wrong with me. You could have sent for a doctor if you had seen blood, then I would have been examined and diagnosed: reassured. But I couldn't see my energy leaking away, along with my sanity, and neither could you: so there was nothing wrong with me and I was being silly, soft in the head, and I had to be strong. That's what I thought. You were always telling me, and so were others, that I had to be strong.

Instead, I was listless and felt as though I were floating, inches off the ground: I was no longer part of this world but some kind of ghost. Suddenly I would feel that I was no longer standing on solid ground, I was floating away, away, light as a feather, looking in on the events happening around me. This happened often, even when I was playing, and it was very scary. It seemed as though I was looking at myself, watching myself float, looking in, and on, whatever I was doing; looking in, from my invisible perch, inches from the ground, at my friends and the scenery; I was not part of what was currently going on. Then I would find myself back on solid ground and playing as I had been minutes before. This floating feeling would just come over me and I couldn't stop it, and I never knew when it would come: it surprised and caught me unawares. I didn't tell anyone, not even you.

I tried hard to work out whether I had died too. I didn't seem real. I asked myself whether I had died, and wondered how I would know. Perhaps we'd all died and yet at the same time I knew I was living as I always did, getting up in the morning, getting dressed, eating, drinking, playing and going to bed again. In bed I lay terrified with my heart thumping and my body sweating, terrified of dying in the night. It was horrible, horrible. And you didn't know. I was only ten and a half.

You said I cried relentlessly in my sleep for months. I didn't know I did, but you said it broke your heart. All I knew was that I didn't want to die, yet I thought about nothing else but dying. We were being told only the good die young because Dad was young: I was young too, and afraid. My head was full of dying. And you didn't know. And it wasn't your fault that you didn't know. I knew that then, how I don't know but I did, and I know it now. I have always known it wasn't your fault. I wonder if you ever knew it wasn't your fault and that I didn't blame you?

My insecurity was made much worse when my Nana, Dad's mother, died only ten months later and I hadn't seen much of her in the meantime. I loved her. She didn't recover from her beloved son's death.

5

Before and After the Second World War

No, I didn't know you'd moved and I can't remember our walk either, well not the walk you are talking about, and I can't remember the care home. How did I end up in a care home? I can, though, remember the many walks we did together years ago: your dad and I loved walking with you and your brother. Yes we did make you walk long distances: it was good for you, strengthened your bones and muscles and in the summer you had lots of vitamin D from the sun to build even stronger bones. We'd seen many of our school friends with rickets after the war because they had been starved of good food. We didn't starve, and neither did you, but good food and sunshine meant healthy children; your dad was a bit of a health fanatic because he'd been a weak sick baby and child and wanted you both to be healthy. Besides, walking helped you to learn about the countryside, nature and natural things: you got to know your local world, your environment by walking it. I remember taking Louise for walks too, she'd walk willingly at first then ask Granda Bob to carry her on his shoulders, and from her high perch she too learned about the countryside. It is nice to know that she is married and has a son, Will. Do you remember your dad's closest friend was Will; he died not long after your dad from a sudden heart attack. You were very upset because you loved your Uncle Will and Aunty Bett. We had lovely Sunday teas at their house and our house, such fun. We walked there and back in the summer; down to Newburn and up Piggys' Lonnen to Lemington Road End, where the road traversed the West Road.

Their house was just off Lemington Bank Top: a white council house just like ours.

Your dad and I were great walkers from the time we met: I was eighteen and he was almost twenty-four. Every summer he used to come to Melkridge on a camping holiday with his friends; they used to camp by the South Tyne between Melkridge and Haltwhistle and they were always popping into Granma's shop to buy their food and cigarettes. Your grandma created the shop out of our front parlour after the Great Depression when your granda had no work. She made the bread, cakes and butter for the shop, staying up late at night to bake, to whisk the cream for the butter by paraffin light. Sometimes she even made home-made lemonade, everyone loved that; she could never make enough. She was up at dawn summer and winter to make sure these fresh goods were in the shop, and enough bread for everyone. We also sold general goods, soft drinks and sweeties for the children.

I used to help out in the shop. One summer day in 1937 your dad walked into the shop while I was serving. He came back every day, and by the time his holiday was coming to an end he had asked me out. He was often accompanied by Peggy, his bull terrier. I was a bit afraid of Peggy at first, but soon learned to love her. Your dad, my Bill, was medium height, had deep blue eyes, lots of dark curly hair and the wryest grin anyone could imagine. He was shy in one sense, confident in another: he walked with a kind of rolling swagger, just like David did as he got older. His right hand, holding a cigarette and his left always tucked in his trouser pocket. He was such a gentle man, so gentle, kind and principled; and remained principled until he died. And he loved cars, talked of little else but getting his own car. All his money was saved toward his car because of course his mother spoiled him terribly: her only son was her precious possession, so she didn't charge him board and lodging so he could save for his car, and by 1939 he had bought his car.

We walked the river paths around what was known as Wall Country; Melkridge was only a quarter of a mile from a Roman

Wall site, with Haltwhistle having its own remains on the hillside overlooking the town and of course only a few miles from Carlisle where the Roman Wall ended, having traversed the countryside from Wallsend as the Roman's fortified their prize lands, building settlements and watch towers along the route. We'd walk over the bridge to Featherstone Castle where you often stayed on church residential holidays. Do you remember being spooked by the castle ghosts at night? Sometimes we'd go up through Haltwhistle Burn, over the velvety green hills where so many reiver battles were fought long after the Romans ruled. We'd walk south to Bardon Mill where we could always go to a dance on a Saturday night: your dad was a good dancer even then. He came summer after summer. Sadly his friend Luke was drowned in the river near Melkridge while they were all swimming together: he and his cousin Harry – you remember Uncle Harry who used to visit us, they were like peas in a pod and couldn't be separated – tried to save him but failed. They never got over the tragedy and stopped coming after that. They used to make their own cricket pitch on the riverbank: your dad was a great cricketer and played for Throckley, his home team. He loved cricket all his life, as much as he loved his football and Newcastle United. He went to every home game he could get to, dressing in his best clothes, his raincoat over his left arm as always.

I grew up in the Saxon village of Melkridge, where there were still wattle and daub houses on the green, surrounded by the stunning scenery of the South Tyne valley and learned to love the countryside, knowing the names of flowers and trees almost before I could walk. I'm glad I was able to pass on that knowledge to you and David. I walked to school, a two-mile walk there and back from Melkridge to Haltwhistle supervised by my two brothers, Bill and George, carrying our lunch, with our break-time snack in a greaseproof paper bag: dried cocoa and sugar. Most times we ate this as we walked; it was gone before we ever arrived at school.

And yes, my Bill was the love of my life. I loved Bob your stepfather too, though it was not the same as the love I had for your father. How could it be, second time around? Nothing can match first love. And yes, the people you talked to were right. I was a happy laughing teenager who was a good dancer, though I wasn't quite as good as my elder sister, your Aunty Ella: all the men wanted to dance with Ella with her dark eyes and skin, her beautiful thick dark hair; her incredible love of life and sense of humour. She had a fantastic figure, and was the wittiest of our family, she was very funny: no matter what was going on Aunty Ella would be joking about it. She didn't worry about a thing and could have had her pick of any of the men around. Of course she had no household skills whatsoever then, and never did learn: she was certainly no housewife.

Yes I remember the radio and how we loved to dance and sing around the dining room and my years in the choir. I also remember you playing the piano and me singing along to *All in an April Evening* and *Sheep may Safely Graze* – these were our favourites along with all the World War Two songs. I know you found learning the piano very hard but you became quite a good player even if you had to be forced to practice: the rows we had over your practice; I was always threatening to sell the piano to buy a washing machine. That got you practising, didn't it? David had a very good singing voice too. Bob's singing was a surprise as he had not shown any interest in singing or music, but when a friend asked him to join the choir he found he could sing and enjoyed it, to his surprise and everyone else's. He had a good bass voice. Aida was excellent and it was packed out every night. Yes, we all loved music, singing and dancing.

Narration was my bête-noire: I could only take so much noise and socialising. I loved it, but also knew when enough was enough. I think coming from a large family, all fighting their corner, I learned very early in my life to fight mine too, and it was a quiet corner. It was hard for me to make my voice heard and so I became the quieter one, although not as quiet as Uncle Bill: he was the quietest along with Tommy. Of course Tommy had already left home during the Depression, along with his elder brother Jack, so I didn't know them very well although we kept in touch, a tenuous thread ensuring some link and affection throughout their life in Epsom in Surrey where they went to work as railway men when they were teenagers, as there were no jobs in the north east. Your dad's family were loud, sometimes very loud, so it was very hard for me to be heard when they were around, If you wanted narration, then the Hollands' parlour was the place to be: our family were much gentler than the Hollands: I found them course and common. I couldn't stand the racket they made, on and on, always in competition with each other, who had the most to say? Nana usually won until you came along: you fitted in well in their house, chattering excitedly with the rest of them, undaunted.

My mother, your Granma Lambert was a gentle soul, a dignified woman who knew her own mind. She was a stalwart member of the Church of England, Conservative, and a leading member of the Mother's Union. She didn't choose to be Conservative and neither did my father: the mine and the mining houses were owned by the Lords of the Manor, the Ridleys, and so the mining families were told how they must vote. Granma was a good neighbour always ready to help others and a member of the Temperance Society, working hard to encourage men, through the counsel of their wives, to control their alcohol intake and avoid drunkenness. The Geordie Song, 'There's a little Fishy' speaks about the drinking problem of the fishermen in the north east; the miners had a similar problem.

Granda, of course, did not always agree with her on this but she kept a close eye on him: he liked a drink and underwent a change in personality if he had too much. His drinking was a constant struggle after the First World War. A kind, gentle, witty man who became angry easily, lost his temper particularly with the boys, even beating them sometimes. Granma could also do 'out of character' things: one extra job she took on every morning, despite her Christian/temperance beliefs, was earning extra cash by collecting all the Melkridge men's horse racing bets. She went from door to door collecting their bets and their money, and then walked to Haltwhistle to put the bets on for them, returning in the afternoon to collect the winnings: she had an agreement for her 'cut' for being the 'bookies runner'.

By the time I was born Granma was worn out by seven pregnancies; I was the youngest child, the reconciliation baby after your grandfather's return from France after the First World War. I was born in 1919 when Granma had a six-year-old (Bill) and a four-year-old (George) still clinging to her skirts, having survived the death of George's twin brother Gordon when he was a year old, alone, while Granda was in France. Consequently my mother didn't have much time or energy for me. After Granda returned there was no work for returning soldiers. He'd been in the coal mine at the end of the street in Melkridge before he left, so he had to do voluntary work around the area as other men were running the mines. This was very hard on the returning soldiers all over the country. They were given a very small pension. Denis Winter in *Death's Men: Soldiers of the Great War*, records that 1919 was the toughest year for those demobilised; demobilisation went on until 1922. 'It was a long time before men regained a civilian sense of time.This problem of unemployment remained an intractable one.' Miners were one of the first groups to be de-mobbed; those over 41 slipped through early in the process with the officers (my father was in this category). Each man could keep his helmet and uniform. He was given a suit at the cost of 52s 6d. If he was unemployed he received 24s per week for the first year with a supplement of 6s for a first child and 3s for others.

My father worked on a farm mending a roof: he fell through the roof and broke his back. The doctors said he would never walk again but with Granma's nursing he did: that left even less of Granma's time for me. That was a very dark time with Granda lying prone in the parlour, in terrible pain, agony, there were no pain killers. Granma did her best with her potions but it was dreadful for everyone, especially him. He was brutally bad tempered, and we had a terrible life then, so my brothers told me; I can't remember. My elder sisters, Violet and Ella, were in service in Newcastle and my elder brother's Jack and Tommy had gone south; so the younger family were almost a separate family from the older half, although I remained very close to Vi and Ella as you know. Aunty Vi, my big sister, became my surrogate mother on whom I relied for all my support. After your Granma died in 1953, just months after David was born, she became your surrogate Granma too. Monica, Aunty Vi's eldest daughter, and Pam the youngest, became my sisters rather than my nieces: I loved them dearly.

We were always proud that our father had been one of Kitchener's oldest volunteers: 37 years old when he volunteered. He was a medical orderly with the Medical Corps Northern Division and his job was to bring in the injured and dead from the Front, taking them to the dressing stations, or on a longer journey to the field hospitals and temporary morgues. He would obviously be at risk himself running to and fro across 'no man's land' with his stretcher and then across active zones to field stations and hospitals. He never spoke of his experience but according to my older brothers and sisters he came back a changed man: he was silent, morose at times, drank, and was unemployed, with no real prospect of work. This is how he came to be doing community work. I was too young to know that my father was a different man from the father my siblings had known. All I know is that he could have very angry outbursts and I was frightened of him as I got older. Granda did not complain, as our house and any work he might get depended on him toeing the line, the Conservative line. He always said he, and we, had to do our duty no matter what our private thinking might be. Our family became split politically: Uncle Jack was a big Labour man as was Uncle Bill. George, Tommy and Aunty Vi were Conservatives, and no one knows what Aunty Ella was, I don't think she cared very much about politics. Your dad was a Labour man and so I was influenced by him and became a life-long Labour supporter. In many ways I couldn't be anything else living in Throckley after Dad and I married: Throckley, having been Liberal for years, became Labour after the First World War.

Mining was not a protected employment during the First World War. Each pit was required to actively encourage volunteering for Kitchener's programme, although any pitman could volunteer independent of this. Pits had to meet their allocation. Your thirty-seven-year-old Granda was one of the first to volunteer along with three others from Melkridge. They all came back with mustard gas damage to their lungs, though it wasn't serious. You might remember the pit was only yards from Granma's back door? He didn't have to volunteer, so in many ways he became the elder statesman in the village; and we were proud that he had. He did his duty, and Granma supported him: doing your duty was very important in Northumberland towns and villages and gained you respect. It was also of course interpreted as God's will: you did God's will too. So between God's will and duty you didn't have many choices.

He never talked about his war service but we have his medals as you know, and his brass box, a gift from Queen Mary, Christmas, 1915. The inscription says *Wishing you a Happy Christmas 1915* with a note to say that the war would be over by Christmas. It was not to be, as Granma and Granda soon learned. The twins were born in 1915: Granma gave birth and buried a child during the first year Granda was at war. His courage was awesome and she was a very strong woman, is what people said of them. Women learned to manage without their men-folk, made ends meet, providing for their families and caring for their neighbours during the war.

When I was a little girl I felt my mother was worn down, and worn out. On top of which she had to deal with an unemployed, bad-tempered man who was suffering because he couldn't provide for his family. Yet they had had, according to my older siblings, a very warm, companionable relationship before the war. Granda played the trumpet and was a great showman, witty and funny, who loved the music halls – they used to travel to Blaydon by train, to go to the music hall. Granma developed a stiff upper lip to cope. I was expected to cope too, they had little time for me; perhaps that's why I loved your dad so much – he had all the time in the world for me.

Aunty Vi also loved music and sang in a choir. As well as being my big sister she was my lifeline. She too was very funny; she had a dry, acerbic, often ironic wit and was able to laugh at herself too. Wit, music and dancing despite all the trauma of war and the Depression kept us alive; we learned the value of music and dance in keeping the spirit alive and kicking. At the start of the Second World War my father was to silently see two sons also leave for war. Both returned unharmed. That must have been a terrible moment for him: he knew exactly what they were going to. I, too, had to stand by and see my two brothers, my protectors and friends, as well as your dad, go off to war. That was a terrible moment. I prayed they would return: and thank God, they did. Your dad returned early because he was ill with dengue fever and stomach problems. He was brought by hospital ship to Wrexham Military Hospital in Wales and then transferred to Hexham hospital in Northumberland. He was not my Bill, not the one that left for South Africa in 1941; he was very sick.

Your dad and I married at Holy Cross Church, Haltwhistle, on 21 September 1941 when Dad was on a short leave before going to India via South Africa. He'd been called up in 1940. Uncle Harry was our best man and Isobel his cousin my bridesmaid. We had a beautiful white wedding despite the lack of money for a dress and flowers; we had both. Granma somehow found the money to make a dress. We had a two-day honeymoon at Aunty Vi's house in Ryton while she went to stay with a friend. Then I had to leave Melkridge to live in Throckley with your Nana, your dad's mother, because that's what women did, they followed their man, doing what their husband wanted. While your father was away I worked as a Prudential Insurance agent. I hated Throckley, I knew that even before I was there permanently, and I continued to hate it for the rest of my life. You know that, you heard me say it often enough. A dirty pit village on the outskirts of Newcastle was all it was to me, and I never changed my mind. I did not get on well with my in-laws, never did, but not at all with your Nana, your dad's mother. Your father adored her and so that was always very difficult. She adored him and you, David too when he came along, but she and I had no relationship at all. I did, though, manage a positive relationship with Dad's sister Isobel and her husband Fred: your Aunty Bell and Uncle Fred and their daughter Sheila.

No, I cannot remember that New Year's Eve. I don't want to say you are lying, but I cannot remember. I can remember being very, very sad; distraught, crying forever, or that's how I remember months and years, not just New Year's Eve. My crying never seemed to stop although I tried hard to stop it, and because I couldn't, to hide it. I realised I had to get on with life and so I would dry my tears, put on my make-up and face the world: I had to pretend I was fine. I wasn't. You are right about the reservoir, it never did run dry. I am sorry that I cannot remember, and that I didn't believe you. I know too, until recently, that no one has ever believed you. It is too shocking to believe, I can see that now. How could your mother be so out of control? How could she be so traumatised that she could think of killing herself – bad enough to orphan your children by committing suicide, but to murder them, well that is unforgivable. I do remember to my horror how many times I threatened to commit suicide by putting my head in the gas oven. I am ashamed of that and it must have been very frightening for you. I am not proud of how many times I talked of committing suicide, actually telling you how I would do it too. There were many times when it seemed to me to be the only answer: to die and have an end to all the misery, poverty and stress. I longed for the peace of the grave – to lie next to my Bill.

How could your mother, I, begin the preparations and plan for filicide, a crime that is beyond understanding? I don't really know, and I suppose because I cannot remember it is easier to believe that I never did; that you were, and are, making it up. After all, children are always making things up, fantasising; their thoughts and ideas can be laughed off, denied and forgotten. These are just childhood fantasies. We get over it by saying that this or that child just wants attention; this was always our answer. Too much attention meant spoiled children and I was never going to be responsible for a spoiled child; as it was your Nana and Aunty Bell spoiled you quite enough.

Perhaps denial was easy for me because everyone knew you always did come out with ridiculous ideas, or so I thought at the time; you seemed never to stop trying to work things out and were forever asking questions. Questions, questions, questions, you drove us mad with them, some of which we couldn't answer. You always did have a strange mind; you seemed to be years ahead of yourself. Your Nana, that ridiculous woman I couldn't stand, used to say you had an old head on young shoulders, that you were years ahead of yourself. She should know, she was a Spiritualist. I didn't believe all that nonsense though.

Besides in those days had anyone believed you and told social services, they would have taken my children away. You know I always had a terrible fear of social services and being taken into a workhouse. You forget that during the war and the Depression in the north east I witnessed many families being broken up and taken to the workhouse. I heard their screams, their terrible crying. I had a pathological fear of losing my children, or being taken into a workhouse. I had no money, no job; I couldn't see how we could survive. If pitmen were killed in an accident in the pit, their family lost their home: the workhouse, or a similar fate, awaited them. Because your dad was ill for so many years and hardly worked, we had survived but we were very, very poor by the time he died. I had worked for the Home Help Service as you know, but that didn't pay enough for us to be able to pay the rent, buy our food and pay for coal. I had no skills to get a decent job. I was out of my mind with worry. Perhaps I thought it would be better that I chose to die with you, than lose you.

I know I had long periods of time when I didn't want to live. I will tell you that. I often felt that dying was preferable to a life without your dad. I cannot remember actually trying to end it all – even talking about it. I'm sorry. I really don't. I remember misery, deep, deep misery and I remember Uncle Fred coming to the door. After that I do not remember anything.

You didn't know either, because you were very young, that I had just been told by the War Widow's Pensions' Tribunal judges that I was no longer entitled to a war widow's pension. I was informed of this not long before Christmas 1959, six months after your father's death, following a long drawn-out hearing; it took months for them to come to a decision. The British Legion provided me with support and a solicitor throughout. Although your dad had had a military disablement pension since 1942, he didn't die of war related injuries or service. He died of oesophageal, stomach and liver cancer and therefore I was not entitled to the pension. We appealed and the answer, despite doctors' evidence that the original stomach problems had been caused by war service, stress and the ravages of dengue fever, the judgement remained the same: no pension. I was beside myself with grief, anger and worry. The workhouse loomed large on New Year's Eve 1959/60.

6

Visiting Grandma, 1952

I'm told I always woke up happy and usually talking fifty to the dozen. Pulling back my curtains I'd peep out of the window to check that outside was still there, and with as much noise as I could manage, jump out of bed, shouting and pestering Mam about which day of the week it was. I loved mornings and still do. If the weather was kind, the order in which the tasks were done during the week depended on the weather: Tuesday was house cleaning, Wednesday we walked to the Co-op (known as the Store) on Hexham Road to buy fresh goods such as cheese and bacon that weren't delivered to our door by the Co-operative van. Mam liked to choose her fresh goods with a great deal of 'umming and ahing' and changes of mind. She was very fussy. Thursdays we usually went to Lemington for the fresh fish and called at the bakers, Mr and Mrs Potter's, for some treats. Potter came twice a week to our door delivering bread and bread buns, baps and stotty cake and I loved running out to his green van and helping him to take off the tissue paper covering the breads. On Friday we went to Grandma Lambert's in Melkridge near Haltwhistle. On Saturday mornings we called at Billy (Joyce's) the butcher's in Newburn to collect the meat for Sunday. These negotiations were fraught with tension. Mam would argue with Billy about the specific cut she required, check it carefully, re-check it before it was wrapped and very often take it back later in the day if she got it home and found she wasn't happy with it. I've known her take it back on Monday just to let Billy see that it was tough, or that it had too much fat, not enough fat, or he'd cut it wrongly! Whatever, if it wasn't right and not as she'd expected then it was definitely Billy's fault not hers. Buying meat stands as a metaphor for Mam's life: it never was how she imagined no matter how hard she tried to make it so. Reality was nothing like the fantasy. Billy must have dreaded her coming into the shop.

Sometimes we went into Newcastle, or to see one of her two elder sisters. Aunty Vi lived in Ryton and Aunty Ella in Gateshead. Sunday was church and Sunday school which I'd started attending when I was two, and I loved it. Unlike my friends I had to go to an afternoon Sunday school and it took me years to understand why my parents were often in bed when I got home. Some Sunday afternoons in summer we went for long walks up the river Tyne to Wylam, to the Exhibition Park or to the seaside at Tynemouth. On most Fridays Mam and I went to Grandma's on the Red United bus, which we caught outside the Co-op.

Mam would tut, flick her head back, and tell me I'd have to learn to be quiet and in the same sentence what I'd wear to go to Granma's. Getting ready to go out was a very important part of our routine. Mam was very particular about her own clothes and mine. We didn't wear our 'old rags' as she called them but our 'best clothes' when we were going out, even if it was just to the Co-op. Our old rags were for indoor and outdoor play and for her housework, washing day or gardening. Her old rags were partnered by rollers in her hair under a scarf tied in traditional northern fashion. Her headscarf was folded corner to corner into a triangle then the long folded edge was placed at the back of her neck and the ends brought up to the top of her head and tied in a knot. The ends were then tucked into and then under the knot, leaving the giant knot resting just above her forehead. I had old rags too, clothes that were past their best, for playing in. In our wardrobes our old rags were kept separate from our best clothes: and I still keep my old rags separate, even now. To visit Granma's I usually wore my kilt and my pink wool coat; it had a black velvet collar. I had clean white or fawn socks, fawn in winter and white in summer, and red shoes or brown suede boots, bootees, as we called them then.

Later, walking to the bus stop, I'd hold Mam's hand tightly skipping and chattering up the hill. '*Stop talking, you're a proper chatterbox, you could talk the hind legs off a donkey. Watch where you're going instead of talking.*' I'd look down at my feet to watch where I was going along the pavement and over the dilly line (colliery railway line). I'd check my white socks and flashing red shoes, keeping my eye on them, doing as I was told, or at least trying to.

I learned to walk looking down at my feet, but I'd soon forget and my feet would jiggle and dance, jump, and skip without me telling them to as we walked along. Mam hated me to get my shoes and socks dirty because she insisted the neighbours judged her by how clean and tidy I was, and if I was scruffy they'd think she didn't look after me properly. I learned that it was very important for me to stay clean but I never managed it for very long. I was always being told that I had to be a 'little lady' but my trying to be this little lady didn't last long either. I'd be running, tripping up, dancing and skipping and when she told me to stop my jiggering and keep still I'd say, '*They just do it Mam, on their own like my tongue. My feet and legs just work by themselves, I don't make them.*' This would make her really mad and she'd pull my arm hard to make me realise she expected me to take notice of her and do as I was told. '*Don't be so cheeky madam. You'll have to learn to control yourself.*'

'*Why?*'

'*Because you'll have to, you're just like your Nana Holland, argumentative, got an answer for everything, you drive me mad.*'

Five minutes later I'd skip off up the hill with her *walk nicely like a good girl* ringing in my ears. But I couldn't walk nicely because I was always excited. Going on a red United bus to Granma's house instead of the usual yellow double-decker bus to Newcastle was always exciting. Red buses took me a long way from home and there was a lot to see as Granma lived in Melkridge, near Haltwhistle, high on the Northumberland moors. Haltwhistle is the penultimate town before Carlisle and the Cumberland border, and travelling north east on the border of Scotland. In the border wars Haltwhistle constantly changed hands, like a prize bull at market, between the Scots and the Northumbrian Border reivers.

As we waited for the bus I'd jiggle and dance around the bus stop, round and round Mam's legs. She'd let me free for a little while and then remonstrate, '*Stop it! Stop drawing attention to yourself. You stand still now, you're old enough to be able to stand still.*' The longer she left me to jiggle around the wilder I became. According to my parents I was always testing to see how far I could go. I never did stand still, or sit still for very long; nothing's changed.

When the bus came I'd climb the steps in front of Mam hurtling down the aisle to choose the seat and start to sit myself down next to the window. '*Don't sit down yet, wait, let me check to see that the seat is clean first. I'll brush it before we sit down, we don't want pit dirt on our good clothes. I'd rather stand than sit down after a workman or a pitman.*'

No matter where we were going this was her constant refrain; she'd embarrass us all by checking the seat and woe betide any pitman or dirty workman that brushed against her. They got the sharp edge of her tongue and probably catch her 'just loud enough to hear' comments, about how trying life was if she had to travel in the same bus as they did. I'm sure she would have had special transport for all workmen (and it was mostly workmen in 1952) if she'd been a politician. She just wasn't born to be amongst muck and I'm sure many backhand 'Lady Muck' comments were shared on the bus behind her back. Most of the workman lived near us, around the houses too so I can imagine their comments to wives and family:

'*By that Mrs Holland's a stuck up prissy wifey. She'll get her cum-uppance someday, somebody'll bring her doon a peg or two.*'

I wasn't allowed upstairs on our own yellow buses. The Newcastle buses for our area, the number 3 and numbers 16 and 17, had an upper deck for smokers. We weren't allowed up stairs even if Dad was with us. I didn't understand this because Dad smoked Woodbines if he was short of money and Players Navy Cut if he'd just been paid. I often went to the shop to buy his cigarettes.

'*But Mam, Dad smokes.*'

'*That's different. Anyway these red buses are easier for us because smoking's not allowed.*'

Having cleaned the seat she'd show me how to sit like a lady. '*Like this, smooth your coat down neatly before you sit down.*' I'd do as I was told, then plonk down like an uncoordinated puppy telling her the seat prickled and nettled my legs. '*Sit still and it won't. Here's the money to pay the bus conductor.*'

We knew some of the bus conductors: Mr Emerson who lived 'up the back garden from us', that's to say his garden backed onto ours, and Mr Teal who lived over the road from us. They knew where we were going and would have a chat with Mam about going home. This always worried me because home was our house and I couldn't understand why she called Granma's *home.* They'd ask me where we were going and I'd ask for one and half to Melkridge. They'd take my money and give me the tickets, telling me to keep them safe because the inspector might get on the bus and want to check the tickets.

I was always careful with the tickets, folding them in half, and half again, clasping them in the palm of my hand. I knew we'd be thrown off the bus if I couldn't show the inspector our tickets and so I became a little bit in awe of the inspector and worried that we'd get stuck in the country, not get to Granma's or back home to Dad. This was my first experience of authority that could do things to me that I wouldn't like. It was also my first experience of anxiety and not feeling quite safe. I gave any ticket inspector a wide berth and rushed past them if I could, especially in the train station or on the train.

The tickets safely in my hand, I'd squash my face to the window to see everything flash by. I loved the whoosh, whoosh feeling as my eyes tried to hang onto what I saw. I swung my legs in time with the hard growl of the engine. I loved noises and I liked to imitate the sound of the engine in my head, brum, bruuuuuum, bru——-m, ow——l, ow——l, ra-a-a-a-s-s-p, ra–sp. It made a lovely sing-y tune as the engine sounds changed when the bus stopped, started, went faster or slower. There was an engine inside my head and only I knew it was there. I loved going to Granma's on the bus watching the countryside flying by.

I'd ask Mam where we were and she'd rhyme off the towns and villages along the route. It was a wonderful journey west along the Tyne Valley. We boarded the bus outside the Co-op in Throckley and drove through Heddon-on-the-Wall, a small village renowned for its run of Roman Wall by the roadside, its blacksmith and farms and now its pub, The Black Swan. It had been a colliery village too and from here I could look over the Tyne Valley to Ryton and Crawcook and see the lazy grey pit smoke rise on the horizon. Leaving the built-up industrial areas, Throckley was just on the edge of these, we travelled from Heddon through Horsley, a beautiful stone village, to Wylam famous for George Stephenson and his steam engine. His cottage sits by the riverside where we often walked on Sundays, Dad telling us about George and his engines and the birth of the railways. William Hedley built his 'Puffing Billy' in Wylam and used it to take coal from Wylam Colliery to the Staithes on the Tyne at Lemington. This was replaced later by his 'Wylam Dilly', which operated until 1862. It was a Wylam born blacksmith, Timothy Hacksmith, who helped Hedley and then worked with George Stephenson on the construction of the Stockton to Darlington Railway and his own engine 'The Royal George' and then of course the 'Rocket'. George overshadowed his colleagues even though they pioneered the way for his own inventions; Hackworth introduced locomotives to Russia in 1837.

From Heddon we wound our way on the A69 toward Corbridge east of Hexham. This was the Roman site of Corstopitum with the first fort built in AD 80 by Julius Agricola. The remains of this fort are visible a short distance from the village. Corstopitum guarded an important crossing of the Tyne at the junction of two roads, Dere Street and Stanegate, and had an important strategic role in Agricola's attempted conquest of Caledonia. When this failed, Hadrian's Wall became his major endeavour and Corstopitum declined until it became a military supply base for the east part of the Wall, housing a civilian settlement with tradesmen and merchants becoming one of the most important Roman towns. Excavations on the fort began in 1906 revealing temples dedicated to a number of different gods, a fountain decorated with statues and fed by a small aqueduct. These finds are on display in the museum along with the Corbridge Lion: a lion devouring a stag, probably a tomb decoration for an officer. At Port Gate, Roman Dere Street crossed the Wall as it continued on to Redesdale toward Caledonia. The Devil's Causeway joined Dere Street at Port Gate and can be traced north eastwards across Northumberland to the mouth of the River Tweed at Berwick.

Corbridge continued in importance during Anglo-Saxon times as it was the capital of Northumbria being the scene of two important battles in 914 and 918 when the Anglo Saxons, helped by the Scots, fought against the invading Norsemen from the settlements in Dublin, Ireland. In the twelfth and thirteenth centuries Corbridge was one of the wealthiest towns in Northumberland and was forever being invaded by the Scots, eventually being occupied by David I of Scotland in 1138, burnt by William Wallace in 1296, by Robert the Bruce in 1312 and David II in 1346. The Vicar's Pele Tower in Corbridge is a strong reminder of this violent history having been built around 1300 from the ruins of Corstopitum.

Leaving Corbridge, travelling west past St John Lee, we stopped to pick up passengers from the market in Hexham: the main market town of South Northumberland or Tynedale. There is little evidence that Hexham was a Roman town but rather its history seems to begin three centuries after the Roman exodus in 674. Wilfred the Northumbrian saint and bishop founded an

71

abbey in Hexham. This had the status of a cathedral, and became a See stretching from the Tees to the River Aln. Later the cathedral and See of Hexham paled into insignificance against Lindisfarne, Chester-le-Street and later Durham Cathedral.

Wilfred, educated on the holy island of Lindisfarne, travelled to Rome and loved the European churches and decided to develop a similar style in Hexham, hence Hexham Abbey and Ripon being the first to use stone, some taken from the ruins of Hadrian's Wall and the fort at Corbridge. Wilfred was a character, flamboyant, highly intelligent as well as educated, and he posed a threat to the King of Northumbria. He was imprisoned and eventually banished to Sussex, converting South Saxons to Christianity. By the time the Normans invaded Hexham, the abbey was part of the See of Durham regaining its independence as Hexhamshire in the gift of the Bishops' of York in the reign of Henry I. The folk song *Hexhamshire Lass* refers to the area's history:

> *Hey for the buff and the blue,*
> *Hey for the cap and the feather*
> *Hey for the bonny lass true,*
> *That lives in Hexhamshire.*

The Vikings destroyed both Hexham and its abbey in 875 when Halfdene the Dane invaded though the Scots remained the main threat and Hexham the target of border raiders. Yet despite the abbey and the town being rased numerous times, continuous rebuilding has ensured our inheritance: a complete historic abbey, or priory church, still stands today with only the crypt under the abbey floor and the Frith or Frid stool in the abbey choir being the original work of Wilfred. The frith stool was a symbol of sanctuary for criminals and refugees as well as the stool upon which Northumbrian kings were crowned: it was probably a primitive Bishop's Throne. Celia Fiennes visiting in 1698, records: '*This is one of the best towns in Northumberland except Newcastle – it is built of stone and looks very well, there are two gates to it,*

many streets some are pretty broad all well pitched with a spacious
market place with a town Hall on the Market Crosse.'

At points along the road I could see parts of the Roman Wall;
the Romans knew how to choose their spot to make them feel
at home. The Northumberland landscape resembles Tuscany without
the sun and Tuscan light but with blustering cold winds and
heavy rain and snow. Of course not all the Roman soldiers were
Roman or even Italian. Many nationalities had been enslaved to
form the Roman army and so it was multinational. Geordies and
Northumbrians are a 'mixed race', indeed, multicultural.

On our journey on the red bus, a few miles north west of
Hexham, we passed the finest remains of the fort Brocolitia a
major site on the Roman Wall to the east of Housesteads with
one of the best preserved temples or Mithraeum, a temple to
Mithras, first discovered in 1949. Mithraism was a form of worship
to the Persian god of life encouraged by the Roman army involving
them in secret initiation ceremonies. Christians were probably
responsible for the destruction of the temple as they strongly
disapproved of Mithraism. A shrine to the Celtic goddess Coventina,
who was worshipped by the local people of the area, stands close
by (known as Vindalanda now).

As the bus continued its journey we were privileged to enter
Wall country (my great-grandparents, maternal and paternal, were
born in the village of Wall) and to pass the Housesteads Roman
site on our left, Chester's Fort, where Hadrian's Wall crossed the
North Tyne via a bridge. The Roman name for this fort was
Cilurnum and it lies on the north bank of the Tyne in the most
beautiful wild surroundings. It is one of the biggest in the Wall
country and housed cavalry regiments. Visiting this site many
times since those early journeys I still wonder at the technological
achievements of the Romans. It has a Roman Bath House with
hot and cold rooms, a sweating chamber and a large entrance
hall, a Turkish bath for relaxation in one of the coldest spots in
Northumberland where the winds in winter howl over the moors
and even in summer can be cool. We are indebted to the classical

scholar and amateur archaeologist John Clayton who owned most of the forts on the Wall and whose house is on the site. Oddly enough in the border war years the Border reivers and mosstroopers protected this site, using the forts as permanent bases, thus preventing the 'locals' raiding stones from the Wall to build their houses.

Our bus took us west through Haydon Bridge, the settlement of Old Aydon. There has been a bridge here since medieval times, one which has often been shattered by the flooded Tyne and barred by the border reivers to keep the Scots out. From here still going west we passed through Bardon Mill watching the smoke curl from the colliery. Throughout the journey I was able to look across the valley to the Durham side of the river: Riding Mill, Prudhoe, the other half of Corbridge and Hexham, then look across from Bardom Mill to Plenmellor, a rich green forested area in which sat the distinct homes of the gentry. If we sat near the back of the bus, and it was a fine day, I was able to look back down the Tyne following its confluence and point out landmarks such as Newburn Pit and the beginning of the industrial landscape of Newcastle. I soon learned by heart the names of the towns and villages. These sites, distanced a little from the road now by the A69 Newcastle to Carlisle bypass, are all part of the UNESCO World Heritage Site. Mam knew her land and its history by heart and I learned all about the Roman Wall on my trips to Granma's. I was very lucky to be able to understand the beauty and history of my homeland and encouraged to be proud of it – and I am.

I tried to remember everything I saw on my journey's to Granma's so that when I was in bed at night I could see it all again in my head. I still do this automatically when I'm travelling. Wherever I go in the world I visualise the beautiful scenery so I can re-run my own video afterwards. I was to remember what I heard as well as what I saw, even when I wasn't supposed to hear it. Mam and Dad called me 'big ears' because my ears were always flapping to hear what I wasn't supposed to hear, and then of course they had the embarrassment of me blurting it out at inappropriate times, often in awkward places. Dad always asked me what I saw on my trips to Granma's and filled in more details about the history of our land, as he loved the Northumberland moors too. So it was very important for me to remember and be able to tell him what I'd seen. I learned to watch and listen very carefully. I am a very visual learner and love observing, although my daughter would say staring! I learned to stare early in my life.

The houses on the journey really attracted me. They were stone and looked strong and hardy as well as warm. If they weren't blackened by coal dust, surprisingly some weren't, they appeared golden. We lived in the White City one of the earliest council house estates built to strict specifications and to look like a private estate. The houses were large with a separate kitchen, lounge and dining room as well as a washhouse, three bedrooms, a separate toilet and bathroom. Some houses had two bedrooms and there were bungalows for older people built around their own green space. We had very large front and back gardens, trees lining the streets and a large green space for playing. All the houses were painted white with different-coloured front doors. We'd moved in when I was two but on my journeys to Granma's I knew I wanted one of these golden stone houses which Mam said we couldn't afford.

Then, as I was enjoying my journey, she would suddenly, or so it seemed, grab my hand and pull me up. She'd dust me down even though I hadn't been anywhere to get dirty, and put me behind her. We'd move forward down the bus as it came to a stop outside Granma's front door. Mam'd step very carefully down one step at a time while I secretly got ready to take a flying leap from the top step onto the narrow strip of pavement outside Granma's house. Her usual retort was, *'Can't you do anything ladylike?'*

Then, on my ready revved-up engine feet driving my engine head I'd break loose and race round the lane, helter skelter into

Granma's back yard. As I hurtled away from her Mam'd shout after me, '*Don't run, don't run, you'll fall and hurt yourself, get dirty, ruin your coat.*' I knew if I fell I'd get smacked for messing up my best coat because it would be filthy from the cinders in the back lane.

It took Mam a while to pick her way through the muck on her very high heels; she always wore lovely high stiletto heels, which she said were window dressing for her good legs. Dad said Mam had beautiful legs, and she did. There was a pit and a pit heap at the end of Granma's lane, another up the hill, and another two in Haltwhistle. The dust and muck from these pits blew along the village road. The neighbours made more muck by tipping their ashes outside their back gate. I found it very funny when suddenly a lady's head, wrapped in a headscarf like Mam's when she was in the house, popped up over her gate pouring hot red and black cinders, sizzling and steaming, onto the lane from a black bucket. I was aware even then that Mam changed when she saw this. Her face became very tight, cross, and she always pulled me away. '*Come on, away from there, you'll get filthy.*' I wasn't allowed to play in the back lane because of the dirt.

Yet Mam called this her home, and told people at our shops, and the bus conductors, that Melkridge was beautiful and how much she hated leaving it. She was always saying that she was going home, wanted to go back, and how much she missed it. I knew from very early on how much she hated Throckley, she said she hated the place, hated our house, and yet when we were in Melkridge there seemed to be things she wasn't happy with either. It took me a long time to understand that she lived physically in one place but fantasised how her life would have been had she still lived in Melkridge.

When we arrived at Granma's she was usually up to her elbows in flour. She would hear us coming and wipe her arms down with the tea towel ready to take our coats. I had my coat off straight away and was quick to find Granda's three-legged stool so I could stand on it ready to help Granma bake. She would roll up my sleeves, cover me with a tea towel and then I'd put my hands in soft white velvet dust. I loved Granma's smell and I melted into her side to help her make things: bread and bread rolls.

Granma never said very much, not even to me, she just nodded her head as Mam talked. Unusually Mam always seemed to have a lot to say at Granma's even though she never chattered at home. I would watch and listen but they'd talk in nearly whispers so I couldn't hear. If Granma thought I might hear she'd turn her head to Mam, nod and say, '*The bairn, Emily, mind the bairn.*'

They had secrets. I knew what a secret was because Mam had warned me I'd get a good hiding if I told anyone that Dad sometimes worked on Sunday: it was a secret. So I told the lady who took me to Sunday school and when I got home Mam asked if I'd told anyone. I must have been naive or stupid because I said I had (I've never lied easily) so I had another good hiding and she left her hand marks on my bottom and thighs.

While the bread was rising big and fat on Granma's hearth I made shapes (buns) with the dough and put them on the baking sheet Granma'd put at my side. She lifted me high up in her arms when my buns were finished and carried them in her other hand to put in the little oven. There were two ovens: one very big one and a small one in the shiny black range in Granma's parlour. When I visited recently I was kindly shown around the house by the present owner and I could still see the scars of the range in the wall. My bread shapes went into the small oven with the heavy handles and big black knobs. Granma told me in her very strict voice that I must never touch these. When she opened the door of the oven we had to jump back because we were hit with hotness. After she'd put my tray in she set me down by the hearth and brushed the flour from my clothes.

'*When'll mine be ready Granma?*'

'*Soon, Pet, soon. Don't fuss now.*' Granma didn't like fuss. She was very kind and gentle but her arms were big and strong and I knew she just expected me to do as she said. The thought of a hiding from those big arms was enough to silence me and prevent me from arguing with her either.

My bread shapes always came out like biscuits and we ate them with our cup of tea. I could hardly wait for the proper bread to come out of the oven but Granma brooked no singing and dancing, I had to learn to be patient. When her bread was ready Granma knocked on the bottom of the tins to check it was done, then she'd drop it out of the tin onto her cooling tray. After awhile she'd carefully slice a loaf and thickly paste it with her home-made butter and we'd gobble it up while it was still warm before we had to leave for the bus home. I was never ready to leave her warm smells: hers, the baking bread or her kitchen.

I'd be very quiet on my way home with my face glued to the bus window. I loved to draw things in the condensation my breath made on the window and reel off all the village and town names backwards. When we got off the bus Dad was there to walk us home. I'd dawdle and trudge down the hill I'd skipped up earlier. Mam didn't need to hold my hand because I walked at her side like a good dog: we had twin golden spaniels, Beauty and Lance, she liked them to walk by her side nicely too. I always felt very happy because I had Granma's smell inside me. Mam had two Granma loaves in her bag.

7

Sounds and Smells of War

It must have been awful for you and for Nana and Granda when Dad's 'call up' letter came: as it was for thousands of mothers, fathers, brothers and sisters between 1939 and 1944, and afterwards too for National Service. You had already seen your brothers leave for war and now your lover: how did you cope with that I wonder? You must have been very, very frightened, your mind running away with you, wondering if you'd ever see your fiancé or your brothers again. How can I know how that felt for you, as fortunately, until very recently, none of my generation had to leave for war unless the army was their career. I wonder what you would have thought about the Iraq war. I think you'd have been against it, as we are.

Bob knew war only too well. He was a young soldier working in radio transmission and one of the last to be taken off the beaches on his twenty-fifth birthday at Dunkirk. The poor man survived Dunkirk, only be to be taken back to Portland Bill for a short rest and training, then ferried back on one of the Normandy landing vessels. From there he climbed the cliffs and walked across Normandy: he said he and his soldier colleagues were starving. They would pull any old vegetable from the ground they walked on and eat it, mud and all. He trudged on toward the French–Belgian border helping to free Belgium. While there he fell in love with a young Belgian woman, married her and brought her back to England. For me, this alone explains his sometimes uncontrollable anger as well as his political rage and will; his hatred of war too.

Your grand-daughter and great-grandson hate war. Will has never so much as looked at army toys, never asked for them and hates fighting of any kind: it is almost as though he knew before he was born that war was wrong. Have his brain patterns been socially canalised, shaped by a long family history of pacifism and hatred of war? Dad was passionately against war: he discussed it endlessly with anyone who came to the house: ranted sometimes too. He was almost demented over Suez, I remember. Every morning he'd listen to the news on the radio and have his paper at breakfast, tracking the developments day by day, discussing it with everyone who came to the house, with his father and friends – it was his pet topic. I learned there was something terrible about war long before I was able to understand exactly what war was. It is possible that brain patterns can change over generations through such experiences: we have not had to sow the seeds in Will. He has never asked for these boys' toys, just ignored them and cannot watch anything about war on the television.

Of course I saw relatives and friends go into the army, but this was in a time of peace and different – very different – they chose to go. Now, after sixty years of living, I have known my own loss and fear at different stages of my life so can empathise with how you might have felt: lonely and scared, lost and frightened. You were engaged and looking forward to a married life together, a future. You must have felt very angry that your future might be jeopardised.

You left me Dad's war records and his health and pension record. As a child I remember you putting these in the hall cupboard, the one under the stairs, wrapped in brown paper, after the tribunal, and I knew you'd lost something important; that you had lost what you wanted and we needed: Dad's war pension. I understood too that we would be poorer without it than we would have been with it. Our security was threatened. At the time, being even poorer than we were seemed impossible to me as we were so poor anyway. Nobody believed we were, as you always put on a show and we never, ever, looked poor, but we were. I always admired the way you could do that: put on the show, especially for the outside world. I found the records when we cleared the house after I so cruelly put you in the nursing home. Some months later I sat down and read them, twice. I have read them many times since, piecing together the facts with my memories, checking and re-checking that my memories are accurate.

David and I had such a row about putting you in the nursing home. He did not want you to go and I had to persuade him, after he had called on you and found you with your skirt on fire. You used to stand with your back to the gas fire in the dining room to warm your back, and you'd got too close and hadn't even felt your skirt take fire, nor smelled it. As I remember, you'd always done this; it was comforting, especially if you had a lot of back pain. The day David found you it was a signal to me and to him, although I was more ready for it, I think, that the time had come for you to be cared for. We'd known for some time that this was coming but he couldn't accept it, so I think we left it too long before we acted for your safety. He found it very hard to come and visit you in the home because he felt guilty that you were there in the first place. He hated the idea and it took him a long time to forgive me; he blamed me for acting before he was ready. Perhaps I acted for myself too, guilty that I was not geographically near enough to you to look after you myself. I lived too far away. I hope you know that I, we, could not have let you have some terrible accident in the house, alone – dying alone. I hope you forgive me for not living near to you and not looking after you, as you believed a daughter should – as you looked after your own mother.

Your GP, the one you liked and we didn't, would not help us to make the transition from home to care because she believed we were exaggerating your condition. Do you remember, we had had a struggle with her when Bob became ill and we asked about the Marie Curie hospice? Her reply to David and me was quite astonishing, shocking in fact. She said that Marie Curie was not a place 'for people like us'. I was so angry. Do you remember that I worked in the cancer field and through my connections I was able to get Bob into a lovely Marie Curie hospice, the one at Denton Burn? Bob chose the time to leave his home, your home; and it was the moment he said goodbye to us both. When we told her that we had a place in this particular hospice, she said, '*How on earth did* you *manage to do that?*' She was simply furious.

You were already in the first stages of dementia and I took five weeks leave from work to care for you and see Bob cared for. I had talked to his consultant on the telephone and knew he was likely to have only weeks to live, at most five. I have never been sure whether you knew what was really happening: I think you had flashes of understanding, emotionally you certainly did. At times you were very confused because you were visiting a hospital and sitting by the bed of your husband, but it was clear you sometimes didn't know who was in the bed, Dad or Bob. We forget that people with dementia feel emotions but cannot always express them, and that they most certainly grieve.

I remember, a few days later, I was sitting with my cousin Sheila, Dad's niece; we had taken you up to bed as you were exhausted, and you cried and cried for hours. We didn't need to ask why but it was very hard to know whether you were grieving for Bob or for Dad, the two were intertwined. I knew the extent of your grief because I had heard it before. You had renewed your relationship with Sheila a few years before after almost thirty years, out of loneliness. I was very glad and it enabled me to renew my relationship with her and her daughter Sandra, a link that helped me discover the truth about you preventing contact with Dad's family. You didn't intend that to be cruel, but it was – your pain and grief dictated your response, you couldn't see them without your own loss being magnified.

I remember being deeply moved as I watched Bob that last morning before we left for the hospice. He was in terrible, unbearable pain and I could see he was struggling with it – it was beyond his control. He tried to hide it but the sweat was pouring down his face as he lay on the settee, while his skin was cold. I tried to comfort him as he wiped his brow with the towels I gave him. After he and I agreed that he should go into the hospice as soon as possible, he raised himself from the settee and knelt down to hug you as you sat in your chair; I had rarely seen him hug you. Only you know what he said to you, but whatever it was you and he knew it was his final goodbye. He was distraught at leaving you because he knew, more than we did, how serious your dementia was becoming. He'd protected us against knowing just how bad it was and by then he had almost taken over. And you sometimes showed great frustration about the loss of your routines and skills. After he retired he gradually took over the household jobs because he didn't know how to fill his time. Then as you became forgetful he became your memory without realising that this would only make the situation worse. You used to cry because he was leaving you very little to do, even taking over the kitchen and the washing, baking cakes. Your identity started to slip away even then, you just couldn't stand up to him. You had always looked after the money and then you found yourself in the awful position of not having any because he took that over too, you had to walk behind him in the Co-op while he chose the food and paid for it, your feisty independence eroded. The little woman walking behind – and you did not like it a bit. I remember coming to see you because you were not well, and you cried and cried because he had taken the change out of your handbag; you had no money of your own. And he thought he was helping and caring; caring is such a delicate process.

He and I said our goodbyes on the back door step, and with a lump in my throat I was able to say that he and I had had a difficult relationship and I was sorry I hadn't always made it easy for him, but I knew he cared about us and I cared about him too. I thanked him for being such a fantastic granda to Louise. He had never said he loved us, your children, although he was always telling Louise that he loved her. He had more difficulty loving Andrew, David's son, as his ongoing health problems became more obvious. Having said that, the day Andrew finally left hospital at three months old, having been so dangerously ill, surviving many awful operations, Bob led the campaign to raise funds for the hospital and baby care unit. There was a lovely picture in the *Evening Chronicle*; he was holding Andrew and you were at their side as you handed over the hundreds of pounds you'd raised. Bob's heart was always in the right place, though he often found it difficult to show affection. He was very sensitively cared for during those last three weeks, which were full of the most terrible suffering I have seen as the cancer ate his brain, fortunately very quickly.

Well, I got my comeuppance because my fight for Bob made it harder for David and me when it came to your turn. Your doctor didn't like the fact that I had gone over her head and would not give us any help whatsoever with you. She said you were capable of remaining in your own home even though we all knew you were not, and if I went against her she would resign as your GP. I could not do that to you. When she visited you were still able to put on the show, and she was easily deceived; so, we had to organise everything ourselves. I have never forgiven her or Newcastle Social Services for their autocratic, authoritarian behaviour because you deserved better; more than anyone, you deserved better. I am sorry you didn't get it. We tried, I even wrote to your friend the mayor to ask him to act as an advocate between the GP and social services. Even he failed. That old social class thing again – it never goes away, though we make a good pretence of believing there was and is equality.

What puzzled me then and still does now is why a Labour-led authority, with a positive history of developing services for its people took such a hard-line position on what was best for you when you were ill. For me being a socialist was always about improving care and conditions for everyone, no matter who they were or where they were. I was very angry and felt very let down by the very services I believed I could trust.

I begged Newcastle social services to let me bring you to Salisbury but they flatly refused. Wiltshire, although a Conservative county through and through, agreed to find a place in a home near to me as long as Newcastle Social Services agreed to transfer the money to them. They were supportive. Newcastle refused with the ridiculous excuse that you would not be able to hear your own accent or see your familiar views. I felt that you would rather hear my voice, Louise's voice, than views and Geordie voices. After all, you were such a snob about accents weren't you? You would not allow us to speak Geordie, as you insisted you were Northumbrian and the Geordie accent was common. When we travelled south for a holiday you told us not to speak on the beach, wouldn't let us play with the other children because they wouldn't understand what we were saying. You should hear David's voice now: he is broad Geordie and loves it, and is more confident than he's ever been. And me? Well I have never lost my Northern twang even though I have lived here in Wiltshire for nigh on thirty years now. Louise, well she can speak Geordie, the Wiltshire dialect and Queen's English, and now the Californian dialect too; she can swap to any of them as need demands. She is, and always was, a very good actress.

Me and my northernness are one, and always will be even though Charles – you remember when I met and married Charles, a Wiltshire man – has always tried to get me to speak more quietly, because Wiltshire people do not have the loud voice I have. He tells people gloatingly that my voice has softened over the years I have lived in Wiltshire. Maybe it has, but he can still feel the full force of my Geordie heritage when I'm cross, especially with him! In your zeal to eradicate my Geordie accent, even though you had little money, you sent me for elocution lessons before I was due to go to college interviews. At least I learned that I could project my voice in different ways and soften the harsher edges of my dialect, which I know helped me. The lessons also helped me with expression especially when reading out loud. Most of all they gave me confidence. Thank you.

According to Dad's military records he was called up on the

19 March 1940 when he was twenty-five years old. He weighed 127 pounds, had good eyesight in both eyes and was 5 feet 4 inches tall, declared mentally sound and category A1 fit. He was enlisted on 18 April 1940 and saw service on 13 May. He had been a sickly baby, almost dying of pneumonia when he was only months old in 1915. That must have been terrible for Nana as she had already had four miscarriages following the birth of her daughter in 1910. He was a desperately wanted son.

At his military health check he was found to have very bad teeth, not surprising as the water was very soft in Throckley; but the main reason was poverty and lack of dental hygiene. It was a long time before I understood why you both had false teeth when I was a little girl. You also didn't teach me to clean my teeth. I was eleven before I learned in domestic science lessons that I had to clean my teeth morning and night. You had to buy me a toothbrush and toothpaste to take to the lesson. Consequently soft water and lack of primary dental care meant I too have had poor teeth throughout my lifetime. I forgive you that, both of you, as you didn't know about dental hygiene. You lost your teeth after David was born because of pyorrhoea, common in those days as the baby drained your body of nutrients and your teeth had not been looked after as a child because your parents couldn't afford a dentist: before the National Health Service was in existence and dental care had to be paid for.

As you know so well, Dad was first deemed ill on 17 March 1942 when he was an inpatient at the military base hospital Drymen, in Glasgow, while training. He'd had stomach pains for seven years, saying they were often severe at night. The military doctors found epigastric tenderness and rigidity when he was examined. He had a barium meal but there was no definite evidence of a gastric lesion so he was treated for gastritis, though he still set sail for India via South Africa as member of the support troops for the Burma campaign. He was a motor mechanic trusted with keeping the military vehicles in working order for the troops to cross the border at any time, night and day.

Dad found himself in a military hospital again in September 1943 in Colaba, where he was diagnosed with dengue fever though he still complained of stomach problems. And yet again on 2 August 1944 he was admitted to the Indian Base General Hospital with the same symptoms. Each time stomach problems were suspected but never really diagnosed or proved until 25 September 1944 when a duodenal ulcer was definitely diagnosed. Only days after your third wedding anniversary he was sent home for treatment, disembarking in the UK on what later, in 1948, was to become my birth date: 24 October 1944; but not before being bombed in the Pacific Ocean by the Japanese. His hospital ship went down but he was safe, and still carrying his presents for you: a red silk embroidered kimono and a set of four painted Japanese eggshell china cups and saucers, which I still have. He disembarked at Wrexham and then travelled north to Hexham General Hospital where the ulcer was seen as more severe, requiring treatment and a medical discharge from the army. By this time he had been in hospital in Glasgow in 1942, Bombay in 1943, Poona in 1944, and Hexham, 1944. He was described by doctors at Hexham as '*a somewhat tired looking man*'. Dad was discharged from service on 15 December 1944 with a military pension amounting to 30% of full pay for a duodenal ulcer aggravated by military service. He had to have three-monthly reviews at Dunston Hill Military Hospital, near Gateshead, then in County Durham. And so began a ten-year intimate relationship with Dunston Hill Military Pensions Hospital. I can still see it in my mind's eye: I can see Ward 7 in detail, all the patients, even now. I could create the scene for a film set.

Recently I persuaded David to take me to see what was left of Dunston Hill. He did not want to go and found it very difficult, but he agreed. The main house had been turned into flats and houses but the wooden wards at the back are still there and are now a day hospital for those with mental health problems. I stood on the ground I had walked so often earlier in my life and remembered. David was distraught. Being five years younger than me when he was visiting Dad in hospital, he has memories too but at that point could not articulate them; he was deeply emotional, and very upset in a David way. You know the David way: morose and silent, head down and mute, followed by what seems like sullenness, but this is David thinking and trying to work things out. The words come later, sometimes months and years later, but they come.

Dad continued to be in and out of hospital though he worked as much as he could when he was well, but it was all a terrible strain on you. He worked at the Air Force base at Ouston maintaining military vehicles, for Thompsons of Lemington, driving lorries. He loved tinkering with any engine he could get his hands on. Unfortunately he couldn't afford a car but he still dreamed of owning one one day, which drove you mad. I think his dream helped him to cope and got him through operation after operation with you at his side. Each operation took more and more of his ulcerated stomach away, until it was the size of a small coffee cup. When he was at home, which wasn't often and usually for short periods of time, you cooked his special diet alongside food for us, and didn't complain.

And yet, in those early years, we had so much fun, there was so much love in our house despite everything. You were both social people and we were always out and about visiting people, relatives and friends visited us too. We had wonderful holidays and good home-cooked food, using our own garden vegetables, every day of our lives. Dad couldn't eat your food, eat what we ate. I have always, as you know only too well, loved my food, so I cannot imagine how he must have felt as we tucked into roast beef and Yorkshire pudding, apple pie and custard; and this only one of your many menus. How could he possibly face, never mind eat, his white tripe in milk? Yet he never ever complained. What did it feel like for you to watch Dad eating his tasteless white diet? Were you ever frustrated?

My goodness, Mam, I have just realised as I write this why I have been so impatient with Charles when he fusses about his food: he is so fussy and has to control what he eats. He doesn't like too much food on his plate, or large servings. He has to have his food arranged as he likes it on his plate. He must know exactly what he is going to eat, how it is cooked, otherwise he cannot eat it. He has never liked wasting food, and I agree, yet he prefers shop cakes and puddings to homemade ones, because his mother's cooking was so awful, so he says. This has been interpreted as home cooking is awful and so he tries his best not to have home cooking. He has to know exactly what food to buy and likes to do the food shopping himself. As a consequence I have lost interest in food and cooking: my cooking skills lie dormant. I am very sad about this. Although it is probably good for my weight it most definitely hasn't been good for our social life. You know how you and I always liked to entertain, how I loved doing dinner parties, well I have hardly ever entertained others around my table over the last twenty-eight years and I have missed that more than anything. If I have, then everything has to be planned the Charles way. Food has become a big problem in our house and I have never found a solution. Consequently, I have been impatient and sometimes very, very angry with him, and with myself. We have rowed over food for nigh on thirty years: food has come between us, and still divides us.

One time, when we lived in Devizes, where you often came to stay even though you thought it was a pretty boring place to be, I had cooked a beautiful French fish dish and a lovely pudding to eat before we went to the theatre. He took one look at it and didn't want it, it was fancy food. Something in me snapped that night. I had the carving knife in my hand ready to portion the fish and, to my great chagrin and shame, I lost my temper and threatened him with the knife just as you had once threatened Bob in the same way. How observed behaviour reasserts itself in times of stress, when there is an instant reaction without reflection. The meal was ruined, we didn't eat the fish, or the pudding, and we didn't get to the theatre. It was a very desperate evening and not the first time a meal had been ruined; and it was not to be the last although carving knives were non-existent in similar quarrels. I didn't know it then but this pattern was to repeat itself lunch times and evenings over the years, and even on holidays. In his mind, even today, I traumatised him. Our relationship was severely threatened and very damaged. Every now and again he brings it up: his wife, the potential murderer, the woman who traumatised him and whom he cannot forgive. He says he has lived in fear of me ever since.

For me, watching Dad eating special white bland food, seeing him watch us eat our lovely food, was torment. If he did try to eat the same as us, and he did sometimes, then he had to leave the table to be sick. The smell was terrible and the upset palpable. I can never forget the sounds of him being sick, nor the smell, and to this day I cannot help anyone who is being sick. I care about their plight but I am useless. Sometimes he was sick even though he'd eaten his special food. Our house was full of sickness.

During Bob's last days I was in the room when he was about to be violently sick. I ran for my life with my hands over my ears, and you got up from your chair and coped. When I returned, you were cleaning the sink and Bob was quiet in bed. I sat in the beautiful garden of the hospice my head in my hands asking why, oh why, did I have to live this sickness all over again? I could not face the repetition and felt I was a coward. You acted quickly because you were back in that other time with Dad. You knew what to do even though on a minute-to-minute basis you hadn't the foggiest idea what was happening. The behaviour for caring for the sick was carved in your brain.

I still cannot eat white tasteless food like pasta, semolina, rice pudding, tripe, plain white fish, coddled eggs, boiled chicken, barley soup and so on. Do you remember when I wouldn't eat the barley soup you'd made and Dad and you tried to force it down my throat because you both believed food shouldn't be wasted and it would do me good? I think I had a cold and it was an old-fashioned remedy for colds and flu. I kept my mouth firmly shut and you couldn't even prise it open. You gave up in the end because we were all terribly distressed.

I remember too the time the teacher in my infant school made me sit all afternoon at the dining table, alone, until I finished my semolina pudding. She lost and I didn't win: how could she have known I couldn't possibly have eaten that white sloppy pudding. She didn't know that was what my Dad had to eat, nor the associations that white pudding had for me. I cried and cried but still couldn't eat it. She thought I was being defiant and naughty and I hated that more than the thought of eating the pudding because I wasn't a naughty child and she knew that too. She made me sit with that white slop until the bell went for going home. I never told you, because I thought you would be cross too, that you'd think I was being a naughty girl.

8

Call Up Papers

I can never think about that morning without becoming angry: you cannot imagine know hard it was when those call up papers came. I was living in your nana's house because your dad and I still didn't have a home of our own. I hated 'living in' as we used to call it, with your Nana. I couldn't bear to let him go and cried for days. My brothers wrote to me from wherever they were in Europe, they had both signed up early in the war so we had some idea how hard it was for them. They both wrote brief letters, those so typical of boys, usually saying they were safe and little else. On a day-to-day basis I didn't know where they were and the time in between letters was particularly tense. I, like thousands of others, was always waiting for that black-edged letter to be delivered by the telegram boy. If I went to bed having escaped the black-edged letter, then that was a good day gone, I could sleep easy that night. Next morning I'd start worrying all over again. Women and families around us were receiving black-edged letters all the time; we just didn't know when it might be our turn. Every day without that letter was a blessing. The joy of an ordinary blue flimsy envelope that I could open without fear was indescribable.

Your dad's letters were very infrequent, having to come across oceans, so in many ways I knew more about my brothers' day-to-day lives than I did your dad's. I was frightened for all of them and worried all the time. I had to work, which helped, and I was close enough to my sisters Vi and Ella to be able to relax sometimes too. I had my nieces for company, my brother Bill's eldest daughters.

We had fun walking your Dad's dog Peggy, and sometimes during summer we even ventured to the beach despite feeling guilty that we were enjoying ourselves while our husbands and brothers were fighting on a daily basis in some foreign land. Aunty Vi's daughters were close by. Her elder daughter was more like my sister than niece and not that much younger than me; we were such good companions, though none filled the empty space in my heart – Bill's place. The most frequent phrase we all used was that 'life must go on' and it did.

My main worry was that my Bill, and my brothers, would come back changed as my father had, or badly injured; unable able to work, walk or dance, to resume the life they led before they went to war. Perhaps they too would come back to unemployment and forced voluntary work, no prize at all after risking life and limb, their lives.

Your dad's father, Will, had been injured in the First World War. He'd been a groomsman responsible for the cavalry horses in France and he'd been badly kicked by an injured horse and so walked with a limp, or that was the story he chose to tell. Who knows what happened to him. I never thought he was badly injured and believed he played on his limp all his life. I always thought he was lazy, that he could have done much more than he did.

Before the war he'd been in shipbuilding in North Shields, he was a ship's plater alongside his father; they were both skilled men. After Granda Holland returned from the war he was a fireman at the colliery, first at Newburn and then in Throckley, he got your dad his first job in the colliery in Throckley when he left school. So, like my father, your Granda Will came back from the first war a changed man too. I suppose I never thought that he might have hidden scars; I was too young and selfish to think beyond the story he told and we all believed. I'd grown up with my own war-worn father, so couldn't take on another worn-out man. Unlike my father your Granda Will didn't use alcohol to heal his soul; he read books and newspapers and educated himself in the Miner's Institute, passing his love of education to your dad, and to you. Granda Will was a very quiet man and your dad's best friend; he was a shadow in his own home, only coming alive in his garden or with your dad and his friends, including his son-in-law, your Uncle Fred. He was a locally respected gardener growing summer and winter vegetables, fruit and flowers; your dad learned his gardening skills from his father.

War drives a hard bargain. Men and women may return from war alive, uninjured, they are the lucky ones. If you can call it luck, after all they have been through in war. And of course some men and women have a good war; they grow from war and mature. We cannot ignore the fact such people exist: war gives them opportunities, and that includes the politicians too. Or they return injured, ill, unable to work; able to work but traumatised or damaged mentally. Many do not return, having been buried in some foreign soil. These are very stark choices for all who take part in war, and for their families. So, yes, my mind did sometimes run away with me but my mother and sisters would not let me dwell on it, and I just had to get on with things as they were.

This getting on with things was much harder for me when I was living with your nana, your dad's mother. She was not able to put anxiety and worry to one side and get on with things; neither could your Granda Will. He worried constantly about his precious only son, as did your aunty. Her husband remained in the mines and she didn't have to worry about him. There was tension in Throckley, just as there was in towns and villages all over the north east between those who stayed to keep the mines going, the Bevin Boys, and those who went to war. During the Second World War there were no quotas so going to war was a more personal decision, although call up papers took some of the sting out of the individual decision making.

I didn't like these choices either, as I could never quite understand why some men could stay in the mines and some chose to go to war. Men who stayed in the mines were often referred to as being cowards.

Every day the Holland family were beside themselves, especially if there were no letters or cards: all day and every day, their way of coping was a sharp contrast to my family's stoicism. Quite honestly, there were times when they were hysterical, especially your nana; no one could do anything with her if she had no news. I thought she was pathetic. She should have had a much stiffer upper lip; or more backbone as we used to say.

She was beside herself with anxiety and fear, because her favourite younger brother had been killed in the last days of the First World War. He was a pilot in the RAF, and his plane was brought down while he was on a German bombing raid. She was not as stoical as my mother by any means, and lived on a knife edge while your dad was away. I think she would have supported him if he'd been a conscientious objector, and believe me he thought about it, she would have done anything to prevent your dad going to war; but duty to King and country came before anything else for all of them – even your father's family.

Your nana was not nearly as conventional as my parents, in fact she abhorred convention in all its forms, took no notice of any rule or regulation, doing just as she liked when she liked and brooking no interference from anyone, so for her to believe in duty was exceptionally hard – but she did, although she didn't like it. No parent wanted their son to go to war but neither did they want their son labelled a coward by anyone and everyone. So the consensus was that men who could fight should support the cause and women should support them. If a man was called up, only poor health or conscientious objection could save him from going to war. We believed, too, that many men chose conscientious objection as an excuse not to go to war because they were too frightened: they, too, were cowards.

You are right, we as a family were not supporters of war, and your dad was terribly afraid of another war. I'm not sure what he had seen in his time while on the borders of Burma, he didn't talk about it, but he was certainly anti-war on his return. None of us would have used the word pacifism, I'm not even sure I know how to pronounce it or spell it. That is your word not ours, but you are not far wrong about us being against war of any kind. Bob, your stepfather, would have done anything rather than go to war again. I think, as he was so much more fanatical about everything than the rest of us, he might have refused to go to war again no matter what pressure was put on him to do so. I have to say though, that for all of us, the bottom line was that if your country needed you, it was your duty to go and fight. We would have been equally unhappy if we had to wave our husbands or sons off for war and yet watch others' sons be conscientious objectors: that would not have been a good place to find ourselves, it was all too difficult.

Your dad could have coped with being a non-violent protestor and he would have supported any conscientious objector but I don't think I could have done so, so easily. I would have been very angry if men had chosen to stay at home during the Second World War or any other war. Your dad suffered, your stepfather suffered, and why should they have suffered when others were able to take the easy way out? No, I hate war but I am not and never was a pacifist. Your dad and your stepfather believed in the prevention of war by political means, through talking and political dialogue; both felt that war should be avoided if at all possible. But if it couldn't be prevented we all had a duty to protect our country, they believed in the idea that some wars are just; we have to fight to protect our country and our way of life. I know you have always thought that all war is wrong and I agree, but when push comes to shove it is not easy to become a conscientious objector either, even if you are a pacifist, or whatever the word is you used. Until you are in that situation, or you have lived through war, it is easy to say what you think you will do, when actually you don't really know until it happens. You always did think you knew best, just like your nana!

By the way, I am not proud that I kept you from Nana and Granda, Aunty and Uncle and your cousin, but I'd never liked them, and I couldn't stand seeing them after your dad died because I couldn't understand why a man should die before his father. It just wasn't fair. Your nana always wanted your dad's attention, and he was always prepared to give it. I know I was jealous but I couldn't help it, and after you were born, Nana wanted yours too.

As usual you have all the right words, and you have fancified the arguments. You always did think far too much, always liked to find an answer, going on and on sometimes until you got an answer, it drove your dad mad sometimes, and he'd say, *'That's an end to it, leave it there will you.'* And you would still try to push it further. You seemed always to need to be one step ahead of the rest of us. Nana never stopped arguing either and that used to upset me, you know how I disliked arguments, neither of you would ever give in until you got an answer or made a decision of your own. I am very glad, though, that you do think seriously about war, and that Louise and her family do too, and that my great-grandson is not a macho boy who likes guns and soldiers. No one should take war lightly and you should always strive to prevent it. After all I tried my best to encourage David not to be macho, and I succeeded. I'm not sure that he was pleased with the way I brought him up but I did my best to make him a gentle male like your father and my brothers. I am proud of that. I don't know what I would have done if David had had to go to war. I can't bear to think about it. It was bad enough when he joined the air cadets and had his air rifle – we were terrified that he'd shoot himself by accident or shoot someone else. He used to hang out of your bedroom window shooting at targets in the back garden. You were terrified in case he got hurt.

You saw with your own eyes and heard with your own ears the results of war: we visited Dunston Hill Military Pensions Hospital every Saturday or Sunday, and in school holidays on Wednesday afternoons too. You saw and heard the aftermath of war in Ward 7, where Dad resided only too often. We knew that he was entitled to his war pension and that I was entitled to it after his death even if the nature of his illness had changed and developed into cancer over the years. The terms of his pension were clear, a duodenal ulcer aggravated by war service. Knowledge has changed since then, now ulcers can be treated with antibiotics, but then they were treated by surgery as well as drugs. Cancer can be the result of stomach ulceration, but ulceration can be aggravated by stress and distress and this was the case with Dad. Yes we were made poorer by the loss of his military pension and I was very insecure constantly wondering how I would make ends meet. I don't think we should have had to be in that position: Dad's medical history was very clear and the doctors agreed. Why deny widows and children to save money? You know that the same thing is happening even in the Iraq and Afghanistan war – oh yes, I know what's going on. I have never forgiven the Ministry of Defence for their decision about my war widow's pension, and it coloured our lives, your life, and our attitudes and beliefs forever afterwards.

As for putting me in a nursing home, I cannot remember being there, nor can I remember my skirt taking fire. I suppose I became very confused after Bob died. He and I had our differences and many rows, sometimes violent, but I was still lonely without him. As for being looked after, it would have been nice if you'd been near to look after me, but I knew you wouldn't be coming home and had prepared myself for that a long time before. I had to move away from my mother when I married so had done the same thing myself. It would have been nice if you had lived near but I understood, probably more than you think I did. I missed you and Louise, we all did, but I understood the need for a woman going where her husband's job was. We saw a lot of you and Louise even after you moved, so it wasn't too bad.

From where my spirit is now I can see it was hard for you when Bob and I became ill, and that you did your best to find a solution. You certainly found one for Bob when he was very ill and dying. I was glad to have you around for those weeks although sometimes you treated me as though I were an imbecile. Do you remember when you were trying to discuss Bob's funeral with David? You both thought I didn't know what was happening until I turned round and said, *'I'm not a child, you know.'* The look on your faces, you got such a shock that I understood some of what was going on. You see, when you slip into dementia you may not always be able to explain what is happening around you, you can't find the right language because it has got lost somewhere, I don't know where, that's what it feels like, your words and thoughts have got lost and cannot find their way home, like Mary's lambs in the nursery rhyme. It is a puzzle where these words of yours go especially after you have had them for so long. You search and search your mind for the right words but you just can't find them, you see things and struggle for the word to describe them, sometimes you even know what you want to say but you just can't find where you have put the words, they play hide and seek with you, some days they are there in abundance and sometimes there are few words available: there is a word famine.

It may surprise you that I had other ways of understanding. I could feel things, especially if I had felt them before. I knew when Bob was sick and it was full of blood that he was very ill, I knew where he was when he was in hospital, I knew there was something very wrong, because I had seen it all before. I knew what sitting by a hospital bed meant. I just couldn't find the right words, but I could feel what was happening. It made me mad that you all assumed I didn't understand. And then sometimes I'd find the right words and you'd all get a shock and realise that I wasn't as far gone as you thought I was. I knew, as soon as Bob was sick in the kitchen, that something terrible was about to happen.

I was very glad that you came home and found Bob a nice hospital because I couldn't do any of that any more: my skills were lost somewhere along with the words, hidden from me. They too had gone walkabout and got lost just like my words. I couldn't manage him at home, he was such a big heavy man anyway, but as you know he was also becoming very violent, his anxiety was very high, he was frustrated, he was very ill with the cancer fast spreading to his brain. And I was muddled up because I didn't know whether I'd gone backwards into the past to your dad, or whether I was in the present with Bob. I had no idea, but I knew what was about to happen. I could smell it and feel it and I could not control my crying even though I wasn't sure what I was crying about. I could just feel sadness and grief creeping up on me like a dark storm cloud. I could feel the threat, a pressure hemming me in, as though the cloud storms were looming overhead and I needed shelter from what would be a downpour.

Do you remember when your dad, David, you and I went to Saltwell Park in Gateshead before we had tea at Aunty Ella's, and the storm clouds gathered and gathered so we began to make our way out of the park? We'd been to see all the exotic birds in their cages. We didn't make it out of the park and were caught in the most awful thunderstorm I had ever been in. It was so frightening and we couldn't hide under the trees because of the lightning. People were screaming and shouting for help; and in the panic a dog jumped up, scared out of its wits, and bit your dad's hand. It was so close and warm too, hardly a whisper of air that day, it made it hard to breathe. That's how I felt knowing Bob was very ill, as I did that day pre-storm, stifled: there wasn't a breath of air. I felt as though my air supply was being slowly turned off and there wasn't a thing I could do about it.

Being the youngest child of a large family was good in many ways as I always had support, protection and comfort over the years as well as a lot of fun, but the downside was the loss of my parents and brothers and sisters, one after the other. Not that long before Bob was ill, my two closest brothers, who'd always protected me, died within eighteen months of each other. From being thirty-two years of age I had witnessed twenty-two deaths, so by the time I was facing Bob's illness I'd already lost all those close to me, except you, David, Louise and Andrew, and my nieces of course. I never expected to be widowed twice, who would, especially as Bob was a big strapping man and always healthy. He'd never ailed.

When I was seventeen my best friend died of TB; that was terrible, and I don't think I ever fully got over it. Death seemed to stalk me, and it depressed me. That changed me from the laughing teenager to a more serious young woman, who knew that young people died, not just old ones. So when Bob became ill, somewhere inside myself I knew what was happening, some imprint in my brain was kicked into action helping me to see the signs, feel the changes, feel the fear, though I couldn't explain. I had a ready template that helped me interpret skin colour, weight loss, smell, all sorts of signs others would probably miss – but I didn't. Bob had also fallen down more than once while out walking David's dog, Holly, and had had to be brought home both times by a stranger. The doctor said there was nothing wrong, couldn't find anything, but I knew there was something and it was only weeks later when the sickness started. My brain, although in some ways lost to me and out of my control, was still capable of giving me signals I did sometimes understand: there was a knowing in me, and an aura around the sick and dying person I understood only too well.

I can understand that David didn't want me to go into a home and that you quarrelled, that's maybe the wrong word, disagreed is perhaps better, because it must have been difficult for you both. As I don't remember I can't say what it felt like for me, except I do remember there was a choir in the home and I loved singing. You were always the big sister, the one who had to take the responsibility, perhaps that was the way it was between your dad and aunty, she was his big sister and your dad thought you should be David's protector, as she had been his. We gave you a lot of responsibility for David, especially when your dad was in hospital. You took him everywhere with you, even to Nana and Granda's and your aunty's in Westerhope; on the bus when you were only eight. When I think back it must have been hard for you not to feel responsibility for him, and of course you were often in charge of him and so he must have felt bossed around at times. I expect he felt you, being the elder, were the one who always had the last say. So, in my case, he felt you made the decision and he had to go along with it. Or did he know that it was the right decision but couldn't face the facts? David was always silent and deep; he was a thinker like you, but he didn't make the noise you did about his thoughts. You were exact opposites in that sense. Everyone knew where you were by the chatter, and no one would know where David was because he was quiet: you overshadowed him.

The more I think about it, the more I realise how hard it must have been for you. You always, as instructed by Dad and me, had to watch out for David's safety as well as your own. Do you remember when he got lost; Dad and I had to go to the hospital, he had one of his medical reviews, and we left you in the charge of a neighbour. You were both playing outside with friends and had gone into the field opposite the house. Somehow during the afternoon you had forgotten your three-year-old charge and he'd wandered off and you'd not missed him. When we got home David was nowhere to be found. Your dad went mad, and after searching we found him half a mile away sitting on the bankside overlooking a dangerous swamp. You had the biggest hiding of your life from your dad. He took you up to the bathroom and slammed the door. He used the slipper on your bottom and legs, you screamed blue murder as he was shouting about your carelessness; it was terrible. I had never seen your father so angry with you. I'd smack you but he had never smacked you as he did that day. You were distraught and we thought you were a very naughty girl for losing your brother. That day you were not very responsible, and we had to let you know that it wasn't good enough.

A year or so later you were in trouble again. You always took David to Sunday school and collected him from the infant class to bring him home with you on the bus. He was four by this time. The infant Sunday school finished before the junior Sunday school and the children were looked after by a Sunday school teacher until their bigger brothers and sisters were dismissed. This particular day, we don't know what happened, but the younger children had been running around and David was pushed over by another child. He badly banged his head on the corner of a chair and split his head, very near his eye. He still has the scar. You brought him home on the bus with only a big hanky someone had lent you to stem the blood. You couldn't stop the bleeding because the gash was down to the bone and needed a lot of stitches. Your dad and

103

I were so mad at the lack of care and safety at the Sunday school and this time we didn't blame you. We blamed them. You see, I can remember facts about the past, but by the time I was ill, very little at all about the present or the recent past. Even then sometimes I'd surprise myself and all of you, by being perfectly aware of the present. I cannot tell you how confusing it was for me, never mind the rest of you.

We expected you to take a lot of responsibility and you were good at taking responsibility for yourself and others. Your infant school teachers made you their shopping monitor when you were only six coming up seven: they gave you the money and a note at lunch time and you had to go to the shop at the end of the road to get their bits and pieces including their cigarettes. At seven you used to walk from home up to Throckley chemist to get your dad's prescriptions. One time you fell down on the cinder path and your knee was a filthy mess. But you still went for the medicine before you came home to have it looked at. Dad had to bathe it in salt to clean the cinders out and then bandage it up. He cleaned it every day for a week until it began to heal. You used to go to Stan Wright's little hut of a shop on Newburn Road to get your dad's cigarettes: twenty Players Navy Cut, or if he was out of money, Woodbines. I used to send you to the same shop to get groceries sometimes too. You could be trusted to do any task or job properly.

I can't remember the doctor you said I liked, but then I had had so many doctors after my own doctor retired: you remember him? You were friends with his eldest daughter before he sent her to boarding school. My doctor was wonderful to me during the years your father was ill, and after he died. Your dad had left my doctor's practice to sign on in Throckley many years before he was ill, but I chose to stay. I moved when my doctor retired, and because Bob was also a patient at the same practice; he'd been with the practice from being a child. I can imagine your clash with the lady doctor: she sounds very forthright and you always fought for what you wanted, especially if you wanted fairness and justice. You were like a bull at a gate if you thought you, or we, were being treated unfairly, quite rightly too, but you didn't back off when others would. No, you'd fight to the death for fairness. And if you failed, you'd cry bitterly.

But then, you'd seen me fight for my rights once or twice. You were stood at my side when I had to fight the Ministry of Pensions when I was on the Home Help. They had docked my pay because someone told them I had worked an extra few hours for an old lady and therefore broken the terms of my widow's pension. I don't know to this day who had reported me but I had done the work voluntarily and not as paid work. Do you remember? We had to go into that official building and there was a large desk with a glass window from the desk to the ceiling and the man spoke to us through a hole in the glass: I was incensed. So, I suppose you learned to fight your corner in terms of justice. You saw me win too, because there was no proof that I'd been paid, the Home Help had no record of extra work.

I am glad you fought for Bob and for me: you were right, I needed care. I would have hated being burned to death, or falling top to bottom down the stairs and ending up with a broken neck; or lying there with a broken hip for however long before I was found. I'd been through enough and needed someone to care for me. I hate to admit that, but it was true. Being widowed a second time was the last straw; it was the end of the line for me, I'd had enough and from what you say my mind had definitely had enough and was giving up of its own accord. I think minds do give way with the stress of the struggle of life; it sometimes feels like you are running the same old film over and over again and you just want it to end: you want the film to end forever. No more film. No more repeats. I was ready for eternal rest, or the promise of it anyway. I had not had much rest in life and I was very, very tired. I'd gone into a world of my own and didn't seem to be able to find my way out.

When I woke up in the morning I couldn't even remember what I was supposed to do. I'd always had such strict routines, cooking, cleaning, washing, ironing, shopping, going to the hairdressers, to the Women's Guild, the choir. But I couldn't remember which came first, or when I should get ready, where I should go, or even how things in the house worked. I couldn't find the food, or remember how to get hot water. The house was an alien thing to me, and the cooker even more so. I'd wander into the garden but couldn't fathom what I was supposed to do there, so I'd knock on a neighbour's door for help. I felt embarrassed by that, especially the day I had to ask a neighbour if she could give me some bread; David was embarrassed too. I couldn't find what I'd done with my money and would search and search, but never find it. And I ended up going out in the weirdest clothes, purple woolly tights; these must have been yours when you were into psychedelic clothes. Maybe I bought them for a fancy dress costume, who knows, but I don't think I'd ever worn woolly tights never mind purple ones. I know someone stopped me and told me I needed my hair done: the cheek of it. My hair was always done as you know. Yes, my life fell apart quickly after Bob died. I remember David rang me one day to say he wasn't well and wasn't at work. I knew what to do then. I filled the kettle, boiled it, filled a hot water bottle, put a towel around the bottle and walked to his house to give him his hot water bottle. But I forgot which house, fortunately he saw me and I could give him his bottle. He was so pleased, he started to cry. I sat with him for a while and then he took me home, as by then, I had forgotten where I was, and where I lived.

I am glad you have read your father's military records and the notes about the tribunal. I knew you would one day and as I have said, I knew you would try to see justice done. We did not have a very good start to our marriage because of the war and living in. I was terrified of your nana, most people were, but to have to live with her without your dad was very hard. He could always get his way with her when no one else could. I certainly couldn't. We had tried hard to find somewhere to live but didn't manage it until you were a few months old. Eventually, after the war, your dad found a derelict cottage by the roadside, where the power station used to be, in Lemington. It was damp and dark but it was ours and we made it as nice as we could. This had not been my dream.

So, throughout the war I lived in with Nana, periodically going home to see my own mother and father, visiting my sisters and often staying with Aunty Vi in Ryton. It was no life but I had more life than some women, and some money as I was earning. I never, ever told anyone what it was like living in with Nana: she was such a harridan. She had a wicked temper when roused, and it didn't take much to rouse her temper, she didn't like anyone telling her what to do or how to do it; she had her own ways of doing everything, and she was no housewife. She thought she was a good cook but compared to my own mother her food was less than second best. I know there were those who thought I was a snob and I suppose I was: my mother had such dignity and I didn't think your Nana had any at all. She was desperately worried about your dad and couldn't put herself in my shoes as he was HER son and I was second fiddle to her, I was only his wife. I really did hate her.

We knew he was not well while he was in India and we were not surprised as he had been a weak child and had shown signs of ill health all the time I'd known him. His mother fretted about him and that made me more nervous too. We didn't know the extent of his ill health when he was abroad, only when he returned to Hexham hospital. We didn't even know that he had disembarked, or that he'd been bombed by the Japanese. We had a telegram to say that he was in Hexham hospital and so the whole Holland family left home to camp at the hospital. I don't think the hospital had seen anything like it: Nana beside herself with worry was not a sight anyone needed to see and the nurses soon knew who was boss. She was hard to persuade to leave, and so I didn't get much chance to be with your father until later that week. Only at the end of the week were we made familiar with your dad's illness. During that time he and I had only very brief moments alone. I loved the kimono and the Japanese cups and saucers he'd saved when the ship was bombed: I am so glad you still have them and treasure them.

107

Yes, you are right, it was very hard to cook his special food and even harder to watch him eat it, struggle to get food down and then have to leave the table. But I had you and then David too, so I had to make sure you were both fed properly and that your mealtime was structured, you finished your meal and had your pudding too. I did not let you leave the table, and Dad always struggled back and sat out the rest of the meal with us. It must have been purgatory for him. He was adamant that your routines should remain sacrosanct and he did his best to ensure they were. Mealtimes were important times and when he was having a good phase we had lovely mealtimes, chatting and discussing; you learned to discuss everything around our dining room table: your dad was a very good debater. I liked listening and never said much. When we had company, friends or relatives for meals, they all accepted that Dad had to leave the table sometimes and it was all done with as little fuss as possible. And yes, I remember the smell and the sounds of sickness. The one thing all of it didn't do was put you or David off your food: you both loved food. And I didn't know about the semolina at school – you never did like rice or semolina pudding and the teacher would not have known that, or what was going on at home.

And as for Charles, I warned you, Bob warned you. We knew from the beginning that it was going to be a difficult relationship: he was so much older than you, and so different. Do you remember the Christmas Bob and I came down to stay and Charles cooked the meal, in your house? That made me mad and I could see where the land lay even then – he was taking over in your house. Well, that casserole, in a half-pint casserole dish for five of us, and no extra vegetables! I couldn't believe it, there wasn't enough even for Bob himself, never mind the rest of us. We went to bed hungry that night, in your house we went to bed hungry – can you imagine that? We were shocked, shocked to the core. Food was the mainstay of our lives. We – Bob and me – had had very little food during the Depression and although I didn't know what it was like to go hungry, I knew many that did and had, so did Bob.

You'd always fed us well, always looked after us and now we were second-class citizens in your home. I couldn't get to grips with what was going on, what had happened to you, we just couldn't believe it, you had changed so much in a few months. And I have never understood why you allowed him to move into your house, you'd fought hard to keep it after your divorce, when your main attention and thought should have been for Louise. It is no surprise to me that you have had rows over food: there would have been a row there and then, that Christmas Eve, if I hadn't left the table and gone upstairs.

I am afraid you brought this on yourself. You must have gone soft in the head. I could not understand how my sensible daughter had made such a decision, and so quickly. I know I was not the least bit sympathetic and remember we ended up not speaking for months after Bob and I left for home as soon as the snow cleared. We spent the rest of the holiday in our bedroom and went out for our meals. I know you thought that was cruel but we were so upset; we hoped you would see sense. You didn't, and life was never the same thereafter, for any of us.

We accepted Charles but we never ever understood why you fell in love with a man so much older and so different from anyone you had ever known. I was angry with you and very, very sad for you. You only have yourself to blame. You should have left Wiltshire and come home to Newcastle as we said at the time of your divorce. But no, you had to do it your way, just like your nana again! When the genes were dished out you certainly got more Morgan genes than Lambert. I will say this though, over the years we realised that Charles was very good with Louise, he always talked quietly to her, I remember saying that to you, he gave her time and never shouted, well not in our presence anyway. I respected that about him. I don't think you were ever the same person, there was the before-Charles you and the after-Charles you, and they were completely different people. If you came home with Louise, just yourselves, then you were the 'you' we knew and loved, full of life and chat, full of fun. We'd do all the things we were used to doing together, shopping in Newcastle, coffee in Fenwick's French Cafe, trips to the coast, walks along the river, sitting for hours in our dressing gowns catching up on the gossip, laughing 'til our sides split, sitting around the dining room table for hours – well *we* did, but Bob would leave after his second helping and we'd be left to our own devices.

I have only just thought of this, but it suddenly makes sense: perhaps you and David felt the same when I married Bob: *things changed*. Oh my goodness, I hadn't fully realised I'd done the same thing to you as you did to Louise! Well I never! I expected you both to accept Bob. I'd never thought of it like that before. I know neither of you did accept him, not as a father anyway; you just wouldn't have it: he wasn't your father and that was that. David tried but it didn't work, did it? I remember saying to you that I needed some life, some fun out of life and you needed a man around: David needed a man around. My eldest sister didn't think so either; we didn't speak for over a year because she thought that I should have waited before getting married again. For the first time in our lives I went against her advice. Loneliness, poverty and jealousy mean we behave strangely; they change our behaviour, as grief does too. In retrospect I can see that now, I couldn't see it then.

9

You Have Appeared in My Dreams Only Twice

You have appeared in my dreams in recognisable form only twice: even though I longed to see you, listen to you, laugh with you, feel you near me, touch you, cuddle you, talk to you. I have wanted to be with you, to know you. You have been ever elusive, though not in my memory. In my head you have walked with me, talked with me every day of my life, still aged forty-four of course, because you have never aged, and I have some wonderful mind-movies of our life together. These have kept you close over the years. Yet I have so many questions I would like to ask you. So many questions I would like to have answers to. Do you mind if I talk you through my mind-movies? You can answer back if you like: I would love that, you and I had a sparky relationship and you were a very good teacher. Come, come close, and enjoy my memories.

The first mind-movie is set in our cottage in Lemington, that old dilapidated place that was your first real married home, as well as my first home, on the road where the power station once stood. Mam had never liked living in with your mother and father, and her ambition was to save enough money to buy her dream house at Throckley bank top, in the meantime to keep the peace you had taken this old cottage. You and I were in the rough garden of the cottage and I wandered away from you and you didn't notice. Then you suddenly saw I was gone and came charging down the garden to find me standing over the old well. You were so angry you smacked me very hard and told me I must never go anywhere near it again. Then you explained what a well was, and why I must never ever go near it. I think you were very scared by your fear and your guilt, realising that you hadn't noticed I was gone. And that's why you smacked me, in an effort to imprint on my childish mind, that I must stay close, not wander, because there are dangers in this life. It was a painful and shocking way to make the message stick. I was about two and half at the time and clearly remember this, and not just because I was told about it often. I have a photograph taken in the garden of the cottage when I was about eight months old: I am sitting up in my pram pointing animatedly, presumably at our dogs, our twin golden spaniels Beauty and Lance. You are cuddling one of them although I don't know which. You are in your usual V-necked sweater and white open-necked shirt. It is a capsule moment with my doting Dad, doting on the dogs as well as me. Were you babysitting I wonder?

Shortly afterwards we moved to our new council house in the White City in Throckley, a deliberately created, and quickly developing mining village just off the main Newcastle to Carlisle road. Your family lived there too, and you must have had a hard time persuading my mother that it was the best place for us to be. Your parents lived in one of the first council houses to be built under the post-war Labour government's scheme to improve housing in the north east after the medical experts' advice proved that parents, and particularly the next generation of children, would be healthier and probably more intelligent if they lived in decent housing: there would be fewer maternal and child deaths too, because squalor bred infection – an evidence-based health approach even then?

Your sister and her family lived directly opposite your parents in Mount Pleasant. You knew and we knew that the colliery owners named their streets after natural phenomena, Oak Street, Maple Street, Ash Street and so on, in a game of 'let's pretend' for those who lived in these houses and for the rest of us who had to look at them. One thing you could not do, and neither can I, was pretend. Mount Pleasant was not pretty then, stark and dark but the houses were usually spotless inside and the gardens pretty, back and front. The coal owners tried their best to encourage everyone to think themselves into being happy and tranquil, using street names so people wouldn't grumble about the dark, black houses they lived in. You had lived in even worse conditions before moving to Throckley with your parents, when you lived in Millfield in Newburn: some of the poorest and most condemned houses in the area. You and your parents were dirt poor. Mount Pleasant was definitely a step upward, a socially upward move but it wasn't 'that' pleasant. The streets and houses were a far cry from the fantastical pastoral idylls in which families lived happy lives a long way from the muck and dirt of the pit and its machinery.

Like your dad, most pitmen were very serious gardeners; it gave them the opportunity to be physically active in the fresh air and the garden provided free healthy food for their families. They also kept animals and poultry to kill for their Sunday lunch. Some even ran businesses from their homes, selling the meat from their pigs or poultry to the Co-op butcher at a good price. They had pigeons and often greyhounds for racing, both were popular hobbies and they'd train dogs and pigeons in the back lane behind the houses or at the bottom of their gardens: working class pastimes my mother couldn't stand. You were not nearly so bothered. They also had a line of 'netties' (outside toilets) in the back lane. These toilets were shared and everyone knew who was in the toilet by their feet. The doors, like women's shabby three-quarter coats, their skirt showing beneath, stopped a metre short of the ground.

Throckley was about four miles west of Newcastle upon Tyne, a constructed village, meaning it was built by the land-owning coal owners, the Stevensons, to house the miners who worked in their three collieries. The Stevensons were benevolent liberal land owners who also built the school and the chapel. Our village nestled at the junction of two farms and a crossroads on the A69 Newcastle to Carlisle road. We moved in to the White City in

February 1950, because you were lucky enough to be at the top of the council waiting list and so qualified for our new three bed-roomed house with an indoor bathroom and separate toilet; a luxury in 1950. It also had a wash-house and large gardens front and back.

'Mornings' remain for me my most precious mind-movies, they're indelible. Mornings in our house were the best of times, the most loving and nurturing times I remember. Mornings in the White City, named as such because the houses were all painted white, a subtle play on the idea that new houses would be spanking clean, free from dirt and grime compared with the colliery houses blackened by coal: this would be a new white dawn. Mornings were the happiest time of the day.

You were both early risers, as I was too, and I liked to climb into your big double bed to bounce up and down like a rag doll, talking fifty to the dozen, while you encouraged me. When you were tired of the game, your sharp, *'That's enough now,'* put an end to our fun. I was never very good at endings and would test your patience while I bounced once more, *'Just once more,'* I'd say. You allowed the 'once more' but then it was very definitely over, *'Or else.'* Or else meant I would be smacked if I didn't do as I was told. I'd push to the limit, trying another bounce and you'd say, *'That's enough now, be warned.'* You were so often torn between your role as a disciplinarian father and that of the doting dad with his little girl. I knew your limits though. You didn't smack me very often but it was your last resort for discipline and you warned enough before it happened, so it happened rarely. When it did I felt physically hurt. I didn't like being smacked, and momentarily I disliked you too. Even as a very little girl I didn't understand why you smacked me, why your anger got the better of you so quickly sometimes, because it didn't always, you could be very, very, patient. When you lost your temper I felt helpless; you overpowered me. Sometimes, Dad, you could seem very cruel.

I know your parents had a tawse, a horrible leather belt with five or six tails; a Scottish smacking instrument was how it was described. Granda eventually gave it to you and you used to threaten me with it, but thank goodness you never ever used it on me. The thing terrified me. Did your parents ever use it on you? I doubt it, as it was always referred to as the belt for the dog in case he got out of hand. That is pretty bad anyway, using a belt on a dog, and the way Laddy was spoiled serves to confirm my view that it was actually a threat rather than a real instrument of punishment – the threat of the Tawse was enough to make anyone behave.

At least your smacking hurt less than my mother's, her hands were so strong they left wheals on the skin; you didn't. I am glad smacking has been banned now for all children under European rules, and at last we have agreed here in the UK too, smacking is an inappropriate punishment. I dare say you wouldn't agree with that. Yet for such a gentle man, and you were gentle, resorting to smacking didn't seem like your style at all. Yet, compared to most children in our street we were lucky, we were smacked rarely, while others were smacked often, and their parents used a stick! They used a stick at school too. Thank goodness you didn't do that. I did smack your grand-daughter, Louise, a few times, only in tired anger, and I am deeply ashamed that I did. She and her husband Larry have never smacked your great-grandson Will and that is as it should be three generations on: reasonable talking and boundaries provide room for negotiation, enable children to learn lessons for themselves.

Once we were out of bed there were familiar morning routines and noises: Mam, once she was up, started her morning banging around in the kitchen in her dressing gown; you went into the bathroom to wash and sing. I'd jump off your bed and rush to the top of the stairs shouting to my mother in the kitchen, checking which day of the week it was. I liked to know because in our well-run and organised house each day had some special significance. Mondays were for washing and ironing. The reason being that the pits, closed over the weekend, didn't really start belching out smoke until late afternoon on a Monday. They continually belched dirt and grime, their smuts flying in the air night and day, until the following Saturday lunchtime. If you wanted clean washing, rather than black coal smut washing, you had to get it on the line on Monday before the chimneys were fired up.

Living on the outskirts of Newcastle upon Tyne the weather paid little heed to Mam's routine, and more often than not ironing spread over to Tuesday and even to Wednesday sometimes. On very wet Mondays, especially in winter, the washing was dried in the house around the fire. The damp crept slowly through the house, and we felt it too, as the clothes gradually yielded up their wetness as smelly suffocating steam and the condensation poured down the windows and walls. Steam ran down the kitchen and washhouse walls leaving pools and lakes on the floor.

I loved the wet-weather drying process because it meant I could play 'camping' in amongst the wet washing on the clothes-horses in the sitting or dining room. It often took two to three days for our washing to dry. My housewife laundry training began when I was four. I was able to iron handkerchiefs and pillow cases standing on a chair by the ironing board, supervised by my mother. She taught me perfect crease extinction and pristine folding; and as you passed in and out of the kitchen you'd add in your military precision on knife-edge creases. Other days had their tasks: shopping on Wednesday and Saturday; going to see my maternal grandma and granda in Haltwhistle on Friday. This varied some weeks, but generally the pattern was fixed.

You were a careful house-husband, unusual for your era and our area. You ironed, cooked, did the washing up, and your scrambled egg was a light fluffy delicacy. You taught me, as I stood on a stool by the sink, how to wash up by efficiently stacking everything in order of size, washing things, draining them, and then stacking them ready to go into the cupboards just as they'd come out. I thought this was a miracle; that you, my dad, could perform miracles. You lifted me onto the chair you'd placed at the sink so I could enjoy being elbow deep in soap-suds. It was such fun; we used to blow soap-sud kaleidoscope bubbles all over the kitchen. I was fascinated by the multitude of colours inside soap-suds; my first science lessons were in the kitchen with you. Unlike most men of your era you had time to cultivate your household skills because you were so often at home recovering from surgery or illness.

Each morning, once I knew which day it was and where we might go, or what we would do, I'd slide down the stairs on my bottom; it was far too slow if I had to walk carefully down each stair. I'd run through the hall and kitchen into the dining room to climb on my chair. My mother wrapped my apron around me and I'd try very hard to wait for my egg to come out of the pan. I rarely sat still for long; I'd get down as fast as I'd got up to run back to mother standing at the cooker, to wrap myself around her warm legs. She'd give me the egg timer so I could see the sand running so I'd know when my egg was ready, when all the sand was in the bottom of the bowl of the egg timer. This was one of my favourite moments with her, I'd watch the pink sand slowly descend, fascinated by its delicate trickle. She'd lift my egg out of the pan on her big tablespoon and place it carefully in my egg-cup, then lift me onto the bench giving me my special spoon so I could break the top of the shell. We'd pour my egg onto the mashed-up bread with its knob of butter in my bowl. She'd help me, her hand on top of mine, to press hard to make sure all the bread turned yellow with egg because I hated any dry bits. Carrying me and my eggy bread back to the table she'd put me in my seat and I'd try to sit still long enough to eat, though I never stopped chattering and she'd tell me not to talk with my mouth full. I'd try very hard not to chatter but the words popped out of my mouth one after the other and I'd put my egg in between them.

While I ate my eggy bread you would appear like clockwork in the dining room, with bits of bloodied newspaper stuck to your chin. Bending down to kiss me you'd say, '*Pull off the paper*

Pet, I've stopped bleeding now.' Very carefully I'd pull off each piece and you'd run your fingers over the cuts you'd made in your face while you were shaving, to check they were dry. Then, picking up your silver armbands and cuff links from the sideboard, they lived in one of the bowls, you carefully put the cuff links in the little holes you explained were specially made for them in your shirt cuffs. Stretching your armbands over your wrists, you'd push them up over your elbows and pull your shirt-sleeves above the silvery bands until your sleeves looked like frilly ballet dresses in the middle of your arms. Then you'd look in the mirror, above the gas fire built into the dining room wall, to see yourself fastening your silver-coloured tie. This dangled around your neck all the time you were seeing to your arms and you took ages to tie it. If I said you were taking a long time you'd say, '*I have to have a perfect knot, Pet. It takes time you know, I have to get it right.*' I loved watching you.

You'd hardly talk when you were busy, and neither did I; I just liked watching you. Watching your gentle, precise movements; your brow wrinkled in concentration especially when you were tying your tie. Your little tugs at your sleeve cuffs as you pulled at them to get your shirt-sleeves exactly where you wanted them. The way you cocked your head to one side as you looked into the mirror, almost as though you were looking more severely with your right eye than your left, to comb your dark, silver-streaked hair. The way you rubbed the Brylcreem in the palm of your hands – to warm it up, you always said when I asked; then carefully hand-rubbed it through your hair to keep it under perfect control. Then you'd walk to the kitchen to wash your hands, drying them carefully with the towel. You took your time with any task, you were so thorough. You'd then take one last look in the mirror to make sure you looked as perfect as you could make yourself, check your trousers and shoes, a quick last look at your hair, touching it to make sure it was firmly in place. I think you were a perfectionist, yet not obsessive.

You'd then, by a quick turn of your heel, walk into the hall for your jacket and your mac; they both hung on the newel post at the bottom of the stairs. You'd carefully pick up your jacket by its centre collar, scrutinise it quickly before putting it on, looking at it quizzically as though you expected to find someone else had worn it during the night. Painstakingly, every morning in the same way, you picked up your beloved fawn mac, scrutinised it too, and then folded it precisely, the sides into the middle, then in half again longways, and then folded it in half to place over your left arm. This was your trademark; your perfectly folded mac over your left arm, even in summer you rarely left home without it; I'm sure it was your comfort blanket. I watched fascinated every morning as you then walked back into the kitchen to give Mam a hug and a kiss on the back doorstep as you left the house. You'd swing me high in the air, over your head, so you could kiss me too; then drop me down, telling me I had to be a good girl for my mother. I loved these same-y mornings.

Sometimes I'd come into the bathroom with you, sit on the floor listening to your singing, watching you shaving; making all the cuts. '*Ouch,*' you'd cry, and send me for the newspaper so you could tear off the clean white edges to stick on your cuts, '*It's the best cure,*' you'd say standing in your white vest, a towel twirled around your shoulders hanging down both sides of your chest so your vest didn't get wet. Your braces hung down over your bottom as though you were a horse waiting to be saddled and reined, raring to go. You loved Alma Cogan and Shirley Bassey among others, and you'd sing their songs as you washed and dressed. After breakfast, having kissed us both, you'd leave for work and Mam and I would run to the living room window. I'd pull the net curtain back so I could watch you walk away toward your friend's house. He'd meet you at the gate, then you turned back, to wave to us before you both turned right up Broomy Hill Road to the bus stop. You worked at Huw Woods on the Tyne Valley estate at this point, as a wages clerk. You'd had to give up your vehicle maintenance work after being ill, you needed a lighter, less physically demanding job.

119

At the weekends your routine was the same except you would eat your breakfast, sit for a long time, quietly reading your newspaper, and we were not allowed to speak to you. Your face was hidden by the newspaper so I couldn't see you, as well as not being able to speak to you. This frustrated me and so I would come and kneel at your feet and knock, gently at first, on your paper door. You would ignore me and I would knock again, you would ignore me and I would persist in knocking until I had knocked the paper in so that it was resting on your knee. Only then would you look over the top and say, '*I am reading my paper, it will have to wait, whatever you want will have to wait.*' No matter how hard I tried you never ever gave in and I'd have to walk away and leave you alone. Only if there was news that annoyed you, shocked or angered you, would you lay your paper down on your knee and turn to Mam, telling her whether she was interested or not, whether she wanted to hear or not, why you were annoyed. If it was about Suez and the Suez Canal you would get very agitated as Mam listened quietly. You perked up quickly, looking over the top of your paper if you heard something on the news that took your interest; our radio was always on in the corner of the dining room. This was usually something about the government, the Suez Canal, war, or the Labour party; politics in general always attracted your attention.

Despite your bad health you loved your garden and working outdoors, and so you persevered with your virgin landscape as contentedly as any squire overseeing his lands. You riddled, raked and manured your soil in your fifties bags and Fair Isle V-necked pullover over a white open-necked shirt. You were slightly built, only five feet four and half inches in height, slim faced with thick, dark, silvering wavy hair and penetrating, bright-blue, sparkling eyes. You suntanned very easily and I have a treasured picture of you that Nana gave me. You'd sent it to her from India. You are in your khaki desert uniform proudly holding a large brimmed hat and your message reads: '*How do you like the darkie, love Billy.*' For such a liberal man this was a blatantly racist comment of the kind you would have criticised others for. You are relaxed, confident, loose limbed; perching on a high stool, looking as though you are really enjoying yourself: proud of yourself. You were known as Willie or Billy, Willie to your mother and Billy to the rest of your family and friends. My mother called you Bill, always: her Bill.

Our new front garden sloped steeply toward the road outside our house. And you wasted no time in turning it into three graduated terraces, carefully measured and levelled. One of my favourite mind-movies is of you sitting on your hunkers (heels) squatting amid your developing terraces riddling and riddling soil until it was as fine as dust ready for your flowers and shrubs. You'd use your spirit level to ensure that the ground was even, inching along on your knees taking precise measurements. Gardening was never an easy task for you as you were frequently not well, your energy levels varied and you were constantly in and out of hospital during this time.

Our back garden was even more of a challenge than the front, as it was set high above the house and had no steps; it was just a rough slope. After we moved in, your first job was to fashion steps from the mud left by the builders so Mam could hang the washing out. Your step handiwork was not the model of perfection seen in your front garden, although your fruit and vegetable garden was. You carved the steps inch by inch from the builder's rubble using odd bits of wood: they were the most uneven and dangerous steps imaginable. I think this was a job that took it out of you; you didn't have the energy, the tools, or the money to do it properly. Nevertheless your steps survived the forty-eight years the house was our home, as did the terraces and rockeries in the front garden. They are still there today. You, and then we, never did improve the back steps, we just lived with them.

Each step of our back garden steps was a different shape and width; we needed to vary our stride and the height of our gait to safely negotiate the journey to the vegetable garden or the washing line – not an easy task in the winter carrying a basket of wet washing, skating on ice and snow. Outside our back door you created what would now be called a patio. The concrete out the back was just the place the dustbin lived, and a flat surface where I could ride my scooter and red toy car along the path and back again avoiding the eight steps down to our gate and the pavement at the front. You, Mam and our neighbours sat out on the back steps on hot summer evenings talking and laughing but you never sat on the flat concrete beside the dustbin. Behind the wash house was a green space, dark and dank, but it allowed me to run back and forth to our neighbours, whom I called Aunty and Uncle, next door. They were my surrogate relations and I spent as much time in their house as I did in my own, except in their house I was thoroughly spoiled. When you were at home life was fun, comfortable, and wonderfully safe.

You both wanted your own house and were very good at saving when you were working, yet you were not able to buy your own house as your war disability meant you could not get a mortgage, nor insurance. You were both very angry at this conditional clause in your pension rights; my mother was furious, and very bitter. You had both agreed on the chosen house at Throckley bank top. Mam had worked with the Prudential Insurance Company during the war conscientiously saving her earnings for her house: she was heartbroken. All through our childhood, as we walked past the house you wanted, my mother reminded us that it should have been ours – yours. It was a handsome house too.

At weekends you'd take me to see your mother and father and I'd walk quietly with you holding your hand until we were very near Nana's house when I'd pester to be let loose. I'd strain at your arm like a puppy on a very tight lead and reluctantly you'd give in, let me go, though you'd caution me to be careful. I'd run up Nana's steps into her always-open back door: summer and winter it stood wide open, ever expectant. Nana, usually in her kitchen, would whoop loudly, '*Hello darlin*,' and sweep me up into her arms as though she hadn't seen me for a long while, when in fact she had probably seen me the day before. When you caught me up she'd encircle us both like a bustling lioness nosing her brood, and lean over my head to kiss you. She had the same greeting for you every time, '*Hello son, how are you today?*' Granda would then silently appear from the shadow of the hall and lift me up with my legs dangling like a puppet down his white collarless shirt and black waistcoat. He'd then rub my face against his stubbly chin; rub his whiskers up and down my cheek and I'd yelp with delightful pain and pleasure. I'd ask him to do it again, again. When he thought I'd had enough, which was always before I had had enough, he'd put me down, then he'd lift me on to the dog's back.

Their dog, Laddy, was as big as a donkey and didn't mind me riding him as my personal steed. Despite his size and girth he was a very gentle dog and he would walk when Granda told him to, with me kicking at his sides. Meanwhile you and Nana would be deep in conversation about your health. She'd check carefully how you were, what had happened since she saw you last, you knew you had to give a running commentary and didn't get impatient with her. You often had to sneak to your mother's, before or after work, because my mother was very jealous of any time you spent with your family. I have often wondered how you felt about that, how you coped with my mother's criticism of your family. It must have been hurtful and difficult, yet I cannot remember you ever chiding her about it, or arguing about it. Perhaps you did out of my hearing, but you continued to be conscientious in visiting your parents as often as you could, which sometimes meant you popped in on your way from the bus stop before you came home to us. You and your dad had a quiet, steady, loving relationship and you'd walk out into the garden together to check the plants, you puffing on a cigarette and Granda puffing on his pipe. You talked ever so quietly and seriously together; you had a very strong bond with your dad.

When you were in the garden with Granda, Nana would give me her full attention asking me what I would like: always a very general question but related to any treat I might want. In the spring it was usually rhubarb and in the winter her ginger wine. She also kept a whole selection of sweets for me. I loved sherbet lemons, dolly mixtures and liquorice. I'd join you and Granda in the garden and ask him to pick the rhubarb for me; I'd help him pick the pinkest thin stalks from his rhubarb patch. Sometimes he had to remove the old buckets to get the youngest bits of rhubarb. You followed the same principle with your rhubarb; you both covered the young shoots with any old rusty buckets or pans you could find. You'd knock out the bucket's rusty bottom so the shoots and the young stems were then protected from early or late frosts, or the birds, while they enjoyed the warmth of the sun.

While I was in the garden choosing my slender stems of rhubarb Nana would make one of her greaseproof conical icing bags. She'd then fill this with sugar and give it to me with the clean peeled rhubarb. I would dip my rhubarb into the sugar in the bag: this was my very own homemade sherbet dip. I loved the stinging, tingling stringiness of my rhubarb and the earthy acid drop smell. In winter I'd ask for ginger wine and watch Nana, her huge blue patterned apron wrapped around her small chunky frame, as she walked toward one of her stone flagons stacked against the kitchen wall. Some were filled with lemonade, but I liked the ginger wine best. As she poured the wine into my glass through her special funnel I'd stand by her side watching, fascinated by the sticky pungent liquid gold knowing the fire in my throat would start as soon as I had my first sip. The smell of ginger wafted around the kitchen, warm and enticing. Nana gave me Spam and tomato sauce in white sliced bread if I wanted it. My mother called white sliced bread white lint, and Spam pink lint, referring to both as rubbish, and food fit only for poor people: I wasn't allowed either at home.

Nana's house was full of magic and always interesting, there was never a dull moment. I loved her bathroom and I liked playing with the Pears soap and its vanishing letters: she always had Pears soap in the bathroom. And in the kitchen, horrible stinging, stinking, carbolic soap used to kill the germs when she scrubbed the wooden table she used for cooking: this was the only respect for hygiene and cleanliness she paid heed to in her house. I loved the smell of Pears soap: custard mixed with Germoline and dolly mixture sweeties. I'd study the letters P E A R S S O A P on one side, and a very long word you said was T R A N S P A R E N T in the middle of the other side of the soap: you'd help me spell it out letter by letter. Then on the other side it just said P E A R S. I'd speak my letters over and over again as I washed my hands. You said the soap helped me learn to read. It certainly helped my love of letters and my attempts to understand what they meant. Every time I went to the bathroom the soap was a different size and the letters got thinner and smaller; this was my Nana's magic soap. It got so thin and slippery I couldn't catch it, nor keep it in my hands, and when the letters almost disappeared, a new bar would appear just so I could start my reading speaking game all over again. Or so I thought.

As it got dark there was more magic for me to do because Nana still had gas lights – gas mantles. You said we were lucky because we had new electric lights in our house but I didn't agree. In Nana's house I could sit high on my granda's or your shoulders, so that Nana could give me a lighted taper to light the gas lights; and I couldn't do this at home. I was allowed to light each cream lacy shade as the gas hissed through. The lacy shades glowed slowly, showing pale, pale, yellow, throwing their shadows on the wall as golden circles with frilly edges that gently waved and moved around: I had my very own magic lantern show. I loved the soft gas-light and the smell. When the lamplighter came to light up the street-lights I'd beg Nana to let me watch from the window. I was mesmerised by the slow circle of light around the bottom of the lamp stand into the road. It was heaven to me, just like the pictures in my Sunday school books when Jesus was taken up to heaven in a golden cloud. I wanted to be a gas lighter magically lighting up the world. I have never forgotten his long pole with the lighted end, he'd reach up to the green street lamp, unhook its little door and then the slow, slow yellow light came through. Gradually a small circle of light formed around the bottom of the lamp, and then it slowly spread, bigger and bigger in a golden arc in the road: so pretty, and so romantic.

You took me to your parents' house every weekend. My mother's reasons for not accompanying us were very clear; as she put it, 'she didn't like them and had no time for them' and referred to them as 'them up the road' so she stayed at home when you and I walked up the hill to visit them. You had an easy-going relationship with your father because you shared a love of gardening, reading and newspapers and you both accepted Nana as she bustled about you seeing you had everything you needed, and I had everything I wanted. When my mother was in hospital, which she was frequently when I was a toddler, I stayed with Nana or my aunty and uncle who lived across the road from her; running like a yo-yo on a string between them, Nana at one side of the road and Aunty at the other. Before I was four years old you had both been in hospital more than once, you with your stomach problems and my mother with a bad back, which she blamed on her long labour giving birth to me.

Do you remember how small your mother was, she was only four foot ten and as round as she was tall, while your father was almost six foot and as slender as his garden rake; they were a strange-looking couple. She had a Buddha belly, a huge mound undulating from her breasts to her thighs. We still joke about her figure as all the females in the family inherited her Buddha shape, which grows or shrinks with more or less food but never entirely abates. We all inherited the gene for short stature, no waist, ripe melon breasts and skinny sparrow legs that buckle under our weight! My nickname in school was Sparrow Legs. She had flimsy yellow hair, an almond-shaped face, grey-blue eyes and thin wire glasses with a nose that was rather too long for her face. My mother said she dyed her hair with dolly blue, the bleach we used to keep our net curtains white. This unruly mop – pictures of her mother show that she too had this wild hair –

was kept a reluctant prisoner in an almost, but not quite, invisible fine hair net of the same colour. Even at weddings and other special occasions her hat was placed on top of this net, this always made me laugh. Women usually took their hairnets off for special occasions but not your mother. Not that it made the slightest difference, her hair and its many fine wiry pins escaped all over the place. She spent a good part of her day with her hands in her hair forever trying to control it, stuffing it bad temperedly under the net.

I was always happy with you at Nana's despite her incorrigible slovenliness and I had a special place in her world, it was my second home. Can you recall how, when you and I left her house to go home, both Nana and Granda would come to their gate to wave. I would walk backwards waving to them, with dire consequences sometimes. On one occasion I turned abruptly and slammed into a lamp-post and ended up with a terrible black eye. You took me back the few yards to Nana's house so she could rub the surrounding skin with butter and vinegar to prevent any bruising. We then set off again and they didn't leave their 'post' until we turned the corner out of sight. I waved frantically as though I might never see them again. You waved too, constantly turning back toward them even though we only lived half a mile away.

10

God Decreed I'd Have a Brother: 1953

I'm staying with Nana and Aunty Bell going between them like a yo-yo bouncing free on its string because my mother is in hospital again. I only have to cross the road, held by an invisible cord, watched on one side of Newburn Road by Nana, and on the other side by Aunty Bell, to change my abode. We've been very busy preparing for the Coronation celebrations: the Coronation of Elizabeth II on 3 June 1953, in two days' time. I am to be a cherry girl, so Nana and Aunty Bell have made me a white dress covered in red cherries and green leaves. My Sunday school class is dancing around the maypole and we have been practising every day for weeks.

The day arrives and I am wild with excitement, jumping up and down, constantly asking when I can put on my cherry dress. I am longing to get going. We have no television and so listen to the radio all morning to be able to feel part of the preparations in London. I am fascinated by the voices on the radio and they encourage my excitement. By the afternoon my hair has to be re-done, it has been done twice already but because Nana can't do it as Mam does, it won't sit neatly. My mother does my hair every night while I sit quietly and patiently in front of her. She winds coils of hair around her fingers and then pins them down with a hair grip: I go to bed each night with my hair pincered to my scalp with steel pins. Before this fad I had sat patiently while she tied it up in rags for ringlets and I hated every minute of both methods. And all because I haven't been born with curly hair, well actually I was, but it became much straighter as I got older. Mam blames the hairdresser for cutting off my natural curls and spoiling what she refers to as my natural wave. This was, and still is, one single line of wave across the neckline!

Nana of course can't do this hair thing properly, even though she tries and so my hair on this special day is raggy and untidy but I don't care. She makes it look better by tying a white ribbon in the front. Then I put on my dress and clean white socks and shoes. We walk up to the green, only steps from Nana's house, where the maypole stands tall and elegant in the centre of the green sporting its coloured ribbons. There are many speeches, lots of clapping and cheering, music by the local brass band, prayers said by the vicar, the National Anthem and then it is the children's turn to dance. I love dancing around the maypole weaving in and out of the coloured ribbons the way we've been taught. When we are finished there is a big party tea on the Green with sandwiches and sausage rolls, cakes and biscuits. The women in this part of Throckley, including Nana, have prepared the sandwiches and the cakes. At the end of the tea the children are given a Coronation Mug and a Coronation Crown to take home: both have pictures of the new Queen on them. I am given two but don't really understand why, but I am as proud as punch anyway.

Next morning Dad comes to collect me, I can't remember whether he was at the celebrations or not. We go down home and I run off to play with my friends. Shortly afterwards I hear him shouting my name and waving me home. There is an ambulance outside my front door. '*Come and see your Mam and your new baby brother.*'

I watch as Mam appears from inside this giant white tin box, that's how it seems to me, as she puts her foot on the top step carrying a white bundle in her hands; I run fast back to my friends. Mam cries. I am hauled back by Dad in double quick time and have a hard smack across my bottom. He says the smacking is for upsetting Mam and for not being interested in my new baby brother: I am not interested in him one bit. All I want to know is where on earth he has come from? This is all I can think about for days and then months apparently. I am used to one or other of my parents being in hospital, on one occasion they are both in different hospitals at the same time, so seeing ambulances at my front door is nothing special or out of the ordinary. Dad is always leaving or arriving home in an ambulance. I am happy during their absences, and spoilt rotten, so I haven't thought much about why my mother has been in hospital this time. As sex and birth are taboo subjects no one thinks to tell me what is happening. The women speak of these things in whispers so children can't tell what they are discussing; they sort of twist their lips to the side and talk out of the side of their mouth looking down at the floor, standing very close to each other. I soon learn this means women's business and is not for men or children to know.

I have no advance knowledge of 'his coming', as Mary had from Gabriel before Jesus was born; this is the only baby's birth I know about. I love Sunday school especially the Christmas stories so this is my only template about babies arriving unexpectedly. Somehow, I think, God and everyone else for that matter has forgotten to warn me about this special coming and I can't understand it; the ethereal telegraph hasn't worked for me in 1953. Instead of being joyful, I am completely puzzled. Where on earth has Mam got this baby from? I am told his name is David William Holland and that he is my brother. I am also worried as Mam goes to hospital often, sometimes once a week; is she going to bring a baby brother with her every time she goes? I did not think this a good idea at all. I also think this baby (or any others she might bring back) might be a sister. I picture our house being full of babies, where will we put them? I can't figure it out and I am not pleased. This is an understatement – my world has been turned upside down and inside out.

I ask Dad where David has come from and I am told he has come from God. '*God decides who has babies*,' is Dad's persistent answer to my questions. But I've seen no angels, nor one particular angel, speaking to me. This is the only means of communication I understand God has from heaven to earth, and especially to mothers. I can't work it out except to think the angels maybe only speak to mams and dads. I didn't think much of that either. Why not me? I know from Sunday school that God decides everything from today's weather to how much food we have and almost every other thing in our life. We have to thank him for everything, every day, and before meals too. So, to a rising five-year-old it makes sense that he provides the babies too.

But I'm not quite satisfied because I can't understand how God makes his decisions about how many babies go where and to whom. I sit in our garden amongst our raspberry bushes thinking and puzzling as well as stripping the bushes bare, too bare, much to my father's later annoyance. Then I tear down the garden steps, red mouthed, my clothes smothered in raspberry juice, shouting, *'Dad, why has Auntie L only got one baby in her house and why has Uncle Bill and Aunty Marie got five in their house and the lady in that house on the corner got no babies in her house?'*

My best friend, a boy, lives next door and he has no babies in his house and I know P's mam has ended up with ten babies in her house but I still can't work it all out. Mam is always saying that Catholics have far too many children and are always poor. My friend is a Catholic and so is P so this didn't seem to work out the way the adults tell me it is supposed to... Mam is always taking our old clothes to P's house to help them out because she says they have far too many children. Well, if she can see that why can't God, especially as He sees everything? We all know who attends which church, how often, and those who never attend. Mam has nothing good to say about Catholics and always gives the impression that she doesn't think much of them. For a start they don't have their Sunday dinner until after their dads have had their drink at the club or pub, whereas we Protestants eat at 12.15 or 12.30 at the latest: the right time for dinner for decent people and our dad doesn't go to the pub.

I can tell Dad doesn't like answering my questions and just

keeps repeating that God sends the babies and He knows what He is doing!

'Don't ask so many questions, you're far too nosey, that's your trouble.'

Mam hardly ever answers my questions; in fact actively discourages these most of my life, but Dad usually does, until he is thoroughly fed up. Then he says, *'Stop asking so many questions about babies, we've told you over and over again where babies come from, make that enough now; you want to know the far end of everything, you always do.'*

My refusal to accept his answer makes me more determined and I worry away at it, thinking about what they'd said about Catholics being poor. If God knows they are poor why does He choose them for the most babies? There is a lady up the road who has no babies. Why is that? We are always taught to share so why didn't God share out the babies. I try to work it out for myself in my childish way. At Sunday school I am taught that God can see everything I do and see other people's actions too, He records everything I do in his Big Book so He can make decisions about whether I am good enough to be allowed into heaven, which is where good people eventually go, and where I will go one day, according to my parents. Every one of my words and actions is recorded and especially when I am naughty. Between my fear of God and the Bogeyman on his rag and bone cart – the other person I'm told, by Nana and Aunty Bell, who takes away naughty children – I can't do much wrong anyway: I am too scared to be very naughty. I make my mind up early on, if it is a choice between being saved and heaven's door being open to me or the Bogeyman taking me away with the old clothes, then I most definitely will choose heaven come what may, as both the Bogeyman and Hell sound terrible to me. Hell, and roasting forever in flames, is something else I've learned from Sunday school. As I don't want to become a piece of roast beef (my only understanding of roasting) I choose being good, or as good as I can be anyway. I do wonder, though, how there is room in heaven for everyone and how He sorts the good from the bad: naughtiness is the only clue. So I set my mind to being good. Hell I am told is underneath my feet, underground, with the devil's fire always burning. I often think about all the poor people burning under my feet wherever I walk, smelling like roast beef.

So, how does He make his decisions about babies? Why were some houses full and others not and would there be more for us? So, back to Dad with another question, *'How do babies get here from God?'*

'God sends them from Heaven. You never give up do you?'

Back to the garden: in the meantime I am not the least bit interested in David. I watch the sky everyday from my hideout in the raspberry bushes. I wait and wait for the babies to descend. They never do and I am very cross. I can't make sense of any of it. It is like watching for Santa Claus, which I do every Christmas Eve, but never see him either. Back to Dad, *'Dad if God sends the babies from heaven how does he do it? Do they come down attached to string?'*

'He has his own way of sending them, now will you leave this baby thing alone for a while, please. For goodness sake we've had enough of this, you're never satisfied.'

You've got it, I spent the whole summer baby watching, looking for babies being dropped from heaven tied to a string.

My parent's absolute refusal to help me sort out the baby thing just made me concentrate on it more and more using the resources I had to try and understand it. I asked myself questions and then answered myself too, creating all sorts of misinformation in my head. It took me years to sort it out. The world according to 'me' became 'the word', and 'law' as far as I was concerned and my concentration on being good became my guide to life. Of course I couldn't keep it up all the time, I was far too irrepressible, but I would be very upset if I was naughty and brooded on it for a long time, lying awake worrying in the night about what God's punishment might be. I drove people mad with my certainty too. If they tried to tell me I was wrong I would argue ''til the cows came home' trying to convince them of my point of view. Just like Nana. I'd work it all out carefully and understood '*my*' world so everyone else's must be like mine. I couldn't be wrong.

This erroneous thinking wasn't helped by the Catholic priest, the hospital chaplin, coming to visit Dad. He sometimes came to the house if Dad was at home and if he was in hospital, visited him there. Mam said he wasn't married when I asked about his wife and babies. She said Catholic priests didn't have wives or babies, they just did God's work. Our vicar, Mr Clements, and his wife, didn't have children and neither did our curate. So, God didn't give his servants (we were taught that vicars, priests and curates were God's servants on earth, sent to help us all) babies and this must be because they were so busy looking after us they hadn't time to look after their own children: simple!

Yet, later, I wanted to marry a vicar and live in the vicarage or be a missionary travelling to sort out the heathen wherever they were to be found. Every Sunday in Sunday school we had to think about how we could look after children in Africa and India and many other countries too. I hadn't a clue where they were but the pictures showed black and brown children with sad faces. We had to give money to help them.

I had funny ideas about clergymen (of any denomination) as a result. It didn't occur to me until I was older that somehow I had got the idea that the clergy were a race apart. As an adult I could not bring myself to see them as sexual beings: they couldn't be. This was a product of my erroneous thinking and I still find it hard to see the clergy as other than asexual. Of course this was related to them wearing dresses and their collar back to front. Other men didn't wear dresses, nor did they have their collars on the wrong way round, even when they didn't wear a tie. I put that down to the clergy being special and thought as 'He' made man in his own image then God 'Himself' must dress this way. My image of God: a man with a long white beard sitting on a throne in a vicar's dress and collar, a black and white dress and collar of course. I believed everything the vicar and his teachers told me, literally too, so I had the makings of a perfect fundamentalist. And I was well into my teens when I realised I'd got it all wrong about babies, I somehow didn't hear all the dirty talk at school – I was a very late developer.

Years later when I asked Mam about my brother's birth and why I hadn't been told she said, '*I was ashamed. Your Dad was very sick and in and out of hospital, often off work, I knew people would talk. What do you think they would have thought about it all, I had a bad back and was in hospital for operations and manipulation. What would they think?*'

She didn't say clearly what she thought even then, that people would talk and assume that if Dad was fit enough to make love then he must be fit enough to work! She was terrified of gossip. But her fears were deeper than just the fear of gossip. She was worried how she would manage with me, and a baby (especially a boy who needed a father), if Dad died. She had shared this with Dad who'd said, '*Some day, David will be a great comfort to you.*'

Her worries were not without foundation. Dad had had a serious operation when I was eighteen months old and between then and David being born he had been in and out of hospital and was under constant review by the army medical board as he had a pension. He still had periods when he wasn't well enough to work, though during the period 1952 to 1956 he had, according to his medical records, better health than the previous ten years. By 1953 he was again having pain-controlling injections from his GP. Mam admitted that she had hidden her pregnancy from everyone as much as she was able to. David must have come as a surprise to everyone when her pregnancy couldn't be hidden any more.

Whatever the ins and outs of David's birth I wasn't happy about it one bit. People often asked Mam whether I was jealous, as I'd been an only child for so long. I've always thought this was rather a daft question to ask a very jealous woman who'd no insight into her own jealousy at all, but of course neighbours and friends may not have known this. Her answer was a very definite no. In talking about this much later I reminded her of my behaviour toward David at the time because I remember it all too clearly and to this day feel ashamed: God's recording activities and my being good fell by the wayside over David, and the green-eyed monster took residence in my heart.

David was the most beautifully formed chubby baby, weighing in at ten pounds two ounces. He was as Gallic looking as Mam, Aunty Ella and Granma; looked as they had when they were babies. Everyone who looked at him said, '*Eeh, what a beautiful bairn.*'

There was no denying this, he was. He had a beautiful skin with soft rosy cheeks, very dark brown hair and a skin that looked as though it had been lovingly and carefully polished with beeswax: his skin shone. Mam was proud of her good-looking boy and the fact that he never stopped crying didn't take the shine off him either. My memories are of him crying incessantly, after feeding, in his pram, in his cot – he was always crying.

I remember Aunty Vi and Mam arguing over leaving him to cry. That was Aunty Vi's advice as per Dr Spock but Mam couldn't do it, she would pick him up. Grandma, who was dying in our front bedroom, the pleasantest room in the house, from bowel cancer, would shout down, '*Bring that bairn up here to me.*' She would put David on her chest and soothe him and I would sit on the bed with her and listen to her soft voice and gentle way with him. He'd soon stop crying and fall asleep. Mam's life must have been sheer hell. What with worry over Dad, her own mother dying upstairs following Dad's long illness and surgery as well as her own back problems and jealous me, she mustn't have known whether she was coming or going.

And, poor David, he was born into a house of stress, repressed emotion and worry. No wonder he cried. I played for long periods of time alone in the front room amusing myself when I wasn't at school. I recently drew a picture of myself then: I'm playing quietly, my little person surrounded by layers of barbed wire. I learned very early on how to amuse myself; after all I always had plenty going on in my head and so I was always very busy. I played with my friends as well but was always perfectly happy alone. I was capable of thinking my way through time: days went in a flash and still do. I observed too; I could record detail as a young child, visually as well as fixing firmly in my head any conversation I heard, and I had my own interpretation of these too. It was as though I had my own camera or video in my head with its own sound track as well. I could play and replay any scenes I wanted any time I wished.

Then slowly but surely I tried to kill my baby brother. My first attempt was to give him my signet ring while Mam was changing his nappy. He was probably about six months old. He put it straight in his mouth. Mam reacted quickly when his choking noises started and threw him over her lap and upside down: the ring came straight out. Boy, did I get a good hiding.

My next attempt came when he was about one. Mam was a ferocious potty trainer. We were both potty trained earlier than most children and she achieved this by sitting us on our potties from the time we could sit up, first being held, and then alone. Her Pavlovian and Skinnerian classical conditioning paid dividends: dry and clean babies who performed on demand. David was never as malleable as me and he would not perform no matter how long she left him sitting. On one winter evening he was on his potty, he had been there rather a long time with Mam encouraging his performance every now and again in between seeing to Granma and washing dishes and nappies. I took my chance and tipped him and his potty into the fireplace. He screamed blue murder and I remember my harassed mother rushing in, wiping her hands on her apron shouting, '*What's going on, oh my goodness!*' And I got a hiding. Fortunately he didn't hit the flames but banged his head on the hearth. He was saved by our brass fireguard.

My third attempt happened while Mam was cleaning the bedroom from which Grandma had mysteriously disappeared. Mam must have been getting the house ready for her funeral yet

I have no knowledge of being told that she'd died although I remember the funeral tea clearly. She asked me to look after David who must have been about eight months old maybe a bit more.

Earlier, I'd heard everybody saying that he was late in walking to which others replied, '*Boys often are, they are lazier than girls.*' So I decided to speed the process up. I carefully positioned him against the arm of the settee instructing him to walk when I took my hand away. I moved my hand, shouted walk, and he fell flat on his stomach banging his head on the carpet which covered a cement floor! He had a huge bump on his head. He screamed and screamed. Mam rushed down stairs shouting, '*What's going on now?*'

'*I was trying to make David walk, you all said you wanted him to walk, I heard you.*'

Later I produced my six-year-old 'pièce de resistance'. Dad always bathed us, I cannot remember ever being bathed by Mam but I'm sure we were. Dad's bath times were some of our happiest times together. He'd run the water carefully so it was the right temperature, put in our toys, and play with us until the water was cool. Then he'd wrap us one by one in large white fluffy bath towels and carry us down stairs by the fire: one in each arm. He'd carefully clean our ears with a matchstick wrapped inside the corner of the towel, generously talcum powder us all over and put on our pyjamas. We'd then play games, tickling games, until we laughed so hard we couldn't stand up straight. Or, he'd chase us round and round the settee, playing hide and seek. Then he'd say, long before we'd be ready for it, '*Now that's enough, you've got to settle down now.*' We hated the fun ending and always pleaded for more but he'd never give in. This was his way of setting boundaries. No meant No.

My murder attempt took place on the evening Dad put David in the bath with me for the first time: David's first bath in the large bath. For some reason Dad left us alone, I expect he had forgotten the towel or something, and I pushed David under the water. He didn't scream, he couldn't I suppose, but when Dad returned it was to find David lying face down in the water. He could only have been out of the room for seconds. Dad was purple with anger and I got a hiding. To this day David has not learned to swim and doesn't like boats either. Did I really try to drown him? I don't know, but whatever happened I'd had something to do with it they all said. I can remember no conscious planning or plotting but these things actually happened and I was blamed so I can only think I was very jealous.

My jealousies melted away before I did any mortal damage and I developed a fierce and protective love for my baby brother which has lasted a lifetime. And I know that at times he has felt smothered by what he has always referred to as his bossy older sister. My bossiness and protectiveness was a disguise for fear: the very real fear he might be taken away from me, that something might happen to him. Later whenever I got home from school my first words were always, '*Is David in yet?*' I could never settle until he was in the house. I was terrified the older ruffians of the area would hurt him. Mam was unkind to David, though not knowingly or deliberately; by not dressing him like other boys she put him in danger of being seen a sissy. He had to be perfectly dressed and his hair, like mine, perfectly coiffed. She managed this using sugar and water to create his quiff. She wouldn't let him be free for the rough and tumble he really needed but I became proud of my Mediterranean-looking brother who walked like Dad.

Another reason why Mam was ashamed of her pregnancy was her own bad back. After my birth she'd been told not to have any more children. When I was two they operated on her coccyx to alleviate pain. This had been caused, she claimed, by her long labour, forty-eight hours, giving birth to me. I was the cause of Mam's bad back. The operation was not successful and she had other treatments including regular manipulation (osteopathy or physiotherapy), sometimes as an in-patient. Delivering a ten-pounder had not been part of the plan. She was worried about the neighbours' gossip, imagining them saying, '*Bad back, cannot be much of a bad back if she can cavort around.*' And the rest!

My birth had been difficult and long and there were many oft repeated myths about it. I was born at Haltwhistle Memorial Hospital on 24 October 1948. Mam reminded me frequently that I was the cause of her bad back. The legacy of her long labour was constant pain and suffering. It spoiled her joy at having a baby of her own and she was ambivalent toward me: fierce love giving way to angry rejection at times. The operations, manipulations and therapy did nothing to alleviate her pain, which continued to the end of her life. I was, and others were, forced to bear constant witness to this pain in the form of her pink National Health Service surgical corset. This pale pink brace was all belts, buckles and whalebones. When she was not wearing it, it was slung ceremoniously over the bedroom chair or over the banister (Mam always hung her clothes over the banister to air). Getting into this brace was a major operation in which we were involved, that is, Dad or me. Once on it became the public symbol of her pain as it curved out from her back under her clothes: a hard, stiff ridge making her blouses, jackets and coats stick out away from her figure. It expressed all her pain in a language of its very own.

And she had much pain, emotional as well as physical. She had had years of worry over Dad's health. She'd experienced her father's death from cancer, followed by her mother's death. In between, Aunty Vi was widowed. She had had to 'live in' with Nana during the war, sit tight while Dad was hospitalised at the other side of the world in India and South Africa, as well as thinking about his safety during the war. She had to bide time without information when his hospital ship was bombed by the Japanese. He was transferred to another and arrived safely in Cardiff or Bristol – it is not quite clear which but he was in Wrexham hospital. She had very poor relationships with all his family and always said that Aunty Bell and Nana were cruel.

I have never felt that I caused Mam's bad back and burdensome injuries. She didn't have the time, the luxury of an advanced education, nor the art or the motivation for introspection. She blamed whoever or whatever was the most convenient for her problems. Life had to go on and gritting her teeth and doing the best she could became her style. From my point of view I didn't find it easy leaving her womb either. What baby does? It is a secure warm place to be and an automatic feeding machine: coming into the world is a shock I should think for any baby. I'm sure Mam was tense and frightened and, without the relaxation classes we have been fortunate to enjoy, probably fought against her contractions rather than breathing into them. Historical knowledge changes one's perspective on birth but also on another's experience. My route into the world was probably a battle of wills, the birth canal narrowed by fear and the baby inching frustratingly forward to view the world. Her cervix didn't expand as it should and my journey was slow and tiring. How do I know? Because I repeated this pattern with my daughter despite the relaxation techniques I'd been taught, the only difference was the weight of the baby: I was seven pounds eight ounces and my daughter was nine pounds four ounces. I, too, had major injuries. They say anxiety can be passed on while a baby is in the womb and obviously the birth myth collusion played its part in helping anxiety and fear be passed on like a beautifully wrapped present at a friendly birthday party. Mam was exhausted by my birth, I wasn't. For the one and only time in my life I was classed as quite delicate.

Throughout her life Mam's back pain became symbolic of all that had, and did, hurt her emotionally: her grief, disappointment, anger and wishful thinking. She referred to it as her suffering and to the end of her life she felt she'd had nothing that was truly hers, or 'mine' as she put it. She believed that all she'd loved had been taken away from her and in her words, '*Everything is always taken away from me, or everyone takes everything away from me; nothing is ever mine.*'

Mam's emotional pain and grief were very real and eventually became the root of her depressive nature which was never diagnosed nor treated properly. I'm sure if you were to ask anyone who knew her well what memories they had of Mam they would say it was the answer to, '*How are you Emily?*'

'*Oh, not so bad you know but, well you know, my back's still bad, I'm in constant pain, I don't know why I have to suffer so much. What did I do to deserve this?*'

Mam's ability to cope with life, her moods swinging high and low, to and fro, was very variable. Despite her back, she would dig the garden, carry heavy loads of shopping, and a shopping trolley was out of the question, '*They are for lazy people,*' she'd say.

She was a very complicated personality to say the least, as puzzling to onlookers as she was to us, her children: a contradiction. She'd walk down the street, her back brace advertising her problems, yet stoically carrying herself proudly, and ram rod straight. She was a very quick walker and moved quickly whatever she was doing, which often belied her physical and mental state. When she was low she would be prostrate with pain, seeking refuge in bed. Her inner turmoil and emotional pain manifest in her physical pain.

I was born in Haltwhistle, as Mam did what most daughters did in 1948, went home to her own mother to have her baby. She was lucky as it was the beginning of the National Health Service and so she could have her baby in hospital rather than at home. She needed both emotional and physical support. Dad was not well. His regular check-ups with the army medical board describe him as being in constant niggling pain and always taking medication. He regularly lost on average five weeks per year of work. Money must have been a problem for both of them. They were disappointed about housing. Mam never did get over her disappointment about the loss of the house she so desperately wanted. I think this was the root of later bitterness against 'the powers that be', not that she really knew who these 'powers' actually were but interpreted them as being against her and Dad personally. The Army Medical Board and the Ministry of Pensions were definitely high on her list of the powerful.

11

Life With Mam and Dad

Often on a Saturday, Sunday or on bank holidays we'd set off from our house in Hallow Drive taking the farm road down toward the river Tyne at Newburn. Crossing Newburn Bridge to Ryton Willows we'd cut diagonally across the fields, the wheat rustling like insects inside a tin can at our ankles. We'd walk over the Newcastle to Carlisle railway line checking for trains as it was an unofficial crossing, and join the Peth leading up the hill to Ryton. Half way up the hill we'd pass the gaily-coloured gypsy caravans in their encampment on the side of the track with no fear of, nor prejudice about, these roaming people. Peth Hill was overhung with boughs of oak, beech, sycamore and ash trees forming a green bower over our heads so we climbed in a dark mysterious world just waiting for the moment when the trees thinned and the sun poured through again. In spring we picked blossom, in summer flowers in abundance and in autumn had competitions with ash keys and conkers.

If it was a hot day we would be perspiring by the time we reached the top of the steep lane, moaning that we were hot and couldn't walk any further. We loved the walk to Aunty Vi's where she often met us in Ryton Park to share our picnic, play tennis or swim: we only swam if we had the courage to brave the freezing water in the outdoor swimming pool. It was the coldest pool I have ever known. I have not found one that compares. We'd stand on the side trying to pluck up the courage to jump in and hardly ever did. If we did manage it we'd only be in minutes before we were out on the side shivering and crying to be towelled dry really, really hard to warm us up, begging for a hot drink. Aunty Vi often walked the other way to our house and almost always alone. Our parents were great walkers and as we walked they'd tell us the names of all the wild flowers, crops growing in the fields and the names of trees, birds and insects too.

I walked to Ryton hundreds of times throughout my childhood, and as an adult, but I didn't know that I was walking on the fields under which my great grandfathers and grandfathers had hewn their quota of coal every day. I walked past Whitewell Lane and Terrace time after time, passing the house they'd lived in: walking in the invisible imprints of their footsteps and the land they'd helped shape just as if I was a time traveller. From the park we'd catch the bus to Aunty Vi's at Woodside, about two miles from Ryton staying for a while, perhaps having tea or supper, and then if it was fine catch the bus to the park and walk home again via the Peth. If we walked both ways we walked about seven miles, '*It's just a hop skip and a jump,*' our mother would say if we moaned.

In winter we usually caught the bus on Newburn Road to Scotswood. We had to cross the road by Scotswood Bridge and wait in a dirty, freezing bus shelter. This had a corrugated iron roof but no sides and so the furious north or north east wind blew right through cutting your face clean in two and freezing you to death. Probably death would have been warmer – at least the grave would have been some kind of insulation. I will never forget how cold I was standing at that bus shelter. We waited shivering and moaning even on summer days for the red United bus to take us over the old Scotswood Bridge to Blaydon and then Ryton. Our return journey was worse, particularly in winter and in the dark, but not much better in summer. The bus shelter we needed to wait in for our connection to Throckley was a huge wooden structure that resembled a large, ugly, badly built cattle shed rather than a shelter for people. It was big enough to hold a rugby crowd and yet rarely were there more than a handful of people waiting. It stank of animal and human urine, was filled with rotting food, old paper and goodness knows what else, had no lights and was one of the most frightening freezing places I've ever had the misfortune to inhabit. The wind roared through its badly fitting slats causing mini whirlwinds in its centre, chip papers and cigarette packets danced like dervishes who'd forgotten when and how to stop their amazing performance. Personal safety wasn't such an issue then as it is now, the world seemed safer even if it wasn't, but in Scotswood Bridge bus shelter it didn't take much childish imagination to feel half scared out of my wits during our wait. Consequently we'd wrap ourselves around our mother's or father's legs for safety. Ten minutes in that shelter, in the dark, felt like ten hours. We shivered uncontrollably from cold and fear.

Outings like this were almost a weekly feature of my childhood, just like the journey on the bus to Melkridge. I absorbed the countryside without understanding or knowing that it was also my heritage, my culture. Now I realise what a wonderful travel opportunity it was: I absorbed the beauty of my landscape, the north and south Tyne valleys with their industrial and non-industrial landscapes. I was frightened of the river Tyne from Newburn down toward Newcastle because it was very wide and slow moving, grey, opaque and often very dirty and smelly.

Neither my parents nor I understood my fear of bridges. When we had to cross the bridge I'd run in front of them, hesitate at the bridge, and then run as fast as I could to the other side. I'd stand on the opposite side bent double with exertion, relieved and panting heavily from my arduous sprint. On the bridge I'd urge myself to run my fastest and I'd turn and watch my parents cross from the safety of the other side willing them on, and the bridge not to collapse. I was terrified the thing would collapse with me, or them on it, and we'd drown. No one, least of all me, knew where my fear came from but in my head I'd pray before I set my foot on the bridge, for God to get me and them safely across. I don't understand why I always had to go it alone, why didn't I just hold their hands and cross with them? The fear of bridges affected me when I was on the bus too, I couldn't look down from any bridge into the water.

I didn't think this river, our river, was beautiful either. The view from Newburn Bridge was spoilt by Stella Power Station, the glass works, ship building factories and industry, guarded over by threatening black hills of coal dust and stones: pit heaps. These were our unnatural mountains, a fixture of our local landscape. I was very wary of these, frightened they'd collapse and we'd be swallowed into their centre. My fears turned out not to be so childish after all but intuitive realism. The world saw how powerful and dangerous these heaps could be in the horror of Aberfan years later.

I watched the rowers from Newburn Rowing Club racing up and down the river wondering how they could bear to be on its surface, if they capsized they'd have filthy grey-river all over them. I couldn't understand why anyone would take that risk. If we walked the other way from our house to Wylam I didn't think like this at all. I loved the river and took a long time to understand that it was all the same river. The water was faster and cleaner and there was no industry spoiling my view. The Tyne sparkled and jumped along with frothy edges splashing on the rocks, shallow enough in places for us to take off our shoes and socks and plodge (paddle).

I was lucky, I realise now, to have seen the beautiful Northumberland villages and scenery often and so early in my life. I absorbed the countryside and it bred a desire for travel, which has never lost its allure, and an interest in landscape and nature that has been and remains an important part of my life. Without realising it then I had the opportunity to learn how important industry was and understand that we needed it to live and to prosper. My father was always emphasising this fact to our mother who hated the industry and the 'muck' as she referred to it. '*But Emily, we'd be badly off without it, Pet. We'd have no money. You can't have money without muck.*'

I saw how industry changed the environment and could see the damage it did to the river environs and the beauty by comparing Newburn walks with Wylam walks (where industry was absent) within a radius of five miles from my own front door: I lived in very contrasting worlds and they were indivisible; a fact of life. You had dirt and smoke on the one hand and clean green beauty on the other and I knew which I preferred and it wasn't industry and muck.

What I didn't understand then was how 'I' – that is the 'me that's me' – was significantly being shaped and moulded by the landscapes I was born into, lived in, and on, just as my parents and their parents had been too. Our landscape was continuously changing. We (humans) were partners in land transformation for our own survival so that we could create wealth, although as ordinary working class we personally had not, did not and would not share in the profits except as wages. Nevertheless I understood that without opportunity for work and employment, usually in industry in our area we were unlikely to prosper or have a future. Industry and humans needed each other and so the wealthy capitalists developed the land they and we inherited and the rest of us became employees in order to earn money to live and prosper. We invented new industries and machinery so we could go on prospering and when what the land had to offer ran out, we started on something else to take its place – often before we tidied up our mess from the last development. We ruined our own landscape with the detritus of our efforts. We left our land scarred with pit heaps; empty factories, derelict housing and a beautiful river polluted beyond imagination near its mouth which happened to be too near me for my liking. We set up, as others had before us, a cycle of invention, use, and destruction in order to be able to prosper and we called it progress. Humans and industry lived and still live in an ambivalent relationship but we are getting better at tidying up and recycling, or at least we are trying. Yet the pit heaps came in handy in an innovative recycling project as practice ski-slopes.

Landscapes and culture are inextricably linked.[1] Legends abound, and as a child I loved the stories about our area: the men down the pits, those in the factories, the farmers, the posh people, the owners and the girls in service. Our parents told us many of these stories and we sang versions of these legends too. 'Keep your feet still Geordie Hinny,' 'Bobbie Shaftoe', 'Blaydon Races', Wo're Geordie's lost his Penker' (marble), 'Lampton Worm' and many more. Aunty Ena (our next door neighbour) played the piano as we sang. Some of the stories and songs were not legends, the traditional literature of an area, but myths about supernatural characters or imaginary people like the Lampton Worm: metaphors for our daily lives. This applies to our own stories, our family stories. I have had to sort out for this story (my memoir) what might be myth and what might be legend. It is easy to come to a version of our (my) story based on myth – the imagined story transformed by memory and often reconstructed by the memory with the gaps having been haphazardly filled in by parents, friends or things partly heard or understood. We can so easily feast on the imaginary and ignore the legends and while we concentrate on the imagined people or events we can ignore the challenge of what really happened, the conjunction of the real people within their history, how to lose ourselves in the real. We have a propensity to wallow in the imaginary or phantasy.

To understand the 'me' and 'I', I have had to free my memory; free the myths so that the legend, the story, can be told as well as it might after such a long time. There is no doubt that in trying to free the legend I have transformed the story, it will not be as it was but as I see it and understand it from my historical and experiential time capsule. This book is my story not theirs. My perception of my family history will shape this story. Our story is rooted in how we (along with many others) designed and used landscape: the rustic versus the industrial story. How in that landscape we developed culture and subcultures until landscape and culture were inextricable. This is my family's story and my story, and I'm pretty certain there is much they'd disagree with.

The myth we created was that there was a creator, something outside of ourselves, supernatural, who created our destiny: God. The legend: we created our own story by the choices we made ourselves and within our particular historical and cultural time. Like all major inventions each time capsule contributed to the design and effectiveness of the next, they transformed the story at each point in time. My great-grandparents and grandparents worked the land and its mineral content to provide them with a living and their values shaped their children's values. Hard work and independence were passed from generation to generation along with a love of the rural and a tolerance of the industrial – canny companions. For my mother such integration was not possible and she remained ambivalent about living in Throckley and a fantasist about her childhood homelands. Consequently throughout our childhood and much of our early adult years we remained ambivalent too. I had a love–hate relationship with my environment tinged with Geordie pride.

Despite the strain of my parents' health and the struggle with money, we had lots of fun. My parents were both funny in different ways. My father could make us laugh by playing games and racing around trees, settees, the garden or the beach. My mother had us in fits of laughter with just the odd throwaway comment; she was very witty. She and we would laugh until we couldn't stop, we'd be doubled up in an agony of laughter, wetting ourselves with laughter. Once any of us mentioned the fact we might wet ourselves, we'd laugh even more and then be jumping up and down in fear of our bladders letting go; we could get drunk on laughter. My parents were social too. We had lots of people in and out of our house, family and friends. We saw Aunty Vi and Aunty Ella nearly every weekend and Aunty Maria and Uncle Bill and their family lived at the end of our road after he moved from Haltwhistle when the Bardon Mill colliery closed, to the pit in Throckley. Uncle George and Aunty Jenny and Colin came from Lancaster every so often and we always had a good time with them. We had wonderful fun times with them in

Lancaster and Morecambe Bay. My mother could be very jealous if they stayed at Aunty Maria's instead of our house. Then she wouldn't let us go out with our cousins if they called, she always made some excuse or said we were ready for bed. We would then watch disconsolately from our front room window as our cousins disappeared on some adventure.

Dad was a very popular man, people just seemed to love him, and so he had lots of friends calling and they'd chat and argue over afternoon tea or he'd go off with them to play cricket. He was a good cricketer and played with his cousin Harry Morgan and his friends as well as his father and brother-in-law (Uncle Fred) and Uncle Jo. Jo was his best friend and we often went to Aunty Betty and Uncle Jo's for tea – the biggest teas you could ever imagine. We loved it. Dad was football mad and if he was well never missed a match at St James' Park as he was a fan of Newcastle United. He'd have his lunch, get dressed up in his shirt and tie, and off he'd go, his mac over his arm. My mother wasn't as easily pleased as our father, nor was she happy with his hobbies: she often made a fuss about his football because she wanted to do something else instead.

On summer days we'd go on the train to Tynemouth or Whitley Bay for the whole day. Sometimes Aunty Bell and Uncle Fred would come too. We'd dress up in our best clothes, take a warm jumper and swimming costumes as well as raincoats. We could never trust the weather so we always packed for each season on every outing. Mam and Aunty Bell would have packed picnics, usually enough to feed an army, and we'd set off hampered by heavy bags to catch the number 16 bus to the Central Station. I loved the steamy smoky smell of the station, the pulsating engines and staccato voices announcing over the loudspeaker where the trains were going, from which platform they'd leave and the time of the next one. I listened carefully for the time and platform of our train because I dreaded missing it and therefore the possibility of less time at the beach. The smell was warm and sooty, as the steam belched out of the engine funnel, the driver hanging precariously out of his cabin as he checked the funnel, the ferocity of the blasting steam, and that all was well with his engines and carriages. I loved these engine drivers with their grimy faces, their black berets or their peaked cap. If a train passed you as you walked along the engine driver would always wave. The trains were glowing coloured giants with polished brasses shining and sparkling in the lights of the station or in the sun. When the train started it gave an almost mighty growl and puff as though it would burst from its metal container with this first effort to get going: the first puff and chuff of the thousands it would make taking us on our journey; chuff, chuff, chuffety-chuff we'd chorus as we rode along. Electric trains were never quite so exciting; steam trains had long carriages and leather seats and the window opened enough for you to see the scenery rushing past and smell the engine fumes. No wonder children are obsessed with Thomas the Tank Engine. No trains, including our fast diesel trains, can compare with the steam train: it is an experience all of its own, and oh, so romantic. I'd dance around my parents' legs while we waited in the station, frantic with excitement in my Sunday best.

This early travelling gave me the travel bug because my father always explained where we going, how long it would take and what we'd see on the way. Every step from my front door became an adventure opening up a new world and new knowledge. Some of my friends find it odd that I don't look at maps very often even if I don't know where I'm going. I think this is a habit I developed when travelling with my father: it was an aural education. Obviously, I find out all about the place, the journey and the times but leave the map reading until I actually need it! It is the planning and the excitement of the journey that I'm interested in. My nose often then takes me without too much difficulty. I was never conscious of being disappointed, nor critical, of where I'd been. I find I get furious if people criticise where they've been for holidays or outings and say they were disappointed. I simply cannot understand. It is the going and being there that is adventure enough for me. As a child I never thought it would be possible to travel around the world as I have done, both with work and in my leisure time, and I see it as a great privilege to have done so. I feel irate when people are disparaging of other cultures or their holiday destination or accommodation.

The beach is where I relocate my soul every single time I'm near one, let alone on it. It is as if the sea air blows gently on my automatic pilot light and re-ignites my soul's dying flame. I can be dog tired, stressed or emotionally upset and within hours of being on a beach – walking, sitting, or playing by the sea – I recuperate and find a joy that is indescribable. This started with our family days at the beach and our holidays by the sea. And it has saved my physical health and sanity time and time again. I have a natural affinity with the sea that began with these childhood visits. It is the most wonderful feeling, those first minutes as you near the sea and smell the ozone, the seaweed, feel the breeze on your face, feel the sting in your nostrils and look out on the horizon line where the land and sky meet: it is metaphysical. The sea is not controllable and has a rhythm of its own, rolling in and rolling out forever unstoppable, humans cannot change its pattern or its will. The sea is the embodiment of free: and it has power. To watch it change colour as the sky changes colour is magic, to see the waves form a long way out and their gathering speed as they head for shore, perfectly shaped and timed is as absorbing as a book. I'd watch the breakers, sometimes small and frail, gentle, other times bold and big lashing the shore. It is its susurration, ssss-ssss-sss-sssssssssss-sssssss-splash, which is so restful, meditative, calming the mind, quieting the spirit. I could listen to that sound day and night and never tire of it. The feel of the sea on one's skin is a cleansing experience, the cold stinging salt is so bracing. It is humbling to think of the world's oceans continuing their immortal pattern day in and day out. It puts life and death into perspective as the oceans will still be rolling and drawing back long after I'm dead and gone. The sea doesn't get bored, its work is its work; its energy its very being. I can sit and watch the sea for hours and feel completely at peace. I love swimming in the sea as it holds your weight and smells better than any swimming pool, I love to feel it on my feet as I paddle along the shore, and I love to be on a boat on its surface. When it is rough and stormy I'm just as happy, enjoying its energy as it smashes its way to the shore and the waves curl, whoosh, and then pull back, pulling the sea itself back into itself, renewing itself. The dark heavy sea of the winter storms is a reminder of the darker side of life: it isn't all smooth and certain. The sea on a sunny day is a jewel that cannot be imitated in any design. It ripples, shines, sparkles like a million diamonds; and moves in its own unique way; its movement embodies the perfect orgasm. The ripples far from shore, part of its very fabric, gently gain strength as the wave develops, stronger, stronger, the ssss-sss-sus-urration gathering pace until it hits the shore with pleasure and energy: satiation; and then pulls back into itself with that wonderful rushing sound; complete.

Throughout my life, especially in my teens, I have had a recurring dream: I am trapped as a tidal wave overtakes me and I try to struggle from its clutches to the shore. It takes shape over my head but I'm not yet in it. I have time to save my terrified self but I'm panicking, trying to find a way to get away from it. I look for the shore, a bridge; help. There is none. Then I wake up. For many years this recurring dream was the same, the cine film stuck, and I'd wake up frightened and sweating, because I couldn't work out my escape as the curve of the tidal wave hung over my head about to engulf me; worried too that it may actually happen sometime.

Later, when I had this dream there was a bridge I just might get to but I never did and woke while struggling to reach it. Later still, I made it to the bridge but not to shore, then to shore in shallow water as the wave receded. I still have this dream but the wave stops short of me and leaves me in the shallows and I can walk ashore by a wooden bridge: this is the current dream. Freudian theory would suggest that I was terrified of sex and especially of being overwhelmed by an orgasm but I don't think so as the dream has changed as I have gained self-confidence and especially as I have overcome difficult situations and been able to cope with whatever faced me: as I learned to deal with fear, verbalise fear, to remain calm and cope with difficulty. The sea is a homoeopathic treatment; even though it can be dangerous it heals me (just as many homoeopathic medicines can be poisonous they can heal) and it has healed my mind whenever it has been troubled. It has taught me, as well as mirroring my anxiety.

The sea on the Northumberland coast was rarely warm enough to swim in but fantastic to watch, paddle in and listen too and with the wind in my hair it made me feel really alive. We'd go to Budle Bay and Warkworth when my father hired a car. He loved driving. We had holidays in Blackpool and Robin Hood's Bay where I skipped along the beach way ahead of my parents and brother happy as a lark until I heard my father yelling at me. I turned and saw him running toward me as I was about to plodge in a stream of water running down the beach. He grabbed me and smacked me hard. I couldn't understand why. Then he explained that it was a sewer I was about to plodge in and that I might get polio. I knew what polio was as our next-door neighbour's son had had polio and it had left him with a limp. I was the last to be inoculated for polio in my school. My mother wanted me to have the vaccine, my father didn't. He was quite neurotic about hygiene and health and they'd argued over this for weeks before he agreed to sign the forms. I think his own ill health made him very conscious of illness and treatments and I don't think he really trusted doctors very much. He certainly didn't trust the science on vaccines.

On another occasion I had bought a secondhand book at a Sunday school sale, it cost me 6d. I brought it home proud of my bargain and he went stark raving mad. My mother and I couldn't understand why but understood clearly that he was about to burn it. Crying my eyes out I pleaded with him not to and so did my mother. He settled for her suggestion that it should be disinfected on the hearth to kill the germs. He explained once he was calm again that paper carried germs from other people's houses and as we didn't know where the book had come from, it could be carrying germs that could cause any manner of illnesses. The book sat on the hearth for two days before I was allowed to read it. This sounds as though my father went over the top but it is important to see it from his perspective. TB was rife, so were polio, scarlet fever and rheumatic fever, and people were very conscious of fleas and nits especially in Throckley as decent people kept their homes clean and healthy and protected their families.

I was a persistent, curious child driving everyone mad with my never-ending stream of questions and constant prattle. My father actively fed my curiosity; he was knowledgeable, read insatiably, listened to the radio and loved learning new things. He'd try his hand at most things. One day he decided to make a coffee table, his own design, hexagonal with a shelf for his books on the bottom. This nearly drove us all mad as he was a perfectionist. When he was finished it he wasn't happy with it at all, he couldn't get it exactly right but it sat in our front room for years. Gardening was the same. He created a rockery from our steep front garden measuring it out, making sure it was straight with a spirit level, riddling every inch of soil. His rockery is still there today and not a stone has moved. The same plants he planted are still blooming. He planted vegetables and fruits and each was paced and measured out, the soil riddled and fed. He had loads of manure delivered and we all had to help to carry it by the bucket load up to the back garden and pile it high for him to fertilise his vegetables. His rhubarb and raspberry bushes still stand today. He didn't go as far as some of our neighbours: they used to shovel up the horse muck off the road and use it as manure. The Co-op greengrocer had a horse and cart as did the rag and bone man (the bogeyman) so free manure was easily available. My parents didn't want to show we were poor so paid for their manure. He wallpapered and painted, but to my mother's instructions. She was the perfectionist when it came to decorating and the biggest most frightening row they ever had was over tiling the bathroom. He wasn't well and was trying hard to complete the job and couldn't. Our mother was furious and it is only now I understand why. I think she was afraid he was lazy, as she believed his father was. This is hard to understand as he was ill but I can understand her frustration. The row was so bad that he sat me down and told me they were going to divorce and that I must tell my brother that we'd be going to an orphanage when we returned from Sunday school. I worried all afternoon about this; I had no idea what an orphanage was but clearly understood we wouldn't be living at our house any more. So I told my brother as we got on the bus for home, he didn't bat an eyelid as he had no idea what I was talking about. We got home to find our mother in bed and our dad silent and stubborn but there was no one waiting to take us away. Their silence lasted an entire week and I knew it was all over when he kissed our mother on the lips again before he left for work: his usual habit. When I reflect on this it seems to me that my father was given to infrequent but furious rages and I believe these were related to his health, his diminishing strength and fear of the future, and when he couldn't do the things other men did our mother was angry, frustrated and frightened too. They rarely had rows despite all the strain. And our mother did want him to do just what she wanted him to do, and in her way too.

One of the great joys in our life was our radio; we were all avid radio listeners: it was on from when we got up in the morning until my parents went to bed, even during Sunday lunch, roast beef and fabulous puffy light Yorkshire puddings in winter, roast lamb in spring accompanied by fresh spring greens or roast pork and apple sauce, not of course if there was an 'r' in the month, a rule Mam took seriously. Her puddings were legendary: crisp pastry apple tarts or lemon meringue pie, the topping four inches high and crunchy, pineapple upside-down pudding, jam or syrup sponges, trifle, to this day my mouth waters when I think of the communion over these lunches and the smell of the kitchen as it was cooking. She had one particular pudding we loved and she called it Nicki tart. This was apple, raisins, currants and ground almonds mixed with brown sugar; scrumptious – and her bilberry (blueberry) tart for the few weeks they were available was something very special. While eating we listened to Forces Family favourites, then Wakey Wakey with Billy Cotton and his band followed by Round the Horn, Educating Archie, and Reginald Dixon at the organ.

During the week I wouldn't miss Mrs Dale's Diary when I came in from school, and on Saturday Uncle Mack's Children's Favourites. I loved and still do the magic of radio and the way it sparks my imagination, far more than television. I could conjure up my own pictures to the text of the radio with Workers' Playtime, Listen with Mother. Woman's Hour remains part of my radio diet now.

When my brother was about ten months old our parents decided to drive to Surrey to see my mother's brothers, Jack and Tommy. Jack was married to Aunty Ann and Tommy to Aunty Peggy. Her brothers had left home during the General Strike and had lived in Ashtead ever since. Dad hired a smart-looking black car and with mother's picnics packed in advance for two days, off we set; down the A1 toward London and then to Ashtead, except it wasn't as easy as that because the car kept breaking down and we had to sleep in the car. Normally we would have been on the road twenty-four hours but it took us nearly forty-eight and our poor father had to keep mending the car with my mother worrying away at him, mostly in the dark with a restless baby on her lap. We thought we'd never get there, never mind back. We did arrive after what seemed a lifetime to a six-year-old, and spent a happy two weeks including going to the races. Aunty Jean was so house-proud my mother was worn out by the time we left for home as she had to watch every move we made and, as she herself was house-proud, someone more house-proud is hard to imagine.

We had a holiday in Blackpool when my brother was two and

I was almost eight, travelling by train, my favourite puffing steam train. The hustle and bustle of the Central Station was an outing in itself and full of smartly dressed people. The huge Victorian portal of the station and the adjoining posh Station Hotel (where incidentally I spent my wedding night by choice) with its grand entrance seemed to me to be entrances to entrancing worlds far from the daily world I was familiar with. The station was a place of people's leavings and returning, greetings and cuddles, tears and farewells, waving, shouting and hurry. It had an emotional atmosphere signalled by hooters, bells and voices. I loved the brown station café and the strange sounding 'Ladies Waiting Room'. I spent hours wondering what the ladies inside were waiting for because there seemed not to be a Men's Waiting Room although there was a 'General Waiting Room'. I didn't understand the conventions of the time; ladies needed to be protected. I puzzled and puzzled about this before I asked. I often did this, I tried to work things out for myself and only if I couldn't, did I give in and ask. I still do this. It has meant I have held onto some hilariously wrong meanings and interpretations in my lifetime and often extremely literal ones which means they come across, once I air them in public, as very funny indeed. It never occurred to me that they might be toilets, as my mother wouldn't let us use public toilets unless we were absolutely desperate which means we hung on, our bladders bursting, long past the time we ought to have done. We always left the house with empty bladders and clean bowels, and we were expected to learn to wait until we had arrived at our destination. We developed inflated bladders and were anally retentive. I understood from that point on that 'ladies' did indeed go to toilets in stations. I found it most odd that they hadn't been taught to wait as we had. Poor things, I thought, fancy having to ask to go to the toilet in public, even worse to be seen to go in public, pity they hadn't had my mother to teach them. It was years before I realised you could just go in there and sit down while you waited for the train.

We were half way on our journey to Blackpool when we stopped at a station and our father decided to get out to buy his cigarettes. I became hysterical as he jumped down onto the platform, his mac over his arm. I was terrified he wouldn't get back on the train in time and he'd be left behind and I would leave without him. I hadn't the wit (as Aunty Vi would have said) to realise that if he didn't get back for this train there would be another and he would still arrive in Blackpool at some time. I hung out of the window tears as big as dewdrop sweets flowing down my face and wetting my blouse. He only just made it and jumped on as the train began to move. This made me very punctual for trains although I'm never very early for anything else.

Throughout this scare our mother was unpacking our picnic; we never travelled anywhere without food. She wouldn't have a flask of tea: she took a flask of hot water, the teapot or coffee pot (or both) the milk jug and sugar basin. She carried the milk and sugar in separate containers. We had spoons, forks and knives, plates, china cups and saucers, and of course serviettes. All our crockery and utensils were exceedingly well travelled. She'd have a small tablecloth on which she'd carefully set everything out, no matter where we were. There'd be egg and cress sandwiches, her famous juicy mince pie, cold meats (not Spam), hard-boiled eggs, cake, apple tart and plenty of fresh fruit: all carefully packed. Relatives laugh at their memories of going on a picnic with her and how she would dictate how the flask was to be filled, the milk and sugar packed. Aunty Jenny made me laugh when she told us about their outing to Southport. They couldn't believe it when mother got out her travelling mini-silver service to the delight of the crowds. Aunty Jenny didn't drink tea or coffee either so had nothing to drink but the flask water.

In Blackpool we stayed in a lovely bed and breakfast hotel with the most wonderful landlady. We had a huge room with two massive double beds in it; my brother and I were in one bed and our parents in the other. I stressed them out because I couldn't get to sleep because the bed-clothes smelled of shoe polish. No one else could smell it but I could. It wasn't unpleasant but I couldn't stop sniffing it: I didn't like the smell. The bed-clothes were white and spotless so I can only think that it was the starch the lady had used. We spent happy hours on the beach even though it was cold, windy and drizzly, walked miles along the prom, went to the fairground and met up with Uncle George, Aunty Jenny and our cousin Colin. One night my father said he had a surprise for us: we were going to go out long after we would normally be in bed. He'd booked tickets at the Blackpool Tower Circus. I was ecstatic because Reginald Dixon from the radio was going to be playing the organ. I stood at the bottom of the tower trying to see the top as he pointed out that we would be climbing hundreds of steps to the theatre at the very top. We climbed and climbed and as we got higher we could hear the organ. It was pure magic and I have never forgotten the sound, so happy and jolly: I danced up the rest of the stairs. The seats were red plush and soft and didn't nettle my legs like the bus seats did. We got settled; Dad with my brother on his knee, with me next to him and then our mother. As the lights dimmed the red velvet curtain slowly moved back to reveal the stage. To very, very loud music the clowns rolled onto the stage shouting, running, jumping. They were everywhere, shouting to the audience and expecting us to shout back. I was mesmerised taking in every detail and then they brought on hose-pipes and started to fill the stage with water, they were rolling in it, splashing each other, the hose-pipes were pumping water at a tremendous rate – and then my brother screamed. His screams got louder and louder even though our father quietly tried to calm him by whispering in his ear but nothing worked. They had to leave and we followed. I was so disappointed.

Our last holiday together, although we didn't know it at the time, was at Budle Bay camping and caravanning with friends. Our father hired a car to take us there. Budle Bay has Bamburgh Castle on one side and Seahouses on another. It has beautiful clean sands and the air is fantastic: healthy windswept headlands. We had a wonderful time with three dads and three mums and six of us playing. When I look at the photographs of this holiday it is to see through my adult eyes how ill my father was; his weight is well below what it should have been, probably only eight stone if that, and the strain our mother was under: she looks very thin and tense. Dad, my brother and I made camps from the dried grass. We played rounders, cricket, tennis, quoits and pig in the middle as well as writing our names in the hard sand in the evening. The dads all mucked in peeling potatoes, cooking breakfast and doing the washing up.

Southerners would find the sea cold but we were used to it: it is just warm enough in summer to risk a dip. When you first put your toes in the water you think you will never dare put your body in, for fear of dying of cold, but the numbing effect of the water doesn't stop you especially when your friends are daring too. It feels wonderful once you're in, cleansing from head to toe, but the secret is don't dawdle, just dive in. The Swedes pay a fortune for their saunas so they can have the same hot and cold treatment: sauna first, and then a freezing dip in the lake for health. The Northumberland coast on a hot day provides the sauna free. Once you are in you don't want to get out, it's worse getting out especially if there is a north-east wind. The shivering starts immediately and your teeth chatter and you can't stop trembling. Our mother always swore that if you relaxed you wouldn't feel the cold so much but I could never do that. Out would come the flasks with hot drinks, and towels, with mothers rubbing their children hard to warm them through. The shivers and goose bumps soon pass and before long you are eager to go back in again: madness.

You can walk miles along the beaches, especially at Amble with its sparkling twinkling sand looking as though bits of stars had fallen from the sky and landed to light it up. There are boats to the Farne Islands to see the wonderful bird life, to Grace Darling's house, to Holy Island, the original centre of early religion, and to taste Lindisfarne Mead, the sweet wine of the monks. Kippers are smoked at Craster and taste nothing like the limp soggy kippers you buy in the supermarket now: their densely dark smoked flesh is a delicacy. The wet fish shop in Seahouses is on a par with any European fish market and they sell almost everything you can think of from crabs, lobsters, winkles, mussels, and fresh cod and haddock, skate, plaice and coley fillet. Our mother would never have coley as she said it was the bottom of the market and only the poor bothered to eat it! She always said that the fish and chip shops used coley fillet and pretended it was cod (and most people according to her didn't know the difference) and so we weren't allowed fish and chips from the fish and chip shop. She made her own and selected her own fish from the shop in Lemington with as much care as she did her meat.

At Seahouses, though, she would give in and we were allowed fish and chips in white paper, then wrapped in newspaper, and we could eat them outside and standing up: a real treat. The fish and chip shop in Seahouses uses fresh, fleshy, white fish, which flakes away from the skin; the batter is thin, crisp and not greasy. The chips are crisp and salty not floppy. Hot fish and chips after swimming taste delicious especially on a wind blown northern beach. Our friends were allowed to eat winkles but our mother wouldn't allow us too, oh no, '*They're filthy things and no one wants to see you poking them out of their shells with an old pin. You don't know where they've been.*'

'*In the sea, Mam,*' we'd say. '*Ah, please Mam, the others have got them, please can we?*'

We didn't win and I've never tried them, not that I ever really wanted to taste them, just didn't want to be different. I must admit watching someone eat winkles is like seeing them pick their nose. It rather put me off. I learned about my mother's worries very well and I still cannot eat shellfish unless I have cooked it myself.

One of the highlights of our holiday was our friend's father who always entertained us at home and did on holiday as well. He was a great tap dancer and magician. We'd beg him to tap dance and when he gave in we were mesmerised as he bobbed about, his grey curls dancing on his forehead. He'd get faster and faster as we watched and then we'd try and join in; unfortunately I had two left feet. His magic was our other entertainment: he'd get his stick and say, '*Abracadabra, sim-salabim,*' and produce some inexplicable trick. He made life seem simple and fun and we loved it.

---

[1] Schama, Simon (1996), *Landscape and Memory*. Fontana Press.

12

To Dad: Legends

I never understood why my mother was so negative about your family, Dad, and how you coped with her being so scathing about them all without losing your love for her: because you never did. Neither did I ever hear you criticise her. I know you had the odd row, but there were few rows in total. You were not a warring couple by any stretch of the imagination. You were loving and close, and when you were at home there was peace and a positive atmosphere. There was only one terrible row I remember when you were going to divorce her, yet within a week you were lovey-dovey again.

As a family we went to visit Mam's sisters and brothers. You had a close relationship with your brothers-in-law; they loved you, everyone who knew you loved you. So, Dad, how did you cope with this rejection of your family? Did you know what it was about? Did you know that your mother and your wife did not get on? I wonder. Or, were you, as a personality, easy going, of the mind to live and let live? You certainly seemed to be easy going; you had such an easy swagger to your walk, relaxed and at home in your own skin, loose limbed as a good cricketer needs to be; yet deeply anxious too.

David is similar, he does not have any snobbery in him, he is accepting of most things and he loves passionately too; his strengths are his ability to love passionately as well as his staying power. He also loves cricket. I have a much sharper tongue at times, learned from my mother, although I think she herself would say

I learned it from your mother, or was it a bit of both? David was determined to keep Andrew, your grandson, at home – you know he was very sick following his birth, and had to be christened in the hospital because it was touch and go whether he would live? His birth problems and illness afterwards led to permanent physical as well as some brain damage – slight, but enough to have disrupted his life, and his life chances. They were the result of blood poisoning. David stood by him and never fobbed him off on social services; this is a credit to him; in that, he is very like you. I have staying power too, but I have only really known one passionate love and have settled for much less. Passion came late in my life and it was an impossible passion at that. I have been afraid, I think, of ever letting myself go in case I was hurt; afraid I'd lose the lover. I missed out there. But I do have the staying power and will see through what I start. Your grand-daughter, Louise, has both these traits of yours, including a belief in passion and romance: she is a real romantic.

Or were you just realistic about your family, loving them in spite of how they were, or how others saw them – unconditional love? It is hard for me to understand my mother's view because I loved them too, so much, and I had a much closer relationship with them, especially Nana and Granda, than I did with my maternal grandparents because they died when I was so young. I know from your niece that Nana had another side to her, she could be extremely unpredictable, but I didn't see that, and I didn't personally ever experience her wrath. Did you?

My visits to Nana and Granda were very different from my visits to my maternal grandparents, who were much more strict and serious. Did something happen when my mother was living alone with your parents, while you were in India? She hinted often enough about something but didn't explain. Was it something to do with Uncle I wonder? Or was it just that 'living in' was such a hard way to start married life, especially when she was alone while you were away? It could simply be that they were so different from her own parents, their ways so alien to her, that she couldn't cope with them. Her family was not demonstrative and yours were; very loving, emotional and loud, well the women were loud, the men quieter. On the other hand we know my mother probably didn't need a reason or an event to stir her dislike; your love for your parents and sister, and theirs for you, was reason enough to fire her jealousy.

She said she hated your parents and made no attempt to hide her feelings from me. They were a sharp contrast, or at least Nana was, to my maternal grandmother, my dignified, strong, reserved, gentle Grandma. Your mother was a character, you have to admit: a strong, dominating personality with a very fiery temper. She could strike enough sparks to set fire to, and to burn down, the Kremlin. Her Willy, as she always referred to you, was very precious. Your whole family adored you, and you adored them. Nana was a matriarch, no one disputed this fact, yet you were happy in her company and so was I. Don't you think that families are very hard to understand: complex, ever changing, hard to keep up with sometimes?

My mother always said that Aunty and her daughter lived at Nana's and repeatedly said, '*You'd think they didn't have a home to go to, they are always wasting time over cups of tea.*' According to her, wasting time was a cardinal sin just like dirty socks. There was warmth and chatter at Nana's as well as endless cups of tea; lots of wasted time, if chatting and arguing companionably is indeed wasting time. Nana had a huge brown teapot called Betty, Brown Betty, as she referred to it, and this would be filled and refilled from the ever-boiling kettle on the range. Mam insisted that Nana's and Aunty Bell's tea was horrid, stewed beyond recognition, over mashed: it was very strong and sour. How did you stand these criticisms? Did you just take it in your stride? Did they not make you cross?

Nana's large table was covered in a balding maroon velvet cloth with pulled out fringes around its edges. I liked to sit and pick at these and see them come away in huge loops. It is true that the family would sit around the table for hours with neighbours, friends or relatives, drinking tea and eating; chattering in competition with the radio battling valiantly with its human competitors. There was never any hurry or routine and always an apple pie or cake; Nana's pastry was thick and sweet. The fire blazed in all seasons so she had hot water for her cooking, and even though she had an old gas cooker in the kitchen she preferred her range. She'd been trained as a baker and pastry cook and delighted in making rich fatty calorie-laden food for the extended family, much of which you, Dad, couldn't eat. There was a bounty of food for everyone who turned up at her door. She regularly produced her very own carbohydrate love-ins: resplendent calorific teas for Granda's clutch of rather large relatives and her sister Esther and her family. Was it her individualism, her disregard for convention, that Mam didn't like? Did you mind?

Your mother didn't like being alone; she hated solitude, so her house was always full of people. You and Uncle, your brother-in-law, were friends since you were young boys so you were very close, along with Nana's nephew, your cousin and best friend, fellow cricketer Uncle Harry, so there was an extended family connection, a tight bond that kept you all together. Did Mam feel outside of this, was she not accepted? Or did she just reject your relatives out of hand? Did you ever talk about her attitudes? These negative attitudes must have hurt you? Was this why you thought of divorce, once?

Nana would take anyone or anything in, animals and people; she'd also help anyone, do anything for you. Did you know the story about a rescued cat my cousin found in the church? She'd promised Nana it would be a good cat because it was found in the Christmas crib yet it turned out to be anything but good; it was a very cunning cat. The cat was forever stealing food, and I remember one occasion when Nana'd made iced cakes for the expected relatives; the prowling cat awaited his opportunity and as soon as she left the room he jumped on the table and licked the cream and icing off the cakes. Nana was demented and chased him around the table, dish cloth flying in her hand shouting, swearing, telling him his end was near, she'd murder him, strangle the life out him. She didn't, of course, and he lived, while she wiped the cakes clean and re-iced them telling me I mustn't say anything or she'd murder me too. 'I'll murder you' is a popular threat in our culture when someone is annoyed. It isn't meant to be literal. Even as a child I knew it was just a chiding comment. The cat wasn't deterred although Nana did become more cautious, putting her beautiful pies and cakes on the mantle shelf above the range. One time the dog Laddy and the cat were watching her every move. Once she was out of the room, Laddy reached up and knocked down the pies so he and the cat could feast. They were both eating contentedly when Nana walked in: all hell was let loose; they did indeed come within an inch of their life that day.

And dogs: she loved dogs. Her idea of a rest was to sit in her rocking chair by the range with Laddy partly on her lap, hanging around her neck by both front paws, scouring his coat for fleas. It was impossible for him to sit on her lap because he was so huge. She'd then throw the fleas on the fire where they popped and sizzled while she ignored everyone who pointed out how disgusting this habit was. She didn't care a hang and did not take the slightest notice of anyone or their opinions. I can understand my mother's horror at such behaviour, this was a particular awful habit, but if anyone had dared to say to Nana that she should stop doing it, this would only have served to keep the habit very alive. Stubborn comes to mind. David is so stubborn and you were too. Ah yes, I know you were very stubborn.

Granda was born into a more affluent, skilled, working class family who owned their own house. He had two sisters, both were tall and broad, Amazonian compared to Nana, but she cooked for them with real pleasure and was on very good terms with them, entertaining them regularly; their supposed poshness and wealth didn't matter a jot to her. In her eyes she was as good as them any day. You were close to them too, as your photographs show, as do your wedding photos: it is your cousin who stands as your bridesmaid, not one of my mother's own many nieces. Your relatives were wealthier than your parents but Nana didn't seem to be jealous of them, rather she welcomed them. She and Aunty were always trotting off, by bus and train, to Stockton on Tees or North Shields to see them, often taking me with them. There seemed to be two-way traffic in these relationships and very strong family ties. Dogs, cats, food and people mingled together and she didn't worry a bit about hygiene. David has some of Nana in him too, a large dollop of Holland and Morgan genes. I have been very much more concerned with appearances. I love entertaining though, in the same way as Nana and Mam, a mix of each.

Nana was the original believer in muck being the maker of a sound immune system. Was this all too much for my mother, as well as too much narration? There was a great deal of narration in your mother's house you must admit. I wish I knew the answers to these questions: we didn't have the luxury of time together, you and I, and so we had no chance to talk about these things, or to put them in context. I have lived in a kind of limbo, not understanding these caustic comments about your family: I loved them and my mother didn't.

I wasn't the least bit afraid of Nana's threats because she didn't ever threaten me and I didn't feel threatened. I knew she was just dramatic, and I was used to her. She would often burst out laughing in the middle of her tirades and we would all end up laughing too. Afterwards she would say, '*Ee, hinny, I didn't mean it!*' She had a very quick temper: all four foot ten of her rose like a large tanker riding a mountainous wave. I have it too and have had to learn to control it. My temper takes a lot of rousing and it is rare, but it has a similar force, at least gale force eight as the weather forecasters would say. The resulting tsunami of Nana's temper could leave others more than a tad fragile.

My Nana, your mother, was larger than life: a Boadicea, tough, dogmatic, terrifying, confrontational and seemingly invincible. Yet kind and loving: myriad personalities tightly packed in her small round body. Perhaps it was her Celtic inheritance, the women ruled the roost in the original Northern Celtic settlements, with the right to divorce; they were magistrates; held power. Was it Nana's periodic emotional incontinence that frightened Mam? After all, her family did not show emotion in public, rarely in private either: they were very controlled. They would all have seen such behaviour as irrational, out of control.

Wherever Nana and Aunty were to be found there was warmth, bustle and constant chatter. I learned to join in, walk, think and talk all at once; no one minded, not even you. You expected me to be polite at home but I didn't have to be polite at Nana's. It was the 'done thing' for us all to be talking at once trying to out-do each other. We'd talk over each other, butt in and argue in very loud voices, and it wasn't seen as being rude. I know my mother found this very stressful; she was intimidated by such behaviour; the constant narration as she called it. Did it bother you I wonder? Did you feel for her, or did you just think she was a snob? What did you think, Dad? I wish I knew.

This is one of my great losses. I don't know your thoughts on many things and I have never been able to ask you. This was my greatest loss, not to be able to put things in perspective by talking to my Dad while I was growing up.

Your mother was anarchic, gypsy-like, and she had known both grief and sadness. She had lost four babies; all were born dead. It is said that these babies were very large and one at least had broken bones. Two of her brothers had been killed: Willy was in the airforce during the First World War and was killed in action, shot down over France when he was only 25 years old. Her second brother Henry was killed in a local colliery accident when he was in his early thirties, leaving a widow and children. She, too, was very frightened of war; she was terrified of losing you too.

Her father had been a journeyman plumber and ran his own business in and around Consett, in County Durham. They hailed from Wales, journeying to the north east for work. Nana certainly did have Celtic looks and her own sense of being a warrior. She left home when she was only fifteen to work in service, where she probably learned her cookery skills. Later she lived in North Shields and Hartlepool, probably working as a servant. She'd moved many times and yet again when she met Granda, and so she didn't live by the same rules as everyone else in Throckley. She didn't intend to learn either; she did her own thing no matter what anyone thought.

In Throckley Nana and Granda were known as 'outsiders' as they were not from the area; he was from Scotland, then Hartlepool and North Shields. The natives of Throckley often drove out outsiders, seeing them as roamers and loafers and a threat to their colliery jobs and houses. This led to the illogical premise that 'outsiders' had no values or morals either. Throckley people, or should I say first and foremost the men, had particular views about women who didn't follow the rules, those who weren't house-proud; they were lazy sluts. No man wanted his wife to be seen as a lazy slut, so housework and childcare were the measures used to control the wives and the women in the village; culturally ingrained attitudes.

Nana was definitely not lazy but it would be fair to say that, by Throckley terms, she was a bit sluttish: she didn't care a hang what anyone thought about her. Did you mind that your mother was eccentric, different? You showed no sign of it if you did. Did Granda mind? He didn't show any sign of it either as far as I could tell; they were chalk and cheese but rubbed along together in a well-worn, favourite-glove kind of way, or that's how it seemed to me then. They were comfortable together even if at times they drove each other mad. He didn't notice the glove on his hand but he definitely noticed when he'd lost it. When she died, he hardly ever spoke again. He'd never had much to say but said nothing at all once she was gone. After you and she died he said nothing at all; he was silent until death.

Is that how you experienced them, Dad? It is so hard for me to know what the truth is, if there is a 'truth' at all. Did you just suspend your judgement about your parents?

And there was another problem with Nana, at least as far as my Granda was concerned: she was a Spiritualist and had trained as a medium but he refused to let her practise because he didn't like voodoo, as he put it. There is a rumour that she was also a back-street abortionist and that a fifteen-year-old girl died following Nana's handiwork. She did lay out the dead and dying, and help women to give birth, but the abortion story remains unconfirmed.

Your mother, my Nana, was definitely different. For people in Throckley and especially for Mam, this alone would be threat enough. My mother would almost certainly have worried about other people finding out these secrets as she would have called them, she would have wanted to distance herself from any controversy. Did you feel the same? I don't think you did; I never heard you say a bad word about your mother or father, or anyone, come to that.

Mam was always telling me that I didn't live with Nana Holland. One of Nana's cardinal sins was her lack of reverence for housework: she wasn't a proper housewife; she wasn't house-proud. She didn't wash dishes until she'd used every last piece of crockery in the house, the sink would be piled high and my mother would say, '*You've never seen such a sink full of dishes as Nana's; she's hacky lazy.*' This puzzled me because my Nana was never still and I thought lazy people sat around all day, another one of Mam's criticisms of people. Worse still she wasn't systematic; she didn't follow the strict household routines expected of the women in Throckley, rules from the men's rule book. She did whatever she wanted to do whenever she decided to do it. She was free, an irritating provocation to Mam in particular. She was also clumsy and forever breaking things. This was another of my mother's criticisms of Nana and eventually me. According to Mam I inherited my Nana's bossiness, her clumsiness, her non-stop chatter and her general eccentricity, and of course, her argumentativeness; as well as her heavy feet. Would you agree with this description I wonder?

I do have many of her characteristics, no mistaking that, but I have been fortunate to have an education as you wanted me to, so much has been educated out of me and I have learned to curb my behaviour in ways Nana could only have dreamt of being able to do. Yet my husband sometimes criticises my louder side. I like the aspects of myself I have inherited from my Nana's gene pool. I have inherited her intuitive qualities though not the interest in Spiritualism as such. I have her build, although I keep my Buddha belly down with constant regular exercise and good healthy food – no pastry. Some would say that I too can be intimidating although I am not always aware of it. Nana and I share the same birth sign, we are both Scorpios, our birthdays only a day apart; we are only just in Scorpio rather than Libra, isn't that extraordinary, Dad? They say Scorpios have a basilisk stare: a threatening stare, perhaps that is what people found difficult in Nana. Was Nana a woman not of her age, rather than of her age, with an untamed intelligence that others misunderstood? Only you know how she was with you. I know how she was with me, and like you I loved her.

My heavy feet were blamed for the cracks in our living room ceiling (lounge was another word not in our vocabulary). If I'd been upstairs my mother would say, '*Look at that ceiling, you made that crack with your heavy feet, just like Nana Holland; it gets worse every time you go up stairs.*' The fact that the ceiling crack was due to the drying-out process common to new houses was neither here nor there, I'd done it, and that was that. Dad, you never said such things but you didn't contradict Mam either. Was your love for your mother unconditional? Unconditional love can survive contradictions, as it says in the Bible, Corinthians 14:

Love (charity) suffereth long, and is kind; love envieth not. Love vaunteth not itself, is not puffed up. Love doth not behave itself unseemly, seeketh not itself, is not easily provoked, thinketh no evil...

Is this the ethical code you applied? You certainly brought us up with these words. Or were they the words that controlled your

176

anger and helped you to be understanding? Controlled your shadow self so that it didn't lash out; so you didn't leave.

Aunty wasn't so accepting; she was often embarrassed by the state of your mother's house. One day, after Nana left to go shopping, she decided to take the net curtains down to wash them; by Throckley standards they were filthy, I have a photograph that bears witness to this: shabby blinds. When Nana returned she was furious, tore down the clean nets and put them on the fire. Aunty was so upset she lost her voice for two days. Her mother, your mother, my Nana, brooked no interference: yet Granda and you accepted her. You could sit silently through her tirades, pleadings and upsets, never saying a word: you worshipped her. Or you would both walk away and commune in the garden, you with your cigarette, Granda his pipe. Sometimes you'd both silently and companionably read your newspapers or books as she huffed and puffed around you both. You had the ability to ignore her.

My Granda loved quietly. He was an intelligent man. He'd been long retired when I was born – his father had also been a shipbuilder. Nana and he had committed a cardinal sin; fornication; she was pregnant when they married and this was probably the reason they had moved around so much. Pregnant young women were not welcome in their own home, they had a choice, make a go of it with the father of the child or take the risk of being sent to the workhouse. Maybe that is why she helped with abortions, because she had few choices once she was pregnant. They had to get married, have a shotgun wedding, sooner rather than later. My grandfather would have had to find work, preferably with a house attached, hence the colliery with a free house. They seemed to move around from colliery to colliery seeking work; their first house was in Blaydon where he worked at the Blaydon colliery, they were in Blaydon at the same time as my maternal grandparents although I am sure they didn't know each other then. They then moved to Newburn colliery, and on to Throckley colliery.

Throckley was built on coal and the village existed only because of coal, the mine owners were non-conformist philanthropists who looked after the men and their families, building reasonably decent housing and paying good wages, so jobs were at a premium. Few ever left the Throckley coalfields as the owners were benevolent, very different to the Haltwhistle coalfields and many others in the area. Most Throckley people had lived in the area or the surrounding areas for generations: they moved from local pit to local pit and were fiercely protective of local men's jobs, hence the strong feelings about 'outsiders'.

Your father got you a job in Throckley colliery when you left school aged fifteen. How did you feel about that Dad, working in a colliery? You'd passed your eleven plus, had a place at the grammar school, but your parents were so poor they couldn't afford the uniform. What a bitter pill that must have been for you, and for them. I have your Shakespeare compendium, the one you won, your school prize, a very substantial prize for the era and a real reward for your enjoyment of literature and your successful ability to achieve and learn. My name is a derivation of Rosalind in Shakespeare; although, I hasten to say, with some of my inherited qualities from your mother, Catherine might have been more appropriate. What do you think about Catherine, Dad? Knowing me as you did? Or did you see a different daughter from the daughter my mother knew?

Were your parent's attitudes your introduction to politics? Were the appalling conditions you lived in, especially in Newburn, your early political education? Certainly, not being able to go to the grammar school left a raw sore you felt all your life: you were forever picking at it. You so badly wanted me to live your dream, be successful for you, and I knew it was important for me to pass the eleven plus. It featured in our conversations from as early as I remember. It was my duty to pass this selective test, to pick up the mantle. Do you know what a burden that was for me, Dad? It has been a burden all my life, being the clever one, the academic one, the one to be proud of. As well as being the good girl. These values have eaten my life away: I have gorged on exams and degrees and attempted success. Fortunately I have enjoyed doing so, but it has left gaping holes in my life at times, especially the gaping hole that should have contained unadulterated pleasure and wanton fun. Being the good girl, the clever girl, left me short on excitement and pleasure; living it up was not a skill I knew how to exercise. I still find it hard. I don't blame you for that, I could have chosen to put it down earlier than I did, and I didn't. I did get the message though, the one you hammered into me; hammering was an epithet for smacking too, girls had to be good, must be good and if necessary hammered into obedience (there was some violence toward women in our neighbourhood, although never in our house or our closest neighbours' houses). I had to be good and clever. My life has been dominated for too long, and certainly too much, by both. Why couldn't I be naughty, different? Why did you have to control me so much?

Like my maternal grandfather, your father, my Granda, was a volunteer in the First World War; he was a groomsman in the cavalry. Both my grandfathers' war records were destroyed in the bombing of the records centre during the Blitz so it is very hard to get actual facts. We have my maternal grandfather's regiment and unit number on my uncle's birth certificate, as well as his brass box from Queen Anne so we know where he was and when. We have no such for your father, although we know he was injured by a horse and had a stiff leg; he dragged his leg and had a slight limp. I do not think my mother ever believed he had been in the war. She used to say, '*War injury, huh, too much sitting around reading books, more like.*' She thought he was the laziest man in Throckley and others have confirmed he was indeed seen as lazy. Was that because he actually liked to sit and read? Men in Throckley might have found that a bit odd, as action, camaraderie, was more their style. Women have certainly found it hard too, it wasn't the norm for working class men, as Hogart's classic, *The Uses of Literacy* demonstrated later. Were these cruel

179

comments just part of the cultural norms of the time? If you didn't conform, others were derogatory about you; this was all too common in our community, even when I was a child and teenager.

Or was your father traumatised? It is possible, of course, that he had not taken part in the war and that the injury was caused in the pit by a pit pony or cart. Did you know the truth, Dad? I wish I knew whether you have the answers to my many questions. I have just seen the play 'Pitman Painters', at The National Theatre in London, about the Ashington miners who wanted to paint, and it too illustrated the great need to learn, but also the angst of the males who stepped out of their traditional role. It was very funny and very moving.

The government instructed each colliery about the number of men they had to release to go to war: this was known as the pit quota; each pit was allocated their quota by the government but anyone could volunteer despite the quota. Mining was a protected employment as the nation and industry required coal. It is possible my Granda was a volunteer, part of the quota for Throckley pit, but equally possible that he remained behind working down the pit with the horses and ponies. If this were true then it would explain my mother's fury. Her father was a Kitchener volunteer and she had no time for those who had not volunteered. Was this what happened? Granda was seen as a traitor, a coward in Throckley, and so became silent, keeping his own secrets? Ashamed?

I always understood that Granda's leg injury was a result of his time in France in the First World War. Somehow I don't think you would have hidden the truth, because I think your interest in war and your view that all war should be prevented by dialogue was possibly the result of conversations with your father and mother; after all she lost a brother in the war. Why then did you put up with my mother being so scathing of your father? I don't understand why you didn't challenge some of her views. Or did you; just not in front of me? You had too much integrity to cover up a lie? I know that without doubt, you just could not have done it, and you would not have had the relationship with your father that you did: a healthy, respectful father–son relationship. I know that much about you.

My mother was a black and white thinker, someone who was easily offended and hurt, with few grey areas to soften her wrath. Some men who did not volunteer, or were not part of the quota, felt guilty and so did their family, their guilt fuelled by community attitudes. Many people did not understand the quota system and shunned those miners who stayed behind as well as their families, because they had lost their own husbands, fathers and brothers to war: there was much jealousy and bitterness and it lasted for years; it became a cultural myth. If a man hadn't gone to war, everyone knew his name. There was little sense that industry had to continue; people were unforgiving of men who had not fought, they saw them as cowards who'd chosen the easy life. Mud stuck, and could never be wiped, washed, or even scrubbed off.

After the war my paternal grandfather educated himself at the Miners' Institute, became well read. He kept up to date politically and kept abreast of the local and daily news. He was very gentle, at least until he became senile when he was very unpleasant and bad tempered. He was a very silent man, a shadow in his own home; and he kept his own counsel. Both my grandfathers were very quiet, often silent, amid all the activity and conversation going on around them. I often wondered why they were so quiet. Were they just quiet personalities, or had their war experience changed them? As senility overtook your father, was he less able to keep his ghosts under control, his demons at bay?

Thousands of veterans were changed by their war experience. Look at Harry Patch, who died very recently aged 111. He refused to speak about his experiences until he was 109. By that time he had lost two sons, been estranged from them; one went to live in America and died there, and the other died of alcoholic poisoning nearer home. He hadn't seen either before they died, they'd been estranged for over twenty years; they died in their fifties and sixties without knowing their father's story. Trauma has far-reaching tentacles; strangling and throttling the voice: silencing, yet leaving vivid memories triggered by the simplest noise – visions.

Did you know Granda's story? You wouldn't have told me if you did because in our day some things were not for children; there were many secrets and children were not party to adult conversation. Did you ever challenge Mam's viewpoint? Or was she right? These are very frustrating questions I can never hope to answer, especially as the records are not available. If the story is true, then why didn't you correct Mam? Or was it that Granda did not talk about his experiences, refused to, told another story to cover the real story, kept his own secrets just like Harry Patch. The story was not for his family either. The more we know and understand about the First World War the more it is possible he said nothing, that none of you knew what his experience of war had been, what mark it left; nor what he thought about any of it. No one knew what he'd seen and heard, just like my mother's father.

If he had been in the mines and not gone to war, perhaps his guilt and the label he then carried, 'coward', caused him such shame that silence was better than justification. No one knew, and he didn't want them to know. Dad, I wish I knew the truth. It would mean so much to know the truth.

As I grew up I understood that both my grandfathers' personalities and their families were blighted by war. There is a family rumour about my Granda that suggests that he had once been a more active and lively man: Nana had given up sleeping with him but when he was frustrated he would chase her around the house in an effort to make love to her – succeeding too, by all accounts; it seems both of them may have enjoyed the game. Photographs of you and your friends almost always include my Granda which suggests that not only was he respected by the young people but that he actively shared their leisure time: football and cricket. You, and your cousin, as well as your best friend, were very good cricketers and played for Throckley. Granda was always there, part of your activities. My Granda never smiles in photographs, and

he didn't in life either, except when he was tickling my chin with
his whiskers. He was a serious person; his face a blank canvas.
He always had his head in his newspaper, or deep in a book –
just like you, like me, just like Louise, her husband Larry and
your great-grandson Will. We are all readers, and this definitely
didn't come from the Lambert genes or culture. It definitely didn't
come from Throckley culture either: men with books; cissies:
'*Bloody cissies*' many would say, out loud too, in gossip over the
garden gate.

It is hard to believe now that you were not always around
when I was a young child: you were in hospital when I was just
over two and then in and out over the next three months, being
admitted for surgery, a partial gastrectomy on 5 April 1950. You
were in hospital until May and discharged on 20 May 1950. You
continued to be ill between then and being re-admitted on 29
June 1952, letters having gone back and forth between Dunston
Hill hospital and your doctor in Throckley as there was little
improvement in your condition. You were unable to work
consistently throughout this time; I was four years old. My wonder
is that we forged such a strong bond despite your absences and
your ill health. I have very good memories of my infanthood and
early childhood with you, apart from the smacking of course, so
you must have worked very hard to make up for lost time. I'm
glad you did. My mother's struggle must have been valiant too,
to provide me with security and love, despite her worrying and
missing you as well as the absence of a regular wage when you
were sick. Between 1952 and 1959 you were hospitalised for long
periods of time undergoing operation after operation, taking a
long time to recover from each.

She too was in and out of hospital three times during my first
four years, having major surgery on her back between 1950 and
1952, the same span of time when you were in and out of
hospital. During those times I lived with Nana and Granda, Aunty
and Uncle, enjoying yo-yoing back and forth: an invisible thread
linking us all in your absences. Did my mother feel indebted to

your family, a debt she couldn't repay? Was I so spoiled that she had a job managing me when she returned and blamed them in due course? Did she dislike needing them? Did she feel guilty that she couldn't look after me herself? No wonder I had a strong bond with Nana and Granda, Aunty and Uncle. They were my surrogate parents and my toddler sanctuary when neither of my parents could look after me. I was certainly not an insecure child, far from it; I was confident, a show-off, so your family did a good job in surrogate parenting. Maybe that was just too much for my mother? What do you think, Dad, so many questions without answers? Questions that can never be answered, only guessed at. Hypothetical questions and answers at most.

13

Questions, Questions

Questions, questions, questions: I didn't know anyone who had so many questions. We couldn't keep up with them, or you. From the moment you were able to talk you never stopped asking questions; you drove us mad. On the one hand I liked you being curious, but on the other I couldn't understand where they all came from. It was as though you went to bed at night and prepared all your questions in your sleep. Every day there were more, and the older you got the worse it got for us, trying to keep up with answering your questions. You wore us out.

And here you are again, wanting to know the far end of everything. Do you remember me saying that to you: *'You want to know the far end of everything?'* And it seems you still do. Why can't you be content with things as they are? Sometimes we just have to be content with life as it is, and as it turns out to be: I had to be content with a short life and an early death I didn't want, and obviously wouldn't have chosen. You still haven't learned, have you? Why can't you sometimes just suspend your disbelief and accept. As much as I loved you, and I did, so much, I couldn't keep up with this aspect of you. There was no satisfying your curiosity.

I was afraid for you, you had such a lively mind and so much energy as well as that insatiable curiosity. It sometimes seemed, as your Nana once said, that you had an inborn sixth sense and you were too old for your years. I was afraid that being a working class child you would end up bitterly disappointed, without the life chances we so much wanted for you. You see, we knew that opportunity for people like us was rare, very rare despite free education after 1944. We encouraged you and hoped, but it was hope rather than belief that you'd have more chances than we did. As it turned out you got off to a good start when we put you into school early, because it was hard to keep up with you, and as it happened the Labour government made your chances of success possible in both education and personal health. For me that was a bonus: a fairer more just society was developing as we'd all hoped for after the Second World War.

The cottage at Lemington was a case in point: yes it was a damp cold ruin, and dangerous, especially for children – burgled more than once during our occupancy and as I was often in hospital the threat to your safety when I wasn't there was always a constant worry. That's why your cousin Sheila so often stayed with your Mam. They came back early one evening and found the place trashed, and I wasn't there, I was in hospital. Can you imagine how I felt when they told me? I was a useless, hopeless husband and father because I couldn't look after my family properly. That's how I thought sometimes; I let you all down by being sick. I know, I know, you will say I was a good father. I tried to be, but through no fault of my own I couldn't be the father I wanted to be, and that hurt and upset me.

You talk about me smacking you and being overwrought sometimes. Well, I was. And my anxiety arose from my feelings of inadequacy. In some senses the hospital, though I hated being there, was a safer option for me than being at home anxious and worrying about how ill I felt. Or worse: the insecurity of being well and wondering when it would come to an end and I'd be in hospital again. My own personal symptom barometer was forever on alert for the changes in my internal meteorology. Would today be the day the sick front would suddenly appear again? I'd become overcast and blot out the warm, sunny, relaxed easy going feelings of being well.

Smacking – well smacking was the way we, my sister and I, had been disciplined; if it was good enough for us it was good enough for you. The worst thing for any family at the time was to have ill-disciplined children: children should be seen and not heard was the norm. They had to be kept in their place if they were to become disciplined adults. No one wanted hooligans in the family. And you were rarely seen without being heard! I didn't mind that at all, everyone loved the life you brought to the adults whenever you were around. But you were a challenge in that you had a mind of your own: you were always thinking, arguing. You knew what you wanted to do, and usually how you would do it too. You needed taming, and smacking was a way of letting you know that you had to do as you were told – something else you didn't always like. In fact even as young as three you let us know in no uncertain terms that you didn't like being told what to do or how to do it. You had your own ideas and these needed knocking out of you sometimes, for your own benefit, not ours, or so I thought. Or, as I sometimes said, our ideas hammered into you by learning the lesson by being smacked.

Now I can see that my parenting attitude was left over from my own childhood, not that I was ever smacked very much, Granda was not that sort of man, too gentle; but he had his moments when he would threaten me with the tawse, or give me a whack with it, to warn me. I know your Mam's brothers were knocked about a bit by your grandfather when they wouldn't do as they were told; he'd take his belt off his trousers and was not shy of using it either. Your Grandma hated those times. I'd go so far as to say that she would have done anything to protect her boys. In my case Nana would protect me and wouldn't let Granda leave a mark on me. I was spoiled by my mother and I knew it. I wasn't smacked much and yet I'd let fly at you when you went too far – well in my mind, too far. I know you found it unjust, I can understand that, but it is what parents did then; all parents did it, and for the best of motives: good children, well-behaved children. And you were beautifully behaved most of the time, and in school too.

Occasionally, though, that other child broke through and you'd do something out of character. Or was it in character? It is hard to know whether we were trying to shape the child we wanted rather than the one we had, and whether the breaking out, and breaking through, of this bold and feisty child was actually the real child showing herself. Or was it the naughty part of you protesting: hard to know for sure which was which. You did learn to behave and acquiesce, and I feel sure we were right in taming your spirit a bit – it was just a bit, remember, we did allow your lively personality to come through.

Your memory is pretty accurate, but then you always were able to paint pictures in your mind. You'd remember something long after an event, when the rest of us had no idea what you were talking about. Then you'd argue the toss and remind us of the detail, help us re-paint events in our minds too. You had a remarkable memory, just like your mother. I, too, remember those mornings and treasured them, every single one of them: they were very special times. I used to run my mind-movies in the hospital where I was often lonely and scared, shut out from my home and family. The movies kept you close, and they were comforting. I'm glad that you enjoy such vivid memories of those years.

Your memories of Nana and Granda and our regular visits with them bring so much back to me. You were a very loved child, and that was partly why we had to be careful, not allow you your own way, because you had so many adults doting on you, including your two adult cousins, Sheila and Eric, on my side, and all those others on your mother's side. You were the youngest of all your cousins, seventeen in all, dangerous for an only child – you might have been spoiled rotten as we used to say. I remember how I felt when I had to walk away, leaving you with Nana when your mother was in hospital. That wasn't easy, but I had to work if I wasn't already in hospital, and you had to be cared for. Of course they ruined you, spoiled you, and you'd have even more to say once you were back home; all learned from my mother and sister. They could talk for England, never mind Throckley, and would argue black was white, and you copied them. My mother never did anything anyone expected of her, and of course it was hard for us sometimes too, she was always out of step, had her own personal rules about living: she too was feisty.

I remember the soap games, the lamplighter and the gas lamps, and of course Laddy. These were good days for all of us, my quiet father in the background, always listening, weighing up what was said but rarely putting his oar in. I was more argumentative than my father but not quite as much as my mother and sister. It was an exciting house to be in: never a dull moment. I enjoyed these times as much as you did, as well as my quiet times with my father. Despite her temper and slovenliness, and her ability to stand an amazing amount of chaos, my mother was the most loving mother anyone could possibly have. We were always well fed, despite being absolutely poverty stricken at times, clean and well turned out. I loved her; I loved her more than I could ever say.

The history of Throckley is certainly interesting. You know how I loved history and how I liked facts to be accurate, as you do now. It was a very safe place to be although split religiously between Protestants, Catholics, Methodists, and Heathens, those who didn't follow any religion. The Stephensons, the benevolent land owners, were Methodists and built the Methodist chapel as well as the school. All those who had some religion looked down on those who had none. We were socially stratified by religion as much as by job or money. Your Nana was a Spiritualist and everyone was slightly afraid of her, partly because of ignorance of what it really meant, including your mother and Granda. It didn't bother me because she would go to church when she had to, toeing the line, so we were not seen as being strange by those around us: different, yes, but not strange. We were not regular churchgoers anyway, unlike your mother's family. As far as I know she was never in any trouble and was always seen to be a helpful neighbour and friend. I don't think she found it easy; she had a topsy-turvy relationship with Granda, loving but irascible, and something in between these polar positions many times a day. I don't think it was the passion of the century but they hobbled along together and they both had their strengths: they respected each other and I respected them both. They were very good and loving parents.

I took you to see them because of my respect for them and

189

because I loved them. You have only to read my letters to them to see just how much I loved them both, and my sister and brother-in-law too. We were a physically attached, as well as an emotionally attached family: we touched and kissed and loved, unlike your mother's family, who as you say were more demure and stoical. Stoicism was not very apparent in our house whereas emotion was; there were mini crises and much niggling, especially between Nana and Aunty Bell, many times a day. We were able to show emotion, all emotions, safely; no one ever fell out, all was mended by the end of the day. Forgiveness was always in the air. And when Nana went over the top as she sometimes did, we coped. We could forgive her, as she was a good mother and wife. As for her being an illegal abortionist, I don't know about that. I do know that women sought her out for all sorts of things; laying out of the dead, help with the sick, so it wouldn't have surprised me if she had helped those wanting an abortion. There were rumours of course, but men did not get involved in women's business, especially in Throckley. The wives had their own businesses and often clubbed together to run successful money-making schemes and the men left them to it. After all, anything they did to bring money in meant less poverty and better-fed families.

Unconventional, yes, Nana was very unconventional, but I was unconventional too, and that annoyed your mother who believed in convention and not breaking social rules. Being busy all the time was your mother's motto, and our family didn't care about being busy – busy for busy's sake just didn't happen in our house, nor routine either. Once I was married I had more routine with your mother and I accepted it: I adored her. Have you got that picture of your mother and me taken in Melkridge by the river? She was eighteen and I was twenty-three, absolutely wrapped up in each other. We always were; she was a beautiful woman with her heart in the right place. I was passionately in love with her and she with me. That never changed despite everything that happened. I am sorry that you haven't found that love. You did once, but it was an impossible love and you walked away. I sometimes wonder now whether being quite so honest is worth it, as life doesn't last forever. Perhaps you have been too honest. I can't imagine saying that to you when you and I were younger, I would have expected nothing but the highest moral standards from you. Now, with what I know, I think you can be too honest and honourable, and miss out on life as a result.

Yes, I was a good house-husband, not that I would have chosen to be, but out of necessity I was, and I enjoyed it. I liked things done properly and efficiently, the army taught me that, and I liked dreaming up ways of doing things and seeing them turn out well. Being in the pit from fourteen years old also taught me to be careful and mindful of others as their life might depend upon my actions. In the Throckley pits this was a safety mantra, as everyone working in each gang had to think about the others, their lives depended upon the others, we were jointly responsible for each other, and the pay structure rewarded this tight bonding and safety. We were paid as a team, so what you earned depended on the strength of relationships and teamwork; the worst sin in the pits was to let your marras down by carelessness or laziness.

Being a house-husband was unconventional, although being an ill man was not, there were many ruined men around following the First and Second World Wars; men who were injured, emotionally as well as physically; we just didn't talk about it. But it was necessary for me to be a house-husband, especially when your mother had to go out to work when I could not. This was hard for both of us: not many women worked then, especially if they were mothers. I felt terrible when she had to work because it wasn't the way things were in Throckley. I felt a failure, weak – a weak man. And no one wanted one of them. It was a stigma in Throckley to be a weak man and I had to live with that, as did your mother: not an easy thing to do. Even those like my father, damaged emotionally by the First World War, did not allow themselves any self indulgence: they stayed quiet and made a life as best they could.

We all knew those men who couldn't manage this charade and

the community helped them and their families: the communal spirit at that time was very strong in Throckley. Taking care of your own, and 'own' meant the collective in this case: all those in the neighbourhood who were suffering in one way or another. Some men had to be watched carefully, because they tried to solve their problems through drinking, some by violence, beating their wives and children, and some would disappear for days on end, no one knew where they had gone: then they'd suddenly return, often having lost their job in the meantime.

We learned the warning signs, and the pit owners were very good at helping these families too. Women and children, putting food on the table came first, and your Nana played her role in helping others, it was one of her strengths. I was always afraid of being referred to as a skiver, it was the worst epithet imaginable – well maybe not as much as being called a coward, but almost. I don't think anyone ever referred to me as such. If they had, I couldn't have lived with it easily. You have to try to understand my family's poverty before and after the First World War to understand some of the family tensions and some of your mother's myths about my family. You also need to understand that Throckley might only have been a constructed village at a crossroads, but it was in many ways a model of community action as well as liberal inter-nationalism: unique, because of its geological history and abundance of coal.

There were many coal-mining villages in the north east, but few with such liberal and socially conscious landlords. I learned so much by working in the mines. I lived history and industrial relations, and these shaped who I was from being fourteen years old, when I entered the pit: it was my university education and in some ways, just because of chance and geography, it was perhaps the best education I could have had, despite my disappointment about grammar school. My experience helped me to be measured in my judgement of others, and understanding of how politics shaped and wrecked lives. You are sharing your mind-movies with me. Let me share mine with you: my history movies will help you understand some of your mother's views about my family and Throckley. She often, in her frustration, said she hated it. I wasn't around to help you with your mother, and I know how you struggled to understand her and care for her. No child should have to do as you did, and you did your best. You did well.

Your mother wasn't an easy woman to understand. Perhaps you will indulge me; let me try and help you to understand some of the tensions you didn't understand then and are trying hard to understand now. I left you prematurely, I didn't want to and I didn't like leaving, it left you vulnerable and lost: but I had no choice. Sometimes there is no choice; we are not in control of our own destiny, as many like to believe.

14

The History Man

I said earlier that I know it was hard for you, and is still hard for you to understand your Mam. Listen, and I will try to explain how I saw her, as well as help you to understand her problem with my family and with Throckley itself. Your mother's upbringing, her village, culture and country roots were very different from mine on the outskirts of Newcastle. It is not surprising to me that you feel you were caught in between. I often felt I was too. Remember, Throckley didn't actually exist before the coal was mined: and it went on being mined for almost fifty years. The village grew from the need for miners; there was no existing culture because there had previously been no village, just a few houses scattered around the countryside.

Your Mam was brought up in the country, surrounded by beautiful countryside and the long imbued, embedded values of the landed gentry as well as visiting royalty. Although the daughter and grand-daughter of pit men, she was perhaps unduly influenced by the endemic landlord/squire domination of her village and the historical market town of Haltwhistle nearby. I met your Mam because I, too, longed for the beauty of the Northumberland countryside as a change from the more industrial landscape I was brought up in.

I knew Throckley as a place at a crossroads between farms, just off the main road to Carlisle to the west. In the other direction on the road to Ponteland and to the east the A1 to Jedburgh: a nowhere place really. Yet Throckley's unexplored coalfield was in the right place at the right time. There was major social and political change going on during my childhood, new ideas were just taking root and so Throckley became a national and local industrial experiment, part of a three-pronged national and international change for the working man and his family, as well as the community.

Liberalism was declining, organised labour movements were becoming stronger and structural change in the mining industry as well as the development of the trade union movement meant new opportunities for my generation and yours. These changes were part and parcel of my life and education as a young school leaver entering the pits at fourteen. This and the ongoing historical change shaped and moulded me. Even though I left the mine when I went to war and didn't return to mining I never forgot my roots, my history, and so my experiences influenced you too. You know, some things are etched deep in our minds. They are stored in places we cannot fathom and unconsciously shape who we are as well as our lives. Living in Throckley meant I was shaped in a particular way socially and politically, and so were you. Your Mam was perhaps already too set in her ways to change or maybe didn't want to change too much. She, too, wanted you to benefit from her experience as well as mine because she had had a more genteel upbringing than me, mostly learned from her mother and elder sister.

She came from a different social system, from a 'doff your cap, noblesse oblige' culture in Haltwhistle set in the Northumberland coalfield. The villagers needed to be deferent to the powerful landowners. Deference was not tolerated in Throckley: not to landowners or church, as it had been in Haltwhistle where she grew up. The landowner–peasant relationship shaped your mother's family, and she wasn't prepared for the different culture in Throckley. She was used to being careful, secretive; keeping her own counsel and doing as she was told, as her parents had had to do whether they liked it or not. Your mother was ripe for social mobility, shaped as she was by the values of the landed gentry and country squires. Moving from Haltwhistle to Throckley was not an upwardly mobile thing to do: it was not an achievement even though she did it for love. She had hoped for more from life than Throckley could provide. I knew that and had always intended she should have it; that is why I made my way from the army to an office job, a white-collar job. Unfortunately my health prevented our plans ever becoming reality. This was very hard on your mother and I always knew that.

From the beginning we pitmen in Throckley had a bargaining relationship with our mine owners: we would have our say. There were no submissive attitudes. Throckley pitmen were feisty but from the first they had a different relationship with the coal owners. That is not to say that Haltwhistle pitmen didn't fight their battles too – they did and were locked out from the pits as they battled for their rights. Their fight changed the pits for the better throughout the Northumberland coalfields including Throckley. It was the culture of ownership that was different. These battles led to a long-term, subtle transformation in the meaning of the word community for the people living in the village. There had been similar developments in the Ryton coalfield during your great-grandparents' and grandparents' time, but this was more social than political change. Throckley was in the midst of, and in some ways a leader, in political change – a little coal village on the fringes of the Northumberland coalfield leading change in the area. We were all proud of that. I was proud of where I lived.

Before 1930 Throckley, like Haltwhistle, had been rooted in squirearchical values: the squire ruled people's lives and not always benevolently either. Haltwhistle was politically Conservative in every sense, including telling the populace how they must vote. If people didn't vote as they were told to vote they could lose their job and often their homes. At the very least they might become pariahs. Other people would not like to be seen with them in case similar things happened to them too. Throckley, on the fringes of Newcastle, was a little bit more liberal as were the surrounding villages; our collective values were grounded in liberal capitalism. During the 1930s the Throckley coalfield was dominated by the paternalism of a single coal company and was a private enterprise. After the Second World War it developed corporate capitalism influenced by the growth of the Labour Party and the Welfare State: Throckley sported some of the first, well-designed council housing in the country. Such development subtly changed and shaped social relationships in the village too.

Your Mam was used to being deferent to those socially superior to her and had learned the skills to survive: she came from a family that upheld conservative and religious values. I didn't, and neither did my parents, especially my mother who didn't kowtow to anyone no matter who they were, or believed they were. Your Mam couldn't understand how quickly the rules for living had changed once she moved in with my mother and father. I understood how hard it was for her but I believed what my parents believed – I believed in the Throckley experiment, a more socially just society, so I wasn't as sympathetic as I might have been to your mother's values; nor her feelings. I, too, thought she was a snob sometimes, even though I loved her. Her mother was organised, a pillar of society, kept a good house and shop, was clean and tidy; she was dignified and quiet. No one, not even me, could say my mother was any of these. She was not. She was domineering, spirited, demonstrative, loud, untidy, and a matriarch. And I was her boy!

My parents had had a very difficult time settling into the village. Sometime after 1909 my parents moved across the river from Blaydon, where they probably knew your great-grandparents, particularly your great-grandfather Lambert who was a deputy at the Blaydon Colliery. They moved to Newburn, living in Millfield where my father had moved for work in the Newburn Colliery. This was also about the time your mother's parents moved from the Blaydon coalfield to the Northumberland coalfield, back to Haltwhistle; home, as it was for them. They had both been born in the Hexham area before their parents left to find gold on the streets in Blaydon; hoping to dig improved earnings and lifestyles from the mines. Your mother's father found work in the Haltwhistle pits, and indeed on his doorstep in Melkridge pit. Probably the coal owners in Blaydon reduced output to increase profits, and therefore made redundancies, so men and families moved on for better conditions and wages, but also for stability and security. My father worked at Newburn, and then Throckley pit.

I was born at Millfield on 21 May 1915, a long-awaited son after my mother's four previous miscarriages. I was a sickly baby, almost dying of pneumonia in my first year. My mother was therefore fiercely protective of me. Eventually, my father moved to Throckley pit after the First World War and was seen as an outsider. Outsiders were not welcome as they were seen to be taking local men's jobs. Throckley and Heddon pits had protectionist policies and these controlled who was allowed to work: local men came first. My father was from North Shields so not local. Your Nana was not local either as she was from the Blaydon area, across the river for heaven's sake, her father having been a journeyman plumber from Wales. Nana had Celtic roots. Pitmen were very parochial in their fight for work.

We were one of the first families to be moved out of the condemned colliery houses in Millfield and moved into one of the newly built council houses in Throckley. Our new house was large with a scullery, a parlour, a second small parlour, which your Mam and I shared when we first got married. She had this small parlour for herself when I was in the forces during my army training and war service. There was a downstairs toilet, three bedrooms and a bathroom. Our house had a long, wide, back garden and a considerable front garden. The colliery owners, like the council, had waiting lists for housing; the council house came up before the pit house and so Granda took this instead. He retained his free coal ration and the rent was low and controlled. Free coal was part of a pitman's real wage and was very important when sliding scales (linking wages to the selling price of coal) were in operation and especially for a fireman who was not hewing the coal underground or living in a pit house (free house) with no rent. It made life just that bit easier for our family.

Throckley overlooks the Tyne Valley, framing Ryton church and Crawcrook, as well as Blaydon in its view. It sits high on the Tyne Bank, and so throughout our lives we could see where our parents had lived their earlier lives; a constant reminder of their past. The west road cut Throckley half: in 1851 there were only 159 people in Throckley but by the turn of the century there were more than 2,000. The successful pits in the area needed recruits and they supported many men and their ever-growing families for years. Coal companies needed to accumulate capital and so the owners invested in the pit and its infrastructure for the community: the community needed to attract labour and in turn the owners supported pitmen and their families; a mutual contract. The owners needed to have some control of their workers, the pitmen and associated workers required to keep the industry functioning, so there were clear rules for both parties. In Haltwhistle there were no such arrangements. The pitmen were employees of the landowners, who owned the pits, the pitmen and their houses, but fought for similar rights too, as all pitmen did in the Northumberland coalfield.

Throckley on the other hand was created by the coal company, which operated in the free market of liberal capitalism and was a thriving community when I was a child. The coal owners saw themselves as social benefactors building up the village, building houses, a Methodist chapel, the Co-operative stores, as happened at the Addison Pit on the other side of the river in Ryton during your grandparents' lifetime.

Pitmen in Throckley organised themselves to prevent exploitation, they created institutions of their own, including a union, to further their own development and interests. Through their actions, attitudes and beliefs they helped to form the values and beliefs of the community, and at the same time remained committed to the community: they encouraged strong social relationships which helped to bind people together. These relationships and bonds helped miners and their families to survive over the years. Part of the new community development was improved housing, a mixture of colliery and council housing in the main, although there were a few private houses at the bank-top and on Newburn Road.

We knew that reports from the Chief Medical Officer of Health, Dr Messer of Newburn Urban District Council, had railed for years (1906–1917) against the poverty and poor housing, blaming these for ill health and degradation in the areas around Throckley. As he said:

There are, in every part of the district, beams and brickbats thrown together in the shape of houses. Naturally they are damp, many ill lighted, badly ventilated – which go to make them unfit for habitation. As for tenants, alas their sorrows in their bosoms dwell. They've much to suffer but have nought to tell.

Social conditions in the area in 1906 were very bad and people were very poor. There was high infant mortality, poor sanitation, inadequate housing and overcrowding. Dr Messer felt that the dilapidated housing was the reason for so many child and maternal preventable diseases, as well as the infant mortality rate. My mother agreed with this as she had lost four babies and then had a very sickly baby, me, in a 'midden' as she would have called the house in Millfield. He believed that the health of the community was in the hands of the capitalist and the architect. In his 1910 report he addressed over-crowding – eighty-four percent of residents lived in housing with fewer than five rooms, and the cause: *'Not ignorance, we know better; the builder is not to blame. For the law allows it.'* And in 1912 he also wrote:

The increase in wealth as shown by the Budget [Chancellor of the Exchequer] *is in the large fortunes of a few, rather than in the diffusion of the nobler possibilities of happiness among the masses. Despite booming trade the mass are no better, and there is always the liability to forget this under the hypnotic influence of big figures.*

These problems – poverty, poor housing and health – served to encourage people to distinguish themselves from one another. They used such conditions to enhance their own respectability and look down upon those who couldn't manage as well as they could. This brought about its own social stratification as people sought a better life. Dr Messer felt that the terrible conditions were both a moral as well as a health threat. Indirectly, and more importantly, women were to blame for the conditions their family lived in, or indeed praised, as the health visitor for the district reported after a survey of 1,444 homes:

A small percentage of homes visited were found to be very dirty, a disgrace to the housewife and a peril to the inmates and to the neighbours. On the other hand, many houses are always beautifully clean, making one realise that the real heroines of England are the mothers who, day by day, are faithfully fighting dirt and disease, sometimes under heavy odds.

The major threat to everyone was poverty and the records for the Royal Commission on Poor Law and Relief (of distress) for Throckley (Castle Ward Division) showed 12,500 in the area claiming benefit in 1901: 2 shillings and 6d for adults,1 shilling and 6d for children, and for really destitute old people it was 3 shillings: a pittance even then. The secretary of this committee, Canon Walker of Whalton, did not see things as Dr Messer did and explained the problems those giving out the Poor Law allowances faced:

The causes of pauperism are extravagance, money spent on dress, in pleasure and amusements. Improvident habit, especially amongst the girls and young women and a feeling often expressed that there is a right to Poor Law Relief; improvident marriages, phthisis and it may be high rents. The housing problem has a serious bearing on pauperism.

The threat of the workhouse was ever present; all working people in Throckley felt its threat and worked to avoid such a fate. I remember this fear being drummed into me as a young child and the message was clear: you had to be careful, work hard, improve yourself and your life chances, and the route to such improvement was the church (Protestant or Catholic) or chapel, and education. I chose education. Cleanliness and pride were an integral part of this package. In the community this led to a supportive culture where neighbours helped each other, looked out for each other through neighbourly deeds, in work, and in political and industrial action.

There were tensions amongst the population of Throckley; political differences, partly to do with the union movement, and there was snobbery. These differences were related to the church and the positions held in church, between the church- and chapel-goers, between Protestant and Catholic. Housing, social standing and self-esteem were linked to where exactly in Throckley you lived, and in what type of housing: social position was *felt* not just thought about.

When I started work in the pit, Throckley was dominated by the 'big house' of the Stephenson family, and the pit itself produced other divisions: pitman versus pit officials (the mangers and deputies). Like your great-grandfather in Ryton, officials earned more money, had a lot of power and influence, lived in larger houses and had closer contacts with the owners. There were also divisions between the pitmen themselves: between hewers and datal workers, underground and surface workers. The differences in wages became differences in social class; ironic when most of us were working class anyway. My father was very poor, as he did not hew coal: he had a static wage as a fireman.

Even though your mother's family were pitmen, she set herself above the pitmen in Throckley, more so once I wasn't working in the pit – yet my family were. The divisions between miners and other workers were equally well known: the steelworkers at Spencer's in Newburn thought the miners 'beneath contempt'. The gap grew between the workers, white-collar workers and the professional classes. Some professions were of course respected, the doctor, lawyer or vicar, but others, such as clerical work and shopkeeping, were seen as soft jobs; and definitely not masculine. As your mother once said of someone, *'He's just a pen pusher.'* The miners saying was *'he couldn't punch his way out of a paper bag'*. And there is the sting; the push to be socially mobile, translated into being disparaging about men in office jobs, who were viewed as weak men because they couldn't do the heavy work of the pitman, steelworker or shipbuilder: pitmen became revered for their toughness and hardiness. There was a lot of confusion. As most miners' wages were similar, most households knew what others earned, there was little to be snobby about, and so ridicule was rife, putting others down became a survival strategy and a hobby: Throckley didn't let anyone get above themselves. Your Mam had also grown up in poverty, being the youngest of eight children and had witnessed her mother having to work very hard indeed to feed and clothe her family. She didn't want that again: she would have liked security and luxury.

Hence 'outsiders' had to learn these rules – unfortunately your mother never did. If anyone did try to be above themselves they were quickly brought to earth with, *'Who do you think ye are?'* The union lodges and employers gave jobs to Throckley men before outsiders: locality was all, and far more important than class. My parents remained outsiders all their lives and never truly integrated into the Throckley community. It didn't bother them, especially my mother, one bit. They had their extended families, they remained close and loyal; they were secure in their own skins. This is why my mother was seen as unconventional in Throckley and why she didn't tow the line: she made it her business not to. Respectability, bearing, sayings such as, 'He has such good bearing', or 'She bears herself very well', became epithets of respect. Honesty, integrity and above all 'the laarnin' (learning) became the long-term goal of many families, including mine and very definitely ours. I agreed with and endorsed your mother's ambition that you would be educated, do well and have the life chances that neither of us ever had.

Women were judged by their conduct and propriety in public and private. A woman couldn't move outside the community rules without bringing upon herself the disapprobation of both other women, and all men: the respectable wife was all. Of course my mother didn't abide by such rules, so she did bring some criticism on herself; Granda and I found this courageous, not weakness or awkwardness. The rules for women in Throckley were very clear: tidiness, cleanliness, looking after their bairns and their man, clean house, tidy garden and a line full of beautiful white washing on a Monday morning which hung on the line correctly. Life was not easy for women and if they let their houses go they were said to live in a midden (a pig sty). These rules were the benchmark against which any woman measured herself; her neighbours measured her qualities as a wife and mother, and other husbands assessed their wives. Falling below standard was the fault of the individual and never the social conditions; these were to be overcome. To be in receipt of poor law funds was the cardinal sin: you were stigmatised. So many in the community gained respectability by taking part in community, church work or politics: these engendered status and avoided the epithet of 'social climbing'. This was a collective village, not an individualistic one.

The Stephensons and the Spencers, local families and respectable business men, were shareholders in the Throckley Royalty. The Stephensons were brick manufacturers and farmers. The Spencers (from Newburn) made their money in steel, running the largest north-eastern steel works, Spencer's Steelworks. There were two other shareholders, J.B. Simpson and E.J. Boyd, both mining engineers. Each share had a nominal value of £1,000 and they needed £18,000–£20,000 to develop the colliery, so they floated the company on the Stock Exchange and began to build workshops, railways, and to sink the mineshaft.

In October 1887 Isabella Stephenson cut the first sod and named the pit after herself; it was known locally as 'the Isabella'. There was already a working pit in Throckley which supplied the Stephensons' brickworks with fireclay and coal, but it was not big or deep enough to produce coal on the scale the owners wanted: it was known as 'the Bobby Pit' and the largest in the area at that time. As more-efficient pumping engines were developed, they enabled the possibility of opening the lower seams in Throckley. There was a secure guaranteed local market, Spencer's Steelworks, and so sinking the pit made good economic sense with low risk.

This was called vertical integration: with a local market there was less risk of the boom and bust related to export that affected much of the Northumberland and Durham coalfield, and your mother's family after the war. Throckley pit, because of this local market, was a peaceful pit compared to many other pits; industrial relations in Throckley were positive. The local community benefitted from the pit and so men were prepared to work hard to make it successful – a new model of community relations.

The pit owners were prominent men on Tyneside as they had connections all over the region and were fully involved in 'civic work' for which Sir William Stephenson was knighted in 1900. They donated money to the City of Newcastle for libraries, with J.B. Simpson ploughing money into higher education in the area. Boyd became High Sheriff of Durham and they all held public office, with Sir William being Mayor of Newcastle. They were skilled in diversification too, putting money into public utilities, engineering and shipping, but they never lost sight of their commitment to Throckley, and as public benefactors they influenced the social tone of the area as well the conditions for a successful and profit-making pit.

The coal owners invested in the infrastructure of the village; they needed miners and miners needed houses. So they initially laid out £8,000 for miners' houses which were of good quality compared with others around the area. In fact the *Newcastle Weekly Chronicle* on 16 November 1872 suggested, '*... company houses in Throckley were the best kind as yet erected for pitmen and have all the proper conveniences.*'

The tenants had to abide by the company's rules – no dogs, because the Stephensons wanted to protect their shooting rights – and poor tenants were evicted if they did not stick to the rules. Allotments were available and the houses had good long gardens: gardening was encouraged by the coal company. Most miners liked their gardens as it gave them time outside summer and winter, a sharp contrast to their life underground. Houses gave the pit owners control of the workers; the owners had the rights: the right to evict sacked workers and widows. In Throckley this control was both benevolent and sympathetic.

Your Aunty Bell (my sister) and Uncle Fred (her husband) lived at Mount Pleasant opposite Nana in one of these pit houses. You remember: it had a scullery and a kitchen/sitting room and a parlour with two bedrooms upstairs, no bathroom and an outside netty. Each colliery row was named after a tree, or a country area, or as in Mount Pleasant, given a romantically fanciful name intended to take the edge off the fact that the pits dominated the area and it was not beautiful: down the pit for hours and then coming up to daylight and home to a house in a street called Mount Pleasant must have had some psychological effect on mood I'm sure. When you were a child, Mount Pleasant was anything but pleasant. Oh, the houses were clean, many spotlessly clean, but the outsides were black and sooty. J.B. Simpson also spent his own money on building a row of cottages for ageing miners at the Bank Top, benevolence taking account of old age too.

The coal owners extended this benevolence to building a school and a Wesleyan chapel, both on the West Road. They also contributed to the building of chapels in Blutcher and Newburn as well as being members of the school board; in fact the coal company was the Management Committee of Throckley School with Sir William a leading light on the Newcastle School Board. If parents' didn't send their children to school, or indeed children truanted, the company docked the charge from the pitman's wage, encouraging parents to behave responsibly and children to attend school regularly. The Stephensons were at the centre of village life, contributing to the pit brass band as well as playing in it. Sir William also took some of the men out on shoots with him and Major Stephenson played in the football team, Throckley Villa. I played in the cricket team, and used the Reading Room, which had a billiard table, newspapers and books, where my father and I read and spent a lot of time. Stephenson's wife visited the sick and helped to advise mothers on child rearing.

The Stephensons were respected and liked; if men griped it was about the coal industry as a whole rather than these specific owners. The company was bound by the agreements between the Northumberland Coal Owners' Association and the Northumberland Miners. From 1879 onwards these bound them to 'sliding scales' as well as joint committees for solving problematic industrial disputes and conflict. This meant the owners had an unfair advantage over the men: they could deflect any problems and did not solve them themselves; they left negotiation and resolution to the joint committees: disputes and conflict, whatever the grievance, was not specific to the Throckley pit and, as Simpson believed, *'This will enable us to obliterate from our dictionaries the terms "strike and lockout".'*

Before these wider regulations and agreements, even if issues arose and pitmen challenged the owners about long service to the company, the owners would say the men had been well paid – this was sufficient in and of itself as an explanation. They were capitalists to a man, no matter how benevolent they might be. By 1900 the owners had also acquired Heddon and Blutcher collieries. In total they employed 1,484 men in the area and subsequently their families. We all walked a delicate path.

There was no working men's club. Instead there were the Throckley Rechabites, The Pride of Throckley, a Tent of the Independent Order of Rechabites. This was the temperance organisation in the village, which had 588 members: 208 adults, 28 members' wives, a female tent of 32 and young persons' tent of 320. It is not surprising that there was some ambivalence in our house about drinking and alcohol; your mother's mother had been a leading temperance worker. In Throckley anti-alcohol views were strong too. Your maternal grandfather took to the drink after the First World War. Both she and your Mam had an abiding fear of drinking: one drink, to your mother, was deemed alcoholism. I often had to sneak away to have my pint.

There was a Home Reading Union and a cycle club, all run by local men. The cycle club raised funds for charity, as did the pubs in the area with local leek and vegetable shows. Men paid a fee to show their produce and a fee to enter the show with their families. If they won the prize for the largest leek or turnip, it was usually something useful. Families and men took these competitions very seriously and spent hours encouraging their vegetables to grow, trying all sorts of new methods and fertilisers to bring them on. The union ran social events and dances, as did the chapel: they had the most wonderful harvest suppers. The Mother's Union was run from the church, an educational opportunity, helping mothers to learn hobbies and skills.

And, on the Ryton Willows, Throckley people shared The 'Hoppings' (the fun fair) with those on the other side of the river. The men had their pigeon fancying and racing clubs and their whippet racing in the back lonnen. Some families, particularly in the Leazes and Mount Pleasant, kept animals in their gardens: pigs, geese, ducks, rabbits and chickens. This was a hobby for the men, smallholdings really, and provided extra food for families. The coal company didn't object to this. Families often had a shed for killing the pigs and geese so they never wanted for ham, bacon and eggs, or a nice roast fowl for Sunday lunch. The women helped the men, as well as each other, and often combined their resources – eggs, bacon, ham, lace work, knitted garments, home-made bread, running small business from their homes or each other's homes. There was money to be made in proggy mats (handmade mats made from rags) and homemade soap. The income they made was ploughed back into the home, or other money-making schemes, and in insurance payments. These were to enable proper burial of the dead, a respectable funeral. A decent funeral was a must in Throckley, as was a decent bottom drawer for potential brides, a good wedding and christening. You were looked down upon if you couldn't manage any of these, or celebratory meals at Christmas and Easter. And of course the Co-op might buy the ham or eggs, providing a good income on a weekly basis.

The Co-op was the main shopping centre and a real emporium, providing all any family needed from birth to death with low interest on loans, controlled prices and dividends. This meant purchases led to savings too: a form of voluntary socialism. The coal owners' 'noblesse oblige' investment in the pits and the village amenities rubbed off on the villagers, and caring for others as well as yourself became the mantra most people tried to live by. It was part of our education to behave toward each other in such a way and I always found it hard to understand individualistic, selfish, self-serving behaviour, and brought you up not to be selfish, but to be understanding of others' needs. I believed, as did my parents, that you didn't need the church to teach you that.

The colliery stood where the old flood plain of the Tyne gives way to the rising valley at the base of the Well Field. It had two shafts, the Isabella and the Derwentwater, probably named after the previous landowner. Pit work shaped us men and our characters: self-respect, toughness, endurance, and underground skills. The work devalued competition and encouraged helping others, as it was dangerous. The coal owners recruited family men, abstainers (from alcohol) in the main, who were chapel and church attendees. Pinching poverty was almost unknown in Throckley in the late 1890s with the Board of Guardians only required to meet the school fees of three out of five-hundred pupils. Steady employment meant steady wages and security. These bred responsibility for yourself and others in the family.

Work underground was hard and dangerous. The pit was geologically placed for men to be able to work most of the seams in the western district of the coalfield and produce coals from these seams: the Harvey, which local men called the Engine seam, the Hodge, the Tilley, the Top and bottom, the Busty, the Three-quarter and the Brockwell seams. Working all these gave the coal company access to several different markets, as the seams produced domestic coal, coking coal as well as steam coal; this last was sold to Spencer's Steelworks and the railway company. Gas coal was sold to the gas company of which Sir Willy was the chairman, a nice bit of nepotism.

The pit was in an area full of old and ancient coal workings which the men would hole into, but it was wet, lying low in the valley from which 1,200 gallons of water an hour had to be pumped out, draining away to the Pit Pond down in the burn, and then into the Tyne. That's why you found our mile or so of the Tyne thick and dirty when you were a child. To the west the coal measures outcropped to the east, below Newburn, and gave way to deep sand and gravel. To the north they were displaced by the igneous intrusion of the Whyn Dyke, a massive fault with a 70-foot displacement, impossible to mine through. The coal seams varied between 18 inches and 3 feet. We miners did not find working these seams easy. We returned from work in the winter, particularly, with our wet pit clothes freezing on our bodies as we walked. I remember your Aunty Bell's house smelling dank, so did ours – wet pit clothes had to be dried around the fire all year long.

The miners at the Isabella Pit used the Bord and Pillar system, using ponies to haul the coal. Groups of 'marras' or mates worked together to work out their own output and thus their wages. Miners need special skills to work in this way as the payment system for underground work was based on the different tasks required to win the coal. In the Northumberland and Durham coalfield there were two methods of working that required the use of 'putters': the bord and pillar system, and the longwall gateway system. The bord and pillar system was at the first stage of working a partial extraction system: from the roadway, entries were made into the coal seam, to form a flat or a district, and made wide enough to allow the passage of a tub. They were known as tramways and there were two kinds of tramway, the bords and the headways, the bords being driven at a greater width than the headways.

Coal has a basic cleavage plane known as a cleat, and workers found it easiest to work at right-angles to the cleat rather than parallel with it. So more coal could be won by working in a bordways direction than a headways direction. The bords were driven at least one yard wider than a tramway travelling in the headways direction. In first working, an area of coal would be locked out, leaving pillars, the dimensions of which were determined by the depth of the coal seam from the surface, and the strength of the coal. About 40–50 percent of coal was won in this first stage and known as working the 'whole'. When a predetermined boundary was reached, the pillars were removed, retreating toward the original entry point of the flat and known as working the 'brokens'. Little dust was caused by this way of working and it was quiet, yet it was wasteful of coal because the pillars of coal had to be left for safety reasons and they had to take out a lot of roof to expose the coal. Machinery such as cutters and mechanical conveyors were the most technically efficient system of winning coal.

This system decided the sequence of tasks (known as task structure) we miners had to use and they demanded complex skills. Knocking out the flats and districts was followed by driving the roadways, which required loosening bottom stone and taking down roof space. Supports then had to be fitted and these had to be cut precisely (a safety factor) and then shaped and the tramways laid down. Drilling for coal using explosives and a heavy pick came next. The miners would undercut (known as kurving) the seam of coal (the jud) and either shoot it down or hack it away. Once cut, the coals had to be 'filled' using a large pan-shaped shovel (known in Throckley as a pan-shull). The filled tubs of coal were then pushed to the main tramways by the putter and then to the pit shaft. The tubs were weighed by the checkweighman whose wages were made up by the men themselves. Any geological problems could affect output; faults, hard coals, crumbling walls or hard stone floors.

Payment depended on output, so to make the workplaces equal they were 'cavelled' for each quarter, this means a random allocation of work places were allocated among hewers and putters. There were separate prices for different kinds of job and these were agreed with the workmen and employers, as a lot of preparatory work was needed before any coal could be hewn.

So as a consequence a finely graded career structure developed from trapper to putter, and then after the age of twenty-one to hewer. I moved through this system as I learned new skills. There was no formal training but skills were learned on the job, often being passed from father to son. We had to get to know where we were in the dark in the pit, learn about airflow, gas build-up, and the dangers of naked flames. We had to know and understand the law. I made it to hewer, before I left for the Second World War. I learned all these skills down the pit, how to work in a team with others, and my wage depended on it. I was a pitman, but of course your mother didn't care to remember that very often. Pitmen were not good enough for your mam: she had other ideas.

The Coal Mines Regulation Act 1872 made many practices illegal. Boys under eighteen were not permitted to be in charge of dangerous machinery, pit cages had to be properly covered, travelling roads had to be provided with manholes, pit props had to be fitted properly, water levels had to be regularly inspected. The miners won these safety regulations but could be prosecuted and fined for violation of them; they accepted that winning rights also brought responsibility, so they were self-determining. The fine would come out of their wages, and the owners had to pay a fine too, so no one wanted to put themselves in the position of paying a fine to them: this would mean losing self-respect and privilege. The Mines Inspectorate enforced all these rules. Pit work is an art and very, very strenuous, so we men had to be sinewy and capable of sustained effort over long periods, stamina was important rather than height or weight. We had to walk stooped for miles underground, dodge rock protrusions, swing a heavy pick, be able to shovel and ram props into place in very cramped conditions.

And we had to understand the precise role of others, to know what to expect from other men: to trust, to acquire an instinctive trust, the ability and willingness to help others below ground otherwise the pit could not function. Most men were proud of their skills and took great care and pride in their work. Comradeship was strong but we also valued our autonomy; hewers had great autonomy, more than the putters. Putters were supervised by the underground officials and so the hewers had experienced close and unwelcome supervision when they were putters. We valued our autonomy and the underground freedom and status it brought. The miner under the bord and pillar system was referred to as a complete miner; performing a composite work role: we were highly skilled men.

We had to develop the canny knack of anticipating danger, and balance our efforts to win coal against the problems of the current situation we were in underground. We got used to the fear and learned to protect ourselves in our taken-for-granted world. Risk of injury was high and death, though infrequent, could come at any time, any day. We became fatalistic and resigned, otherwise we'd not be able to go on. My uncle, Nana's brother, was killed in a pit accident so I knew the reality of these safety measures. Throckley had a good safety record but miners were mindful of the consequences of accidents too; there were no pensions so poverty was the result. If they were killed their family would be evicted from their colliery house within days. We watched as my uncle's widow and children were evicted. I never forgot that scene and neither did my parents.

Men underground were concerned to keep good relations with each other and be able to negotiate with the officials, but we did not tolerate laziness or sloppiness: these endangered too many others' lives. We valued men who pulled their weight. These relationships, some of them strong friendships, encouraged self-discipline at work. Any unexplained absence, slipshod work, slackening of pace and effort would bring rebuke: we valued our independence and this is how we ensured we retained it. This spilled over into our everyday lives; we disliked dependence on anyone, and especially charity or 'skivers'. Discipline bought independence and freedom; it was a form of self-defence too, keeping management at bay.

Underground working had a very complex system of payments and appeals, with agreements made by the joint committee (the coalmen and the overseers), and these determined how the coal was hewn, the price paid to the men and the wages we shared (hewers were paid as a group once a fortnight and shared this between them equally). Ultimately if your marra let you down then you had less of a wage: wives would be most unhappy about this. Obligation was the key to a decent wage.

Throckley pitmen worked a six-hour shift, and the lads an eight-hour shift, with the hewers fore-shift (earlies) starting at 4 a.m. and the back-shift hewers at 10 a.m. All hewers had to change at face, meaning we came up in the cage and then the new shift went down, exchanging information as we went. The lads (the trainees) went down at 6.30 a.m. and rode (came to the surface) at 4.30 p.m.

Back-shift men had to ride after the lads, and the pit commenced drawing coals immediately the lads went down. All ceased work at 4.30 p.m. On Baff Saturdays (the day after pay-day) the pit would hang (start) at 4.00 a.m. and cease at 2.00 p.m. For this discipline, if they didn't live in colliery houses or lived as the hewers did in rented houses (private or council), they were paid two shillings per week house rent, if they worked 10 days per fortnight. Those working less only got fourpence per shift. Their deductions for coal were sixpence per fortnight and water rate fourpence. Broken lamp glasses had to be paid for at sixpence each. We recouped the cost of the repair of our drilling machines and if we lost our tokens we had to replace them from our wages. On top of this we had to pay for the cottage hospital, our union fees, pick sharpening by the pit blacksmith, and buy our own powder for blasting from the coal company. We had to be canny with money to remain in work. Our wives needed to be prudent and careful with the wages.

Our wages were based on the yardage won by each man separately and agreeing the price to be paid for that job there and then, with putters being paid by the yardage they had to push their tubs. Some faces were miles from the roadways and the distance pushed had to be compensated for by cavilling rules and price arrangements. In a way, we were all self-employed, the equivalent of the modern consultant. Of course these arrangements caused dissent and conflict, with constant arguments and haggling over distance and difficult faces – some not being profitable enough to bother working in. If these disputes could not be solved at pit level, which they usually were, they were referred to the joint committees of owners and men and these had the right to appoint referees who would go to the pit and investigate. They had the power to settle it too. It was this bargaining that shaped the miners' political consciousness including fairness and justice: we had to be aware of the wider world and economic situation otherwise we would be exploited. There was subterfuge, collusion, double standards, manipulation and conflict in the system, intensifying and decreasing according to coal prices and the owners' profits. It was in our self-interest to be acutely aware of our economic position and how it related to the wider economic situation throughout the country and in Europe.

The owners delegated the running of the pit to their agents, and in Throckley the owners managed to remain peacemakers in such disputes; often men ignored the agents and deputies and took their grievances straight to the major. The system of officials, over-men and deputies was not always a happy one with the miners either, and in Throckley we were not very tolerant of the officials: we didn't always respect them. The way the agreements were struck between the Northumberland Miners' Association and the Northumberland Coal Owners' Association made conflict underground inevitable and there was a powerful resentment of supervision. There was a general hatred of being 'stood over'.

Miners could be sacked by the deputies (your great-grandfather Lambert, Uncle Fred, and Charlton Thompson, your step-uncle were all deputies) for swearing or breaking safety rules, which the deputies were there to enforce. It was hard for them too, as they'd be friends with the miners in the social sense, living in the big house at the end of the street which caused resentment anyway, and they had extra perks that the men didn't have. Naturally they'd be damned if they did and damned if they didn't: they couldn't possibly win. Uncle Fred and Charlton were popular deputies: Uncle Fred managed this difficult relationship by smoothing his way drinking with the miners (his marras), and Charlton because he was just such a nice man and well respected. All of us had to be respectful underground, so it was easier to make this transition. Their role was a difficult one.

Most miners were union members, and fathers encouraged sons to join. The meetings were held in the store hall every two weeks, or if there was an emergency by the side of the pit heap. In 1900 only half the men in Throckley pit were in the union; by 1914 three-quarters had joined with rapid growth before the First World War. This followed the national union as a whole. The Northumberland miners shifted their allegiance from the Liberal Party to the Labour Party and joined the Miners Federation of Great Britain, and in 1912 took part in the national miners' strike over minimum wages. Industrial action was coordinated because of conflict and growing unrest with railway workers and the docks. The rise of the shop stewards' movement, syndicalism and the maturation of the Labour Party greatly challenged Edwardian society. For the Northumberland miners and those in Throckley, this struggle was over the Eight Hours Act and the minimum wage dispute. This made the miners reconsider joining the Miners' Federation of Great Britain and thus the possible dismantling of all district bargaining agreements and conciliatory practices. The leading lights in Throckley, members of the Council of Northumberland Miners, were George Curwen and Bob Huchinson and they discussed the wider issues of unionisation with the Throckley miners. Northumberland miners joined the MFGB after the acceptance of the Eight Hours Act in 1909 and accepted nationally negotiated agreements, although Throckley had voted against it, as it ended the traditional six-hour day. This was a big change for the men, as six-hour days had allowed them ample time for their allotments, whippets and pigeons as well as their smallholdings; often men had more than one allotment. The owners also tried to use the act to stop free coal. They didn't succeed. The strike (lasting six weeks) did achieve a victory against the coal owners in that miners' wages should not be linked to the fluctuating price of coal. The miners gained little, as the minimum wage (five shillings per shift) was below that for many miners anyway.

This led Throckley miners to demand that their own voice be heard through their own newspaper, and those from the Maria pit pushed this through, as well as a resolution advising branches to set up Labour Party branches, so they could field candidates for parliamentary seats. At this point Throckley became internationalist, supporting German miners with funds, free trade, and fighting for better conditions in the mines in South Africa. They were critical of government policy toward China, and supported domestic policies, free school meals and pensions. They were very critical of the amount of the Exchequer Fund being spent on war as they viewed paying for war as putting more of a burden on the poor. The Executive passed an anti-war resolution in 1906:

Recognising that war destroys life and wealth, that it arrests the consideration of social politics and the development of industry, and that it brings untold misery upon the human race, the members of this Association desire to raise their protest against the expansion of armaments; the encouragement of militarism; the loaning of money to belligerents, and the tactics of contracting syndicates who for selfish purposes promote colonial conquests.

Men in Throckley found it difficult to see the German man as an enemy – your Granda struggled with this: capitalism was the enemy. But many of them had no choice but to sign up with Kitchener's Volunteer Army. Recruiting was brisk with some 52,000 men from the Northern Division becoming soldiers, and it cost £70,000 per year to keep the families left behind. The coal owners in Throckley remunerated the wives of those who signed up at the rate of seven shillings per week, with an extra shilling per week for each child under 16. In the first round of recruitment 81 men left, of whom 37 were married, my father being one of them. This left the pits in a difficult situation, but the export in coal was also collapsing, and so this encouraged some miners to choose war – being paid and in work was certain in the army.

On the broader front, war changed Throckley and mining: it further politicised the community, especially as the death telegrams began to appear. Horses from the mines were also requisitioned,

Churchill was deemed a 'war monger' and he bred an intense dislike of the Tory party in the area. This further reinforced the work of the unions and the Labour Party, stripping the veil from people's eyes, especially about the bosses, the owners, and the capitalists, showing just how important the ordinary man was in terms of creating wealth. The coal controller in 1915 had agreed that 21,000 young miners be recruited by the war office: the quota from the Northumberland pits was 955 men and 15 from Throckley, this on top of those who had already volunteered. The miners fought to have taxation removed from wages under £15 per annum and fought for the Conscription of Wealth Bill to pay for the war. A sharp class consciousness was developing in Throckley.

Miners were encouraged to play their part in the war by literally keeping the home fires burning. The union membership grew with a lodge request to force non-union members to join. Men wanted to strike to be able to do this, and to press for the nationalisation of the mines, taking the mines out of the hands of the capitalists. Many fathers would not let their sons join the Boy Scouts as they saw it as training in militarism. The war had far-reaching social effects in Throckley. After the war, under Lloyd George's coalition government, with 338 Conservative MPs and 60 Labour Party members, the largest opposition, the idea was to create a land fit for heroes. It was agreed at a Lodge meeting in 1919 that all pits remain idle on 21 July to protest at the government's use of soldiers in Russia, continued conscription, and the six-shilling per ton rise in the price of coal.

The leading councillors and Labour men in Throckley were respected; Dick Browell and Danny Dawson. They were the new breed of local Labour leaders (even though they'd been schooled by the Independent Labour Party before the war) active in the union but also founding the Newburn and District Labour Party of which we were members. They affiliated with the Central Labour College in partnership with the Throckley Co-operative society (I think some people didn't know, nor understand, that the Co-op was not the Labour Party) to send two students per year to the college and also start an educational class in Marxist Economics in the Co-op Hall.

This was the post-war ideology in which my parents, my sister, your Aunty Bell, I and my friends and neighbours lived. It was the ideology of the pits. So different from your mother's more genteel experience, the conservative atmosphere in Haltwhistle: the more conservative culture of their pits, and their doff-your-cap attitude. They were also told how they must vote if they wanted to keep their jobs and houses. Dick Browell, a councillor since 1905, was chairman of the Newburn and District Labour Party, Danny Dawson was secretary and Bill Graham treasurer. They were affiliated to the Wansbeck Divisional Labour Party and through that to the League of Nations. They set the tone for internationalism in a colliery village, they believed in international parliaments long before any talk of a European Parliament. My father and I were in favour of these changes. Browell firmly believed this was the way forward and we believed him. Your Mam was uncertain about the Labour Party at that point.

To live in Throckley was to be political, directly or indirectly; there was no choice in the matter. I learned all my political knowledge through being a pitman; it shaped my loyalties and my moral development. I passionately believed in the internationalist message and the antiwar message. I was not weak, but I was not a typical male either, no more than my father was: we were not misogynists or dominant males. I'd like to think we were thinking men and ahead of our time. I had to fight in a war as a non-believer in war: that was one of the hardest things I ever did. The war changed your Mam's mind about conservatism too: she became a labour supporter. Her brother Bill, also a pitman as well as having served in the army, also influenced her political change of mind.

220

15

Fantasies

You see, there were many tensions between your mother and me, between our different family cultures. Tensions that could not always be stated in words, or dealt with in action: they had to be lived with day in and day out. After I was released from the army it made us different as a family. I was different from other men around me. I loved cooking and caring. I think it suited me and if conventions hadn't been a problem I would have been happy to run the home and do the childcare. It was a constant battle between things as they were, and things as they should be, and too often things as they should be won through, causing immense stress. I was also a bit of a perfectionist. Naturally, as a pitman, then an unwilling soldier who was trained as a motor mechanic, a team player in football and cricket, doing half a job or a job badly meant possible life and death to my fellow soldiers or colleagues. It was not an option, and so when I cooked I brought some of that conscientiousness, as well as my eye for detail to the task. I really enjoyed doing a good job no matter what the job was, or what type of job it was.

I was very particular about my appearance; I loved dressing well and looking smart. I like to think I had my own style to match your mother's: she certainly had style. In the mornings I was always aware of your intent gaze: your eyes upon me, watching my every move. It was one of our closest times together, free from the jealous gaze of your Mam and a time when you were quiet, very quiet. I always knew this was the other side of you: the reflective child and daughter, the daughter who took everything in. As we said, you didn't miss a thing, ever. You observed, stored quietly, and then regurgitated actively and noisily; usually with pertinent gesticulation too. It always seemed to me that the things you decided to watch quietly became etched on your mind, stored safely for some later date. You could go hours without speaking if you so chose: you played quietly, often alone, although of course you played outside with others too, first with boys as they were the first other residents, and then girls when they too moved in.

It was always hard for me to align these two aspects of your personality: the quiet observer and reader, the independent child and the noisy boisterous child. It was as though we had two girls wrapped in one skin, both had a strong will, both needed to determine their destiny. You showed that trait from a very early age and we were proud of you, both your grandmothers were similar although your mother's mother was never noisy though very determined. You were a girl who could be friendly, outgoing, yet introverted and shy: too much social contact and you became shy and retiring. You always were able to stand back amid activity and watch. Have you still got that photograph of our holiday where I am building a grass castle for your brother and you are licking an ice lolly, observing, almost challenging the very idea of a grass castle? *'You stupid boys, what are you doing?'* is written all over your face. Your gaze was penetrating and intimidating even as a child. There was, like my mother, a 'knowingness' about you. Things just didn't escape you as they might other children and I wonder if that was more about our circumstances, the fact that both your mother and I had been in hospital so many times during your first few years. I think this was sad for you: you were forced to grow up too quickly, we used to say. This was said of you by others too.

I'm glad my terraced garden outlasted me; that must be one of my great achievements. I'm sorry about the steps: I had big intentions to have proper steps but of course they never materialised because of my health and lack of money. But I did love my garden,

I really did. Granda and I had our most loving moments in his garden; we were often to be found silently pottering around, or sometimes working hard digging and planting, pruning and nurturing his plants and mine. We communed intuitively and there was a close companionship. We didn't need to talk, we just liked being together, in tandem as it were. I loved my father and I know he loved me; I know that because he was always there when I needed him and he was the same with Uncle Fred and all our friends. Not many fathers were accepted by a young man's friends; in most cases young men didn't want to have their fathers around, but I didn't mind and as you can see from photographs he is often with a group of us, a quiet presence who respected young men as we respected him.

We both loved the outdoors and sport, so summer and winter we had shared interests. I learned all I knew about gardens and plants from him. My father was a quietly confident man, one who had no need to show off or boast: these he couldn't abide and didn't like braggers around him. He had enough to cope with having my mother and sister around, they made all the noise and he let it go over his head – mostly. Occasionally he would protest, but it was only occasionally, because he got a vicarious pleasure from their antics. I think they helped him 'come alive', brought life into his house and garden. He came from a quiet family, his sisters were impressive in size and build but reserved and quiet, dignified.

If we were together in the house we would usually sit in opposite chairs. We'd either read the paper or our books: we discussed the news and politics. Your Granda was very up to date with international events but he wasn't actively involved in politics, neither was he a hot-head. He was more of an observer, his own views clear, but he had no need to force them on anyone else. It was not unusual for men to sit and read books in Throckley because the Miner's Institute Reading Room was there for that specific purpose, to provide books and newspapers free, to provide a space for working men to read. I used to join him there sometimes because I was also educating myself using their resources. We might have had little chance of further formal education but the reading room provided what we needed to be self-taught. Both of us shared a vision of a better world, a fair and just world, and above all a more peaceful world. That was often our main topic of conversation.

Granda had hopes for me, despite my not having been able to take my place at the grammar school: he was mortally ashamed that he could not afford to send me when I passed the eleven plus but I understood the reasons why: I too wanted fairness and justice but I also knew I had ability and was trying to find my niche.

Granda had been a skilled man, as his father before him; he probably could have been in management but his war service took the stuffing out of him and like many men he had to take what work there was. His dragging, limp left leg made it impossible for him to work underground in the colliery or return to his shipbuilding work. He was a fireman, a poorly paid job in the colliery, yet one of the most harrowing jobs there, one that meant protecting other men's lives, and at times saving men's lives. After the war many families were homeless and journeying to find work to keep hearth and home together, so Granda was no different from many others, nor was he different from your mother's father either. The work was not there when they returned from war and the great Depression made things so much more difficult. Men took what they could in terms of work. You know work does not define a person, and Granda's work did not define him: he was a kind and intelligent man who kept his own counsel and made the best of things, even as an outsider, and he never grumbled.

I can't answer your questions about your mother's dislike of my family: I think it is very complicated. I can offer some insights. I had enough experience of her feelings and thoughts about my family over the years to be able to hazard intuitive guesses about her reasons, but remember, your mother didn't need reasons – often her remarks were a manifestation of her own frustration and anger and were best ignored. I couldn't always ignore them but most of the time I tried to do so. Yes, of course they hurt, but I also knew your mother well enough to understand her frustration with my family.

I also feel that perhaps I should not have made her – and I did make her – come to live in Throckley while I was away on training and duties during the war. Hindsight always reminded me that I had displaced her at a crucial point in her life; left her in an urban environment so unsuited to her temperament and needs, and alone. We men called the tune then, and it is a call I regret. I was not a man who needed to be in control of a woman, you know that, but it was convention, and my work was in Throckley so it seemed best at the time. Your mother wilted in Throckley and had an endless struggle to survive emotionally despite her sisters and brother being near at hand; her natural bloom faded and she struggled to retain it. There was no work in Haltwhistle anyway, so in some ways there was no choice, we had to be where there was work and money to be earned. Free choice was not an option for us.

Your mother, as you know, needed lots of approval and love and expected others to demonstrate this freely and copiously. Even I got tired of propping up her self-esteem at times. I can only say that her brothers doted on her and her mother but she had not had a lot of attention from her father: he too was damaged by his service in the First World War. She was attractive to men and a bit of a flirt: she liked flirting and men liked her, so she needed continual attention. In my family no one got that much attention, we could be disparaging of each other, yet we were closer in many ways than the bonds between your mother's family: less conventional and more accepting.

She was raised more conventionally than I was. Her views were formed by her experience of being raised in the Church of England, her very Christian mother, and this meant she found herself at sea in a family who did what they liked when they liked, and said what they liked too: we lived in a happy state of chaos much of the time. She was too easily hurt when no hurt was intended, though I could never convince her of this, no matter how hard I tried. In your mother's defence, my mother was domineering. She didn't always take people's feelings into account: she didn't mean to hurt anyone but she often did, especially other women. They forgave her because she was kind and loving, but your mother could not forgive: it caused many rows between us.

Your mother was not a very forgiving person. Yet she was great fun, had a feisty sense of humour and I loved her. There are always tensions in families and you should not take it all too seriously, although I know that you were very aware of the tensions at times. It is very difficult for children to appreciate the relationship between their parents, the intimate aspect that doesn't include them. Equally it is difficult for wives and husbands, as adults, to appreciate the depth of love and relationships between their parents and their children. I had to be very open-minded and forgiving, concentrate on your mother's strengths, her family's strength, to be able to go on loving her: and I did. I had no difficulty with that, though I was frustrated at times, because I loved her and wanted no one else. Besides, she was suffering. I had to make allowances for her frustrations; those caused by me being in the army, war, and then ill. Nothing is ever one-sided.

The house we wanted to buy is a point in question: she desperately wanted that house, so did I. I wanted to be upwardly socially mobile as much as she did. I wanted to provide her with her dream, but it wasn't possible. You are right, she never did recover and always dreamed on: one day she would have her house. Circumstances robbed her of her dreams, and everyone needs a dream. She never did recover from that blow, perhaps the most pertinent one too, even more devastating than my illness, I think. Your mother always wanted to be somebody. I don't think for one minute she knew who, or what, but she wanted more than she was able to have and she was bitter because of it. Bitterness rots the soul, and although bitterness didn't destroy her, it was always there under the surface, eating away at her self-esteem and dragging her into imaginary taunting worlds, disturbing her, because they could never be hers. Her depression was the result. She was born at the wrong time, in the wrong place, as far as she was concerned.

Why did she dislike my father so much? I really have no idea. I am not sure she even did dislike him. I think he was such a contrast to her own father because he kept his own counsel, read, was quiet, was very close to me, had his hobbies, loved you, and she had not had this from her father: this wasn't her fault or her father's fault. He was damaged by his war service during the First World War, terribly, and didn't talk about it, but was not the same man who left for war. You have already discovered that. She didn't know anything about it. She didn't know why he was bad tempered, why he drank, why he didn't talk: she was born after he came back, her personality shaped before she could even ask any questions. He died long before any of us understood the damage some men suffered during the war, and he had no physical injuries: his were all emotional injuries, trauma.

My father had his dragging lame leg – we could see it, knew how he got it. Her father had invisible mental scars and no one knew they were there. My father was marked by war emotionally too, but she interpreted his sitting around, as she called it, as laziness. He wasn't lazy. He made his life and ours as comfortable as he could but joy was something he rarely showed and he didn't converse much either. It was my relationship with my father that she was jealous of because she did not have a strong relationship with her father.

Her young brothers, Bill and George, paid her a lot of attention but her parents could not, not in the way my parents paid me attention. Love was in the open in our house, in your mother's family it was assumed, but not demonstrated; always implicit but not explicit. She was frightened of her father and resented that: I was never frightened of my father. She had little attention from her mother, stalwart and courageous as her mother was, but she was too busy keeping hearth and home together.

I think it is quite simple: your mother probably never knew the truth about her father's war service, how much he had heard and seen, and how much he suffered from nightmares and relentless replays of those sights and sounds. She probably didn't really know that he had been extremely brave to volunteer aged 37, after all he didn't have to at his age. That, in itself, was something to be proud of, but their family didn't talk about things: they had secrets. And the biggest secret was your grandfather's drinking to cope with his trauma. They were all ashamed of this without understanding its origin.

Your Granma was a brave and courageous, gentle woman, but lived by the mantra of respectability, so nothing was in the open: all was bottled up to ensure the family's survival. I loved your Granma and your Granda, but they were always in sharp relief to my family: we seemed very rough, noisy and ebullient in comparison even though both were mining families.

Your mother was emotionally neglected through no fault of her own. Her brothers, Bill and George, made up for that as they adored her during their childhood and continued to do so in her adult life, and so she expected all men to adore her, to love her, or she needed them to. I think she was simply jealous that I was loved and then, when you came along, you were loved too, demonstrably loved by my parents and family – and she could see what she hadn't had. New experiences unconsciously raise old hurts. She didn't know she had a sore, so she couldn't heal that sore, even with my love.

On top of this she had a husband who was sick, and her life was not as she'd wanted it, expected it to be, and she found that hard. We all did. She cannot be blamed for that. She was demanding, yes, but it didn't stop me loving her and it hasn't stopped you loving her either, you know that. Like her mother she was a survivor, and ensured you survived as best she could, even at a time when she was not surviving emotionally herself: when she was lost and grieving.

Of course my mother was the antithesis of her mother: a harridan, your mother would have called her in comparison, and of course your mother recognised some of those traits in you. You were never going to be demure and undemanding, never going to accept without question, never controlled by others. I think she would have preferred it if you had been more like her mother and elder sister, more like her. Instead you were a complicated mix of my mother and sister, me, my father and her own wayward sister, Ella, as the family thought of her, as well as elements of her too. You didn't look anything like your mother either, especially around the eyes; you were definitely not a thoroughbred Lambert. You had those Holland eyes last seen in my grandmother.

I think, even as a baby, you took attention away from your mother, attention she badly needed, and so she was ambivalent about you, loving you and resenting you in equal measure. You were not the child she had expected and never could be. Your mother was a romantic, and romantic personalities suffer a great deal, especially if life does not treat them as they expect: fantasies and dreams cannot always become reality. Your mother grieved for what might have been, and in some respects she was justified in doing so. Life battered her and although practically she was a good survivor, as her mother and elder sister were, emotionally she was not so tough. Your mother didn't want anyone stamping on her fragile self and my mother wasn't always sensitive enough to see that. Our sense of humour could be disparaging, but it wasn't meant to be, and it hurt and annoyed your mother. Sometimes when you were little, when they teased you, it hurt you too. My family dealt with stress by throw-away comments and black humour: too much for your mother to cope with.

And of course your difficult birth caused her injury and she was often separated from you as they tried to help her with her back injury and life-long pain. Your attachment with your mother was disrupted many times in those first few years, and it was my family she had to rely on to look after you. I think she resented that – and of course you were learning their rougher ways, something she definitely wouldn't have chosen in a million years: another Nana and Aunty Bell in the family was not what your mother had ordered. Such is life: we think we have control over it and then find we do not. Your mother had a hard time in that sense.

16

Visiting Dunston Hill Military Pensions Hospital

I am very familiar with the journey to Dunston Hill hospital and was so long before David was born; after he was born our lives were inextricably linked with travelling on buses, changing buses in Newcastle, over Scotswood Bridge to visit Dunston Hill Military Pensions Hospital. We did this journey summer and winter to see our Dad. Visiting Dad in hospital at weekends and school holidays, as well as living with and coping with our mother, was an inimical education. Dunston Hill became the focal point of our week and has only been as famous since as the birthplace of Gazza, that rascal Geordie footballer. In my childhood it was famous for its inpatients: the victims of two world wars.

From the outside it looked what it was, a lovely old country house with a fine front entrance, a grand formal gateway set in beautiful, restful grounds. We approached the front entrance through the open gate and crunched our way up the mellow yellow gravel drive. I always felt as though I ought to arrive in a carriage in my party frock covered by my fur coat. Once inside we followed the very familiar passageways that led to the wards: these were wooden and linked by corridors to the main house and offices.

Inside there was an eighteenth-century staircase with fat turned balusters and a wide handrail in the rear wing under a high-quality stucco ceiling. All the main rooms on the ground floor

231

had stucco ceilings. The later staircase, the one we admired on our visits, had more slender banisters than the original and a ramped handrail. The stucco ceilings were still in evidence in the main buildings. I loved looking up the staircase and running my hand down the rail. When I was bored – I loved Dad but I did get bored – I wandered. I often wandered to the main entrance to indulge myself in princess fantasies, walking down those stairs in my party frock just like Cinderella.

Dunston Hill became a hospital during the First World War, commandeered as so many estates and houses were by the Ministry of Defence. Hospital buildings and wards still remain today. I persuaded my brother to take me to the remaining site recently: it is now a short-stay hospital for those with learning difficulties and mental illness. The house has been derelict for many years but has recently been repaired, currently being developed as apartments. The wooden wards where Dad so often took up involuntary residence are long gone; they have been replaced with new townhouses.

I was barely two when I was first carried to Dunston Hill in my mother's arms, and when David's turn came he too was carried to see Dad. Mam was working on the Home Help Service as we called it then, in the morning, leaving her free for visiting times at the hospital. 'Home Helps' visited older people, who were becoming infirm, were ill, or who'd begun the long weary journey into senile dementia. They shopped, cleaned and cared for these older people, washed and ironed their clothes; they sometimes even collected their pensions. When I look back now I cannot imagine how Mam coped physically, never mind mentally, with the demands of her life. Her physical and mental breakdowns are witness to the fact she sometimes didn't: yet there were often long periods of time between these breakdowns when she was courageous, hard working and strong. For nearly twenty years she was under continuous stress and she slowly metamorphosed from a buxom wench into a stick-thin, black pencil woman.

Dad always wore his silver badge, the sign he was both a war veteran and disabled from his service: he swapped it from jacket to jacket: it had 'war disabled' in tiny letters around its rim. It was many years before I understood what this badge was for and what it meant to him and others. When I was first conscious of visiting Dunston Hill I was about five years old; I became aware of the other men in the ward. It was difficult, after those first excited moments with Dad, lots of cuddles and kisses, not to get bored. If he was well enough Dad played with us: board games and later billiards.

We sometimes walked down to the canteen for tea and cakes, my favourite being iced fancies, particularly white or pink ones. Other times we would walk in the grounds. Inevitably, I would ask lots of questions. I was told to stop asking so many, to mind my own business, to go and play. Where on earth did a child go and play in a hospital? Don't adults say the most ridiculous things to children sometimes, particularly when they are interested in their own business!

So instead of playing I would wander around, drift about, with purpose. As David got older I'd take him with me, dragging him along beside me. There was plenty to see in the ward. I became a child voyeur, alert, watching with amazement, fear, listening to the sounds and sights of that ward. These were not nice sounds; it was not a pleasant place to be. It is still hard to think about what I saw and heard. I have very vivid memories. There were men with no legs, no arms, men in wheelchairs, some blind, some with no eyes, patches where their eyes should have been. Men with burnt faces and arms, men crying, men screaming, men moaning, and some men silent humps in their bed or wheelchair. There was a man I have never forgotten, and remember with much distress: he seemed to be hanging from the ceiling in some kind of basket, his face distorted, moaning continually. Another rocked and moaned incessantly. There were men being fed by nurses as they couldn't hold a knife and fork; men who shook uncontrollably. And they all had one thing in common: they all wore the same pyjamas if they were in bed; blue striped pyjamas. If they were able to walk around as Dad sometimes did, they wore blue serge suits. I couldn't understand why they were all dressed the same, why there was such a horrible smell and why there was such an awful incessant noise. I tried to ask my parents but was fobbed off with the usual entreaty to mind my own business and to find something to do.

Parts of the hospital were forbidden to visitors and I couldn't understand this either. I'd wander down the corridor from Dad's ward trying to read notices on the way, but of course I couldn't make sense of many of these until I was older. There was one that I eventually learned said 'No Admittance to Visitors'. I was fascinated by its closed doors and small covered windows. I longed to know what was behind those closed doors. I was insatiably curious and horribly nosey. I think now these hid the most terrible burned and maimed victims and perhaps injured women. I have always wished I'd been told, because I imagined possible sights through the years anyway.

Such sights put me off hospitals and I made up my mind I would never be a nurse – I didn't change my mind. The smell of Dunston Hill has stayed with me: the hospital smell was urine, feaces, blood, bodies, sweat and cheap disinfectant all mixed up with carbolic soap and cheap oil-cloth. These spoke the acid sickness of human decay and misery. I often felt sick as I wandered. The horrid, cold, cheap oil-cloth echoed every foot step, I'd watch the visitors' faces as they came up the corridor: their look of hurt and pain etched in every pore. This has haunted me for a lifetime, although I was an adult before I knew what these sad anxious people's faces meant. They would venture slowly up the corridors, watchful, fearful, looking carefully into the ward before they fully entered, checking what today might bring, before they started their walk down the ward, took out their smile from its hiding place, stuck it on their face and quickened their pace, waving and falsely hollering, '*Hello hinny, how are you today, eeh its lovely to see you,*' or words to that effect, all rather too loudly and dramatically. When I visit anyone in hospital now I still do the creeping slow walk to the ward door, holding my breath so I cannot smell the smell, then peep around the ward door before I have the courage to enter; a social skill learned as a child and one I could have done without.

Worse by far was the smell of chrysanthemums in their stinking green slimy water: rotting, dusty, decaying rats in a stagnant sewer. I hate chrysanthemums, or as we called them, crysanths. I detest their shabby, flaky dullness, their garish colours: they speak to me of life's detritus. Rubbish dump flowers. They are a metaphor for all that Dunston Hill stood for, spilt blood, spleen, guts, brains, eyes, arms, legs, gangrene – stagnant and wasted life. The hospital was full to the brim with destruction, the human and spiritual destruction of those unable to live again. I only saw men, no women, yet I am sure there were women in Dunston Hill.

I was fascinated by the activities the men who still had their arms and eyes had to do. I was puzzled by the fact that sick and ill men had to be kept busy, to have hobbies and interests. Later it did make some sense to me: the hospital staff had to help combat boredom. Many of these men, even Dad sometimes, were long-term patients and the others were definitely not going anywhere. The rest of their life would be spent in Dunston Hill. Dad was a great reader of books and newspapers. He liked to follow the football, cricket and racing. He played billiards, snooker and cards so he didn't need to have imposed activity but he didn't seem to mind embroidering his tablecloth using delicate cross-stitches. I have his beautiful tablecloth to this day, carefully preserved. It has an intricate pattern of cross-stitch and a drawn thread border. He had immense patience, and delighted in making his cloth perfect, every stitch is in exactly the right place and the colours co-ordinated. He taught me how to do drawn thread work. Others made lampshades, knitted jumpers and those who'd been blinded made cane baskets. The hospital almoner organised all this production. What I couldn't understand then, and still can't now although I will be accused of being sexist, was why these men had to have hobbies that were viewed in the 1950s as women's work. They had fought, handled guns, been bombed and probably did some bombing, been in charge of battalions, and yet when they were deemed unfit for service they had to do 'women's work'. I am very glad that Dad did make his tablecloth as it is a very personal memento: each stitch is a tiny bit of him that lives on, a cross-stitch story of long weary days in hospital yet also a mark of his pride and creativity.

But I didn't mind visiting Dunston Hill. I loved seeing Dad, telling him what I'd done, where I'd been during the week, and especially all about school. I'd lie cuddled up to him as Mam perched on the edge of the bed. I liked it best of all when he was up and about in his blue serge suit. These suits looked rather like prison uniforms, wide trousers and a round-necked jacket, quite loose and straight. The material was rough, a bit like horse-hair. We'd walk through the corridors to the garden, wander the grounds or sit in the sun. The canteen was always a very busy place with relatives escorting patients in wheelchairs, some with crutches, some hobbling and others walking. They served good tea and lovely cakes. The tables were metal with matching chairs painted cream, not comfortable but spotlessly clean. Having tea in the canteen gave Dad and his visitors a break from the wards, a break from the stress of being surrounded by invalids and sick people. It was a deeply private time where others were too busy to take much notice of who you were. Mam and Dad could be themselves and so could we: we relaxed more than we did on the wards. Visiting times were two hours on Wednesday, Saturday and Sunday afternoon, and children were welcome unlike the National Health Service at the time. Had Dad been in an NHS hospital we would hardly have seen him for the best part of our childhood. We were very lucky.

I missed Dad at home and yet I wasn't conscious of pining or yearning for his presence. I think I had come to terms with his longer or shorter absences when I was quite young and so got used to the routines when he wasn't at home. I knew where he was and why, and knew I only had to wait for a few days each week before I could see him and talk to him.

Yet despite his absences he was a major influence on my life, on the way I think, and especially about understanding the importance of school. Mam and Dad wanted me to do well at school. Education, as far as they were concerned, was the key to life. Without it you had no chance to better yourself as they put it and so it was drummed into me very early on that I had to be successful at school. This wasn't difficult, I loved school from the day I started and was indeed doing very well: always on the top table, interested and motivated, I believed the world was my oyster. I missed Dad most when I was with other families or watching other families out for the day. Then I wished my Dad was there too. I never talked about it, nor was I jealous, but I acutely felt his absence. I also felt it when friends talked about their dad, or when both their mam and dad came to school plays or other functions. But I didn't get upset about it, not noticeably so anyway. Perhaps my feelings were repressed.

As Dad became more ill I remember my teacher at the time, Mrs Carnaby, taking a special interest. Every day she'd ask me how he was, how Mam was. No one had done this before. She took a special interest in me too. She made a point of showing she cared: this was unusual as she had a reputation. Most children were frightened of her as she was strict and tough. She thought nothing of picking up the window pole and using it to hit some recalcitrant on the head to remind them they should be concentrating, or remind them they were useless. She'd stand poised with this pole at the back of the classroom waiting for her victims. Yet I loved her, I learned with her and wasn't frightened of her. I also had my first serious illness while I was in her class. I had not missed a day at school, in fact I would not miss a day at school, I loved it so much. Fortunately I had not needed to worry about missing school, as I had been a very fit and healthy child: slightly overweight but strong. Just after Christmas I had a funny pricking in my throat when I swallowed, as though a piece of glass was stuck in my throat, it really hurt and I knew I didn't feel quite right. I can't remember how long I persevered with this feeling but I knew it was getting worse. I didn't say a word to my parents: Dad was at home for a while. This was a familiar pattern, as he convalesced he would come home for short periods and then return to the hospital. The broken glass feeling got worse and worse, and still I said nothing and continued to go to school, until one afternoon I was in a state of collapse with a very high temperature. I managed to get home but collapsed when I got through the back door. By the next morning I was delirious and my father was terrified, absolutely terrified. So was my mother.

They sent for our doctor who came immediately – Mam, David and I had a different GP to Dad. He diagnosed suspected scarlet fever and wanted me taken to hospital. Dad flatly refused and said he would treat me at home; there was no way his child was going into hospital. So I was prescribed penicillin every six hours. The doctor said he would give this treatment forty-eight hours, and if there was no improvement then it would be hospital. Dad moved into my bedroom (David was moved out as we shared a bed) and set up his alarm clock, towels, water, just as though he'd suddenly completed his nurse training and I was his first patient. He sat by my bed sponging me with warm water to cool me down and when the alarm rang he gave me my next tablet. He continued this throughout the night. I think one reason he moved in with me was to allow Mam to get her sleep as she was working.

I only remember this time vaguely, knowing he was there, hearing the alarm, seeing him in his blue knitted jerkin, one Mam had spent hours knitting for him. It had a very complicated neat cable pattern up the front panels, a zip and a collar. David had the boy's version in the same colour. I would see his image standing at the bottom of my bed, the tea towel over his arm in place of his mac, just watching me. At the time I didn't know whether he was real or not. Life was very blurred for many days. Sometimes I didn't know where I was, I seemed to be able to move around the room, the walls moved too: things were crawling on the ceiling and animals climbed the walls. After forty-eight hours my temperature was stabilising and on the fourth day I started coughing and thought I was going to be sick. Dad fetched a bowl as I was retching badly: but I wasn't sick. I coughed up the most horrendous hard, almost perfectly round, ball of pus and blood the size of a walnut. They kept this specimen in the bowl under my bed until the doctor called: he'd been calling each day. I'd had a quinsy throat. It was three weeks before I was back in school, very thin and very weak. Perhaps it was just a chance infection, but I think that possibly the stress of Dad's ill health and absence had come home to roost. I was prone to throat infections from then until I had my tonsils out aged 21. Dad was an excellent nurse.

As he became more and more ill he was in hospital for longer periods of time and I remember him becoming yellow, sallow and bed-ridden. One evening Mam sat with us cuddled up to her, she was very distressed. She told us that our father had cancer, and that he would only live for a few months at the most. I was distraught. I couldn't take it in and it remained on my mind every minute of the day. I felt torn into small pieces, nothing about me fitted any more. I was a mess. And then began the vigil with no known end. No one could be precise about when he would die. I stopped sleeping. I'd toss and turn, thinking it might be tonight. If it wasn't tonight it might be tomorrow, and so every day I expected the knock at the door. And we went on visiting Dad, not saying anything about what might happen. I don't know if he knew he'd been given a death sentence.

We visited him as usual on the Saturday. He was bed-ridden, very quiet and yellow. He was sleeping so we walked to the canteen for some iced fancies and I kept a white one for Dad. When we got back to the ward he was awake, just, and I told him I'd kept him a cake. He turned his head slightly, looked at me and said, '*That's lovely Pet. You keep it and have it tomorrow.*'

He then turned his head back into his pillow and sighed deeply. I wrapped the cake up and took it home.

17

A Knock at the Door

It is a very quiet Saturday evening after we return from the hospital on 25 July 1959; and it is an even quieter Sunday. Aunty Vi is looking after us while Mam goes to see Dad. We go to Sunday school as normal on the two o'clock bus and return at four. Mam comes back from the hospital looking tired and pale at about seven. We are sent to bed at our normal time of eight o'clock. The house is very, very quiet. Mam and Aunty Vi talk in whispers. I can't sleep and lie awake, frightened and anxious. At about eleven o'clock there is a knock at the door: it is the policeman. I can't hear what is said, but know somehow that Mam has gone back to the hospital. There are more knocks at the door and neighbours whisper with Aunty Vi. I know my Dad is dead. I don't cry, or shout, or ask for confirmation: I just know. I lie quiet until morning. Mam comes back in a taxi in the early hours. I don't sleep. I hear her desperate crying.

We are called next morning – we are always called, awake or not, at 7.30 a.m. even in school holidays. Mam is in the kitchen looking white as a sheet and dishevelled. Aunty Vi tells us, before we sit down to our breakfast, that our father has died. I grin and grin, trying to prevent myself from laughing. I am frightened by my need to laugh. I don't say I know. It's as though I know that they know, that we all have to play a game of charades, look and behave as normal. There is no obvious emotion just a prolonged eerie silence. And, even though Dad has been in hospital for months and not at home, there is a great yawning empty space in our house this morning. He'd always come home before, but now he will never come home again.

Aunty Vi explains that Aunty Bell is coming to collect us, to take us to stay with her. We have no say in what happens. I cannot imagine how Aunty Vi feels as she is reliving her own experience of her husband's death, with her own two children aged the same as David and myself now. She is supporting and guiding Mam. It cannot be easy, yet I feel a strong sense that she needs to keep control of everything, including prohibiting crying and any scenes: we are never told that we shouldn't cry, but we understand it is not the done thing. There is palpable fear in our dining room: the fear of a scene.

Aunty Bell and Uncle Fred arrive in their car to take us away. That's how it feels for me – I am to be taken away from my own house and have to pretend that nothing has changed and that this is an ordinary day. I can't imagine how Aunty Bell copes. She adores Dad. He is not mentioned during the next few days. I can't remember what we do, or where we go. I do think a lot about the knock at the door: I knew it was coming and just waited for it to come. It feels strange being told something I already know, yet not being able to say, '*I know.*' It strikes me as very odd, when I am only ten nearly eleven, that the adults around me think I don't understand what is happening. I can't say, '*I know I heard it all, I know what's happened because I heard it all.*' I have been on red alert for weeks listening to the adults talk around me: I inform myself from their conversations while they pretend I can't understand what they are saying. They say I'm too young.

I still wonder at their assumption that children have neither eyes nor ears once they are in bed and thought to be asleep. I wonder how they thought I could sleep? After all, Mam had told us Dad was going to die.

I don't know how long we were at Aunty Bell's but I remember very clearly that we were brought home for a few hours to be able to see Dad in his coffin in the little bedroom upstairs. Aunty

Bell said we should both go to see him and she tried to take my hand. I was sitting on the chair in the dining room in the corner by the kitchen door. It was the chair Mam usually sat on, and if she wasn't sitting on it, it was covered with folded washing awaiting ironing. Aunty Bell got down on her knees to try to persuade me to go upstairs to see my dead Dad. I wouldn't go. She attempted to pull me off the chair and I screamed blue murder. I did not want to see my dead Dad. There was a lot of persuading and attempts to force me to go – she wasn't cruel but obviously thought it was best for me. I knew differently. Eventually she gave up and took David (aged six) instead.

It was twenty years before I ever entered the little bedroom again: I refused to go in, or sleep in, that room. Only a few months ago, after a major trauma in David's life, he told me that he has seen Dad lying in his coffin, tiny, shrunken and yellow, every day of his life: the image is as clear now as it was then. He described it to me and I was shocked that he'd carried this picture with him throughout his life and never said a word.

Through these difficult days I have my grin to protect me. If anyone says anything about Dad I grin like an imbecile but inside I want to laugh, and laugh, hysterically. In my attempt to prevent this happening – I know it is not appropriate and will upset everyone – I grimace so hard and so much that I begin to look like a demented child: this thin-lipped, on the verge of laughing but trying to control my laughter grimace-grin becomes my mask. I am demented – by fear and grief but I don't know it. What I can't understand is the adult behaviour that is going on around me. First we are got rid of, presumably because children and death don't mix, and we are to be kept out of view of adult emotion: and yet bizarrely we are taken back to view the dead body. As I grow up I understand that adult emotions are out of kilter in grief and that all the adults around us are trying to do the right thing 'for the children'.

Our mother, in her white blouse and pencil-thin black wool skirt with the split up the centre back and her black stiletto heels, is fashionable in her grief. She is a vague hazy figure in the background of my bad dream. Her black skirt has a beautiful matching jacket. This has a neat revere collar, three buttons and a nipped-in waist. In her skinny fleshless state she wears her widowhood and sadness elegantly because her dress sense hasn't died with Dad. Only her hair gives away her inner turmoil, as it sticks like rats' tails to her skull: it has somehow become thin and bedraggled. Her hair is her pride and joy, usually lush and thick, well cared for, and now it is flabbergasted at her neglect. It just doesn't sit right on her head and seems to know it no longer fits her scalp: without her help it hasn't a clue how to behave itself. Her face is haunted, thin and pale: it too is surprised by its sagging hang and how quickly it has aged. It doesn't belong on this paper-thin scrawny neck or shrunken skull either. Our mother has aged fifty years overnight. The suit has been bought to fit on the day after Dad dies and that's why it looks comfortable when everything else about her doesn't. It is the custom that widows go shopping for their mourning clothes after the death, so they will be appropriately dressed when people visit or they have to go out on funeral business: it is a mark of respect. She's become so small and frail it seems impossible that she can remain upright. But upright is what is needed so the neighbours don't think she is weak. We are expected to be upright too.

I can't remember much about this week other than it seems very long. Aunty Bell delivers us to my cousins on Newburn Road on the morning of Dad's funeral. In the absence of adults my older cousins (one two years older and the other a year older than me) are to take care of us by taking us to play tennis: they are supervised by our male cousin who is somewhat older than us. I do not want to go and play tennis. I want to see the cortege (I didn't know that was what it was called of course) come out of our street. Uncle Bill and Aunty Maria's house is opposite to the entrance to Hallow Drive so it is easy for me to perch in the window to watch. Every time I go near they drag me away. We spend the morning at the tennis courts where I am listless and unable to think of anything except what is going on elsewhere. I have no idea what happens at a funeral: I try to imagine it and of course I make it up. I explain it all to myself and picture it as I think it will be.

This has a long-term effect. I am unable to go to funerals, even those of relatives and two of my friends: I just can't go. It is to be over twenty years before I attend a funeral. When one of my best friends dies, aged 21 after a rugby club party, I cannot get out of bed. They get the doctor and he doesn't know what the matter is. I stay in bed for a week because my legs won't hold my weight. I don't eat. Then I get up and go back to work. I can't tell the doctor that my friend died after leaving the party: he got on his motorbike and he hadn't been wearing his crash helmet, even though I reminded him before he left the party, asking him to put it on. All his friends and mine go to his funeral, but I don't. I don't cry either. I can't.

We are taken home in the afternoon to find Aunty Vi waiting and Mam in bed. She has managed the funeral without crying, got through the niceties of the funeral tea and then collapsed. She is proud she's walked with dignity and ramrod straight. She hasn't let herself down, or the family either. I can't remember anything at all about the next three weeks. It is school summer holidays, warm and sunny and some days are really hot.

Aunty Vi thinks it will be a good idea for us to go with her to her daughter's in Scotland for a little holiday. Monica and Bob live on an army camp just outside Edinburgh. He is a sergeant in the Royal Signals, they married two years before and I was a bridesmaid. We travel by train from Newcastle to be met by them both at Waverley Station in Edinburgh. Mam is in her black suit and white blouse, which for the next year she doesn't take off except to wash her blouse and replace it temporarily with a similar one. Bob is very good with David, and Mam is comforted because she has Monica, whom she loves as a sister, as well as Aunty Vi around her. I play with the girl next door. As we play one morning I fall over the shoe cleaner outside the back door and hurt my wrist. No one thinks it is damaged, only wrenched, but they take me to the chemist to have it checked – it is badly sprained. Next morning I hear Mam telling Aunty Vi and Monica that I cried and cried all night in my sleep, never stopping for a moment and it has nearly broken her heart. She doesn't know whether it is the pain in my wrist or grief. I have no recollection of crying, yet I can remember sleeping in a made-up bed on the floor. This crying goes on night after night – so I'm told, but I have no recollection of it at all.

The highlight of this holiday was a trip to the Trossachs and to the Edinburgh Tattoo. I loved the Trossachs and the Tattoo left me with indelible memories. To be seated in the illuminated yard of Edinburgh Castle overlooking the huge central stage and out over the main gardens and streets of Edinburgh was magic. I was mesmerised by the bands, the music, the colour, the costumes and especially the Greeks. On the bus home some of the Greek Army bandsmen got on the bus. They were so tall and wore little white pleated miniskirts, silver bands across their chests, white boots and white hats. I had never seen anything like it. It was a really amazing experience. We stayed at Monica's for nearly three weeks. David was then taken to Cornwall on holiday with Aunty Maria, Uncle Bill and our cousins: he came back looking like a perfect shiny conker he was so brown.

In the meantime my wrist did not heal and I had to have an X-ray. This established that it was a hairline fracture and so my arm was put in plaster for five weeks. Fortunately it was my left wrist so I wasn't much hindered by it. Then, it was back to school to an important year: the year of the eleven plus. It was my second year with the same teacher, the headmaster's wife Mrs W. I did not like her at all and she disliked me, as they say in Wiltshire, 'from the first go off'. She was not a very good teacher either, not compared to Mrs C, although violence in the classroom from handy implements was not a problem in Mrs W's class: she had a poison tongue, sarcasm. She could make you wither with just a comment.

Mam changed her job from the Home Help to school meals so she could be home in time for David coming from school and have the holidays with us. Our weekends were taken up with visiting the cemetery to put flowers on Dad's grave. We'd either walk to Newburn, and up Piggy's Lonnen, entering the cemetery from the gate in the Lonnen, or we'd get the bus along the West Road. It was my job to collect the water for the flowers using the special jar from the headstone flower-pot. The water tap was quite a walk from the grave itself and I was always afraid I'd forget how to get back. This is another indelible memory. Recently I had to describe the place to the Co-op stonemason, who was in the cemetery trying to find the grave so he could give me an assessment of its condition and a quotation for engraving Mam's details on the headstone. He was on his mobile phone in the cemetery and I was in my lounge in Wiltshire on the landline. I had to describe in detail how he might find the grave. He had the number of the plot but still couldn't find it. I described exactly where it was and within minutes he rang back to say he'd found it. I have an internal map of the position, learned from fetching water, and I have never forgotten it.

It was at the end of the summer holidays I first started to float. I didn't sleep very much. It took me a long time to settle in bed at night. My heart would race and pound as though it would jump out of my chest. I'd call Mam and she would try to calm me but it was impossible. I believed I was going to die, that my heart was going to stop. I'd sweat like a pig and the pounding of my heart in my ears was like an earthquake. I knew I was going to erupt. Long into my frightened night I would settle down, only to jump awake with my heart pounding all over again. This went on for years. I was tired and distracted. Mam wandered the house in the middle of the night making hot milk drinks for herself so she didn't sleep either. The first time I felt I was floating, I was playing with my cousins on our front doorstep. Suddenly I felt I had left my skin and was looking in, and on, the scene below me: watching myself and my cousins play. I was simply terrified, but said nothing. Within what was seconds, but felt a long time to me, I was firmly sitting on the step again, quite normal.

Not long after Dad died a lady who lived further along our street was walking past our house with a wreath in her hand. Her son had died from leukaemia. I felt very sorry for her but at the same time knew exactly where she'd walked. For months I avoided walking on the same side of the path she'd walked on. This was followed by an obsessive fear of walking on the joins between the paving stones. I must not stand on the joins, so when I walked I was in my own personal hop-scotch game. All these things were in my head and I never spoke to anyone about them. I just didn't air my strange thoughts and behaviour. But in my inner dialogue I knew exactly why I was doing this: if this lady had walked on these stones, or the joins, then she might bring me bad luck – bad luck being the death of someone else I loved. I also started knocking my teeth against each other. I had to repeat this over and over so many times before I could stop. I would do this teeth-knocking business when I looked at the panels in the door, and do one knock for every corner of the panel alternately, one on one side of my jaw and one on the other. If I made a mistake I'd start again. I could be at it for ages. I did the same with the ornaments on the mantelpiece. No one noticed my demented behaviour.

The worst, though, was my dying to go to the toilet. I would suddenly want to go to the toilet for a wee in the most awkward places, like on the bus. I would be frantic trying to keep it in. My feet would be tap, tap, tapping on the bus floor, I would be jiggling up and down and just longing to get home. This went on for months and I thought there was something very wrong with me but didn't tell anyone. I dreaded going anywhere, as this performance was agony: I was terrified I would wet myself in public. Quite frankly I knew I was going mad. Yet everyone around me continued to say I was a good girl, a brave girl, and wasn't I doing well. No I wasn't. But nobody could see that I wasn't. I was falling apart at the seams. I was quite literally coming apart, like a worn-out dress, tearing apart from the inside out.

It was our second successive Christmas without Dad at home and I cannot remember anything about it. I have absolutely no recollection of it, just as I have no memory of the previous fatherless Christmas and other fatherless Christmases.

Christmas when Dad was at home was wonderful. We didn't get lots of toys but simple things, our stockings full of fruit and sweeties, small gifts. We'd get one main present which was always a surprise: we were not allowed to ask for things. It was the preparation for Christmas that was important. These were the highlights: Mam making the Christmas cake, the mince pies, the lovely smells, shopping for the chicken and the vegetables, making the stuffing. Buying the tree and dressing it. The coloured lights that didn't work and had to be mended with much impatience. Dad always plucked the chicken of its feathers very carefully, as though he didn't want to hurt it, even though it was dead. He'd then singe each little hole where there were now no feathers with a lighted match. This made a little fire burst and sizzle – it is the smell I remember most, and his patience while he did this. While he was doing this Mam was tying the pudding up in a white cloth ready to steam the next morning. She'd then start icing the cake and I was allowed to help. The kitchen was warm, full of the smells of Christmas – happy.

I slept fitfully ever afterwards; I'm not a good sleeper even now. I was insecure, anxious, scared and sad. Although my sadness didn't show on the outside it was seared deep on the inside: locked tight inside me so no one could find it, not even me, its owner. I became my mother's little mother, her helper and supporter. I watched her constantly, needed to know where she was and what she was doing. I couldn't let her out of my sight for a minute while at home. I worried about how I might find her mood if she was at home and I had to go into the house, having been out. When she was sad I tried to talk her out of it, combed her hair, which she loved. I stayed close so she had company.

She became my project: my aim was to make her happy, heal her sadness. For weeks she had howling outbursts. These are very hard to describe, the sounds seemed to come from the bottom of her boots. She made sounds that were very hard to listen to without crying myself. Tearing sounds, very low-pitched with much spluttering, coughing and snot. There was a choking sound with a kind of panic as she caught her breath between sobs. Sometimes it was a high-pitched noise, screeching almost. It went right through me: it was her primeval howl.

18

1960–66

Most weeks our life had been structured around visits to the hospital, work, school and housework: hospital visiting times had been our mainstay. Suddenly the purpose of my mother's week had been taken from her, and this exacerbated her grief; it took a long time to establish a new routine. Weekends were awful as we had long days stretching in front of us when Dad's absence was most keenly felt. Life, though, has its own way of helping out, springing surprises when least expected and off you go again with a new routine, other joys and problems to please or frustrate you.

Not surprisingly with all that I was involved in, and my own grief playing maddening tricks with my sanity, I did not pass the eleven plus. I was absolutely devastated and this single failure dominated my adolescence and consequently much of my adult life. My sense of failure has unconsciously driven me on. I was, though, given a second chance: I wasn't a complete failure only a borderline failure. I had the opportunity to re-sit the eleven plus in February 1960: this was called 'an interview' in those days. A number of us sat the eleven plus papers again. I remained borderline: this meant I had to go to the secondary modern school as my main base, though I could attend the grammar school for maths and French. My mother was furious and once again she challenged the powers that be. All her previous angers, and they were many, found their target – Mr and Mrs W, the headmaster and his wife.

She was told during her conversation with them and two governors of the school that I was too emotionally upset to be able to cope with the grammar school at this point in my life. What could she say to that? They had noticed the change in me, and deserve credit for their observations, but they did nothing to support me. In fact Mrs W treated me more harshly than ever in an attempt to get me 'back to normal' as she would say. These were two good people and I know they were sincere in their beliefs, but they had little empathy or sympathy, which was no different from the general attitude at the time – 'pull your socks up and get on with life'. Mr W explained that he and the governors (the school board) had the final say about whether I attended the grammar full time, or went to the secondary modern school using this special arrangement (there were four others in this arrangement: two pupils who were also borderline would come from the grammar school to the secondary school, and two of us from the secondary school would take their places at the grammar school for maths and French, passing each other on the way). This was a bizarre solution for borderline cases of success or failure then, and seems just as silly to me now. What on earth was the purpose of such an arrangement? After all, we were neither in one place or another: borderline wanderers, temporary refugees.

This arrangement was only possible because our schools were part of a government experiment to dilute 'labelling' (and any sense of failure) of children by the eleven-plus selection process. This was to be the first step in the dismantling of the three-tier educational system policy of the time, toward a comprehensive system. The three-tier system in our area consisted of grammar, technical and secondary modern schools. Northumberland Education Authority, as it was then, had been selected to run an experiment, one of thirteen such experiments in the country to establish a new model of education. They built three new schools, all on the same site: the grammar school sandwiched between the two secondary schools and referred to as Walbottle Campus, now a new academy. Our badge then was of a Roman Mile Castle, the remains of which could be seen in the garden of a house on the boundary of the school grounds. Allocation to each of the secondary schools was by area and address. The rationale for these experiments in education was laudable: to give more children the chance of reaching their full potential. It was well understood at the time that many borderline pupils did not fulfil their potential because they ended up in secondary modern schools with a restricted curriculum. Some who passed for the grammar school could not cope with the overly academic curriculum, having little academic input at home. We didn't know then, nor until many years later, that each pupil's scores for the eleven plus were 'weighted'. If they hadn't been weighted many more girls than boys would have made it to grammar schools, as they performed better than boys aged 11. In 1960 the perceived (rather than real) gender differences between males and females came out in boys' favour: boys were understood to be more intelligent than girls. Cyril Burt, whose research lay behind this thinking, had a lot to answer for! How else could the male population hang onto their power and authority?

I was not only very, very disappointed, I was ashamed – so ashamed that I had failed. Even now I find it hard to think about how I felt at this time. Words are inadequate tools to explain my feelings then. I felt I had disappointed my parents, especially my father who had an infallible belief in the fact that I would go to grammar school and make up for the fact that he had been unable to take up his place. The shame ate away at me day and night and I was in meltdown. This 'interview', as they referred to it, meant absolutely nothing to me. I thought it a stupid idea then, and I still do. If I'd failed, I'd failed, and nearly being successful was no help whatsoever. Those of us who lived this 'experiment' didn't belong to one school or the other – in each place we were seen as belonging to neither. This didn't help our street-cred either: we were in the grammar school for too short a period of time in the week to make friends, and our friends in the secondary school were suspicious of our dual educational nationality. For me it was destructive: this was a time when I badly needed to belong, to feel safe, and I just didn't. I was emotionally upset, grieving, overly responsible for my mother and her emotional state, for my little brother and running the home. I became the little mother, and at school I had a foot in two camps. I had no sense of belonging anywhere.

I enjoyed my lessons in the grammar school and hated the school I was in for the rest. I hated it with passion and I can still feel this now: I was in a desolate land. I had plenty of friends both male and female, joined in activities, but I was awkward, not the 'me' I'd once been. When I first started attending Walbottle West as it was known (the other secondary school was Walbottle East, what unimaginative naming), I'd arrive at school each morning, by walking around the grammar school first and then around the back to the West School on the pretence of going to see my mother in the grammar school canteen where she worked as a dinner lady. She worked full time, with regular bouts of illness and sick leave, making and serving school dinners so she could be home in time for us returning from school. By this circuitous route I could kid myself for a few precious minutes that I too was going to the grammar school. I don't think anyone fully realised the shame and failure I felt, nor my levels of fantasy.

In conversations during my childhood, based on school reports and parents' evenings, the teachers had been in no doubt I would pass the eleven plus. I felt I had let my mother and father down – he would have been disappointed and shamed. I had let down the teachers I'd loved and respected in infant school and junior school. My mother was disappointed, ashamed and angry, her anger increased by the headmaster's admission that he had the final say. I think she believed that he might have erred on the side of caution because of the events of the previous three years and the summer in particular. She never forgave him, and I became a great supporter of comprehensive education.

I came to accept that I was not as clever as everyone had thought I was: I was mediocre. My self-confidence took a dive and my self-esteem plummeted. My pre-pubescent body didn't help either. I grew plump, with what seemed to me to be enormous breasts especially when measured against my still-flat-chested friends. I walked with my shoulders humped over to hide my inflating chest balloons: my breasts appeared larger every day and in my imagination they were enormous. I was the first girl to wear a bra in junior school and I was mortified. I'd inherited both the Lambert and the Morgan breast genes: combined they were a proper nuisance and so embarrassing on my body! Or so I thought. Once in secondary school I wasn't quite so alone in my miseries, but I still used to hide my bra in my satchel after PE showers so I didn't have to been seen putting it on again. Loose, my breasts were not nearly so problematic: I could hide them more easily.

The school doctor had advised my mother to tell me about menstruation as he thought this too was imminent. He was right and I was again mortified. I'd also misunderstood what Mam had told me, as I thought she'd said periods lasted for a month. She'd been embarrassed about telling me and so I'd become all muddled up. She stood by the fire in the living room surrounded by the clothes-horse full of wet washing so my brother wouldn't see or hear us, and tried her best to explain, stammering, stuttering and blushing throughout. So at the first sight of blood I thought my life was over because I would have this awful thing for a month! I didn't want to live. She said this was a woman's secret and that no one must know. She handed me the ghastly sanitary belt – the female equivalent of a badly designed Elizabethan cod-piece, all belts, buckles and ties. The cod-piece was supposed to be protective and appeared sexual; the sanitary belt and equipment certainly did not. These items were topped by pink rubber lined knickers, frilly around the edges. After these had been washed a few times they crackled once dry. So, terrified, I'd sit on the edge of my chair in lessons, afraid of crackling pants, blood and becoming smelly. My self-image was in tatters.

In music with Mrs R in particular, where she shouted and

conducted violently, putting those not singing outside the door to await her later punishment, I felt nothing like the delicate dancing trout we were singing about. We were listening to the Trout Quintet and had to make up songs to go along with the music – the trout she said jumped in and out of streams like a delicate ballerina. So I would be no delicate ballerina! I was the ugliest, fattest fish in the stream, or so I thought. Photographs do not bear this out. I wasn't as large as I felt, or as I remember. I was feeling the blubber of my puppy fat. I had always been taller than most of my classmates but after my father died I didn't grow another inch. Everyone thought I was going to be tall but it wasn't to be.

Greasy hair was my bugbear. My hair changed from being thick and shiny, bouncing on my head in time with my breasts, which bounced even with my mother's Triumph bra armour. It now hung in lank lumps as though I'd rubbed it with lard. My once-admired tendrils looked like flaccid greasy chips. If my hair was my crowning glory, as I'd been told throughout my childhood, I knew there would be no coronation for me! I was an oddball, a geek. Nothing would bring my hair back to its former glory. No shampoo, rollers, setting lotion: nothing at all. To look like a greasy chip was my destiny and no boys would ever run their fingers through my hair, my *greasy rope* as my mother called it. I started to wash it every day, much to her annoyance as she said it would make it worse.

And then I sprouted spots, massive eruptions across my chin and brow. Spots are often tiny but to be host to them means they seem like mountains, in this case mountains on my face. I was most definitely rotting from the inside out. I can't remember ever disliking myself quite so much as I did between the ages of twelve and fourteen. By fifteen the trout scenario was just beginning to be a possibility. I would yet be able to skip and jump, dive and dart around with grace. My mother was often furious with her bulky, sulky, stooping daughter. We'd be walking along, me as the hulk at her side and she'd say,

'*Stand up straight, be proud. You have a lovely figure, show it off: be proud.*'

Proud, *you must be joking*, I'd argue with her. I certainly couldn't see any '*good figure*' as she put it. My mother was always proud of her figure, her 36C breasts and slender waist. She always had a cleavage and was happy to show it off. When she was skinny after my father died, she still managed a semblance of cleavage. I didn't feel the same although she tried hard to encourage me.

Despite my freaky flowering I resolved to work very hard at school as I, and we, knew that six pupils would be chosen to go into the GCE (as it was then) class when we were thirteen. We didn't sit an exam though; the aggregate of our summer examination results was the measure of our worth and success. The competition was fierce, more so than in junior school, as others like myself had come in from schools around the area. I was pitting my wits against others who'd been in more competitive and higher-achieving junior schools than mine.

It was also the time when boys made their way into my conscious mind. My friend and I had a foursome with two boys in our class, and even then I recognised the love one of these boys had for my friend. I don't think the other boy felt that way about me but we remained friends for years afterwards. My friend was still breastless, spotless, periodless and slim. I didn't even try to enter the competition and never have done. We'd meet at the swings on the green after school. My heart had been lost earlier to another: a boy who'd come into our class from the south of England. He wasn't the least bit interested in me but if my mother sent me to the Co-op I'd go the long way around on the off-chance of seeing him. I wanted that boy to want me so much, and was devastated that he wasn't interested in me. I'd always got on with boys as a younger child: my first friends were boys and we played for hours together. Maybe it wasn't me they were interested in but my red toy car. We'd take turns driving it along the path at the side of our house. My mother could see us out of the kitchen window, as could my friend's mother from hers.

One day they both pushed me rather too hard, and the car hurtled along the path and straight down our eight steps with me hanging on for grim life then flying out of the car at the last minute to hit the gatepost when the car came to a stop. I had a broken nose and to this day the bone is more prominent on one side of my nose compared to the other.

I'd also become friendly with a boy who'd come from London, as the teacher had asked me to take care of him. We got on like a house on fire. We sat at the back of the second row. We were streamed then, and Mrs W had moved me out of the top row into the second row. Throughout junior school I had been one of four on the top table in the top stream: I'd fallen a long way! Only the first row was coached for the eleven plus. He and I had great fun as Mrs W coached the top row. We chatted and wrote notes to each other, played games and were generally silly, having fun together. This was sheer joy at the time, light relief. Mrs W got so annoyed with us that she moved me to the front row to sit next to a boy I'd sat next to in Sunday school. He became my first serious boyfriend and later my husband. Our friendship grew from school and Sunday school as well as youth club.

During my second year of secondary school I had a paper round because my mother couldn't afford to give me pocket money. My brother helped on a milk round by the time he was ten for the same reason. My round was very big and I had a large, heavy bag especially on Sundays when there were supplements with the paper. The boy I liked and went out of my way to try and see eventually asked me to the pictures. No dressing up, no make-up: I just had to go as I was, paper bag in tow. Not a glamorous sight for my first date. To my horror, my knicker elastic snapped on my round. It was terribly difficult to push papers through letterboxes, keep the bag on my shoulder and hold up my knickers at the same time. So I stopped, let them fall, picked them up and put them in my pocket. I was knickerless on my first date at the pictures with a boy! It mattered not a jot: we were shy, innocent and knew nothing of sex except for the love life of worms and birds. He didn't ask me out again and I wasn't bothered, as we were so horribly shy: crucified by embarrassment.

During this time my mother's health was like a yo-yo. She would be energetic and coping one minute and back in bed the next, weepy, depressed and weary. We were told it was her weak heart. She was taking sleeping pills and rarely came off them. Barbiturates: I think she became addicted to them, as many did in the sixties. It was common then for doctors to hand out sleeping pills to unhappy women no matter what the underlying reasons might be. There was no time for the 'reasons or what they might be'. When my mother was ill in bed I took over all the household chores. The boundaries were clearer when she was ill than when she was well. When she was supposed to be well she could be moody, sad, and this was more difficult to cope with than her being in bed. When she was ill she would say she was past caring – and she was. It wasn't long before the word depression entered our vocabulary: she was very depressed for long periods of time.

And, of course, when she was ill she couldn't work and so our income dropped as all she had was her widow's pension. It was always a question of getting her stabilised and back to work. Her doctor knew this and knew that her illness was becoming cyclical. She'd get well, her sense of humour and fun returning, and then become run down, depressed and bad tempered: sad in a never-ending cycle. W didn't understand these ups and downs at the time but the effect on my brother and me was devastating – we couldn't please no matter what we did. She would reject our attempts to love and support her, birthday and Christmas presents were rejected. She cried and cried, withdrew into herself and we just had to cope by ourselves. At the worst times she would threaten to commit suicide, or to 'end it all' as she referred to it. I didn't know what I would find when I returned from school when she was in these depressions. She'd say she was going to put her head in the gas oven or throw herself in the river. I believed she might do this. When I came home from school I'd approach the back door with trepidation, terrified of what I might find. She had no company throughout the day and the depression always worsened when she was alone. I came to expect that one day I would indeed find her with her head in the gas oven. It didn't happen but it left my brother and me afraid of her moods, afraid she might leave us and afraid of finding her dead. We were often threatened with abandonment, although she had no perception that we saw this 'possible' effect of her words and behaviour. These threats continued until we left home and she used them to control our behaviour and our life. I didn't tell anyone what was going on at home – when I did try to tell a neighbour, and it took courage to do so, she didn't believe me. I never tried to tell anyone again.

Soon, to our surprise, our hospital visiting routine was restored to us. In the spring of 1960, while our mother was still in the middle of an appeal for her widow's military pension, her older sister Ella was suddenly widowed too: her husband dropped dead from a heart attack. He was nearly twenty years older than Aunty Ella (Isobella after her mother). He was a character, 'dapper' was the word used of him, a barber, a good dancer and liked his alcohol. He once, to my parents' chagrin, left me outside a pub while he drank inside. My father came looking for us as we'd been away for such a long time. He went stark raving mad with Uncle Bob who was never allowed to take me for a walk again. Now the three sisters were widows, while their brothers remained happily married until they died, all dying before their wives and in their late seventies.

Aunty Ella was a known beauty in Haltwhistle according to the neighbours, and the best dancer in Bardon Mill and Haltwhistle. Apparently the guys queued up to dance with Ella. She could have had her pick of the young men but married an older widower who had three young children aged between 3 and 12. Ella was the wild sister and certainly didn't live by the same rules as Vi and Emily: she was not hindered by religion or needing to be good, nor did she need to be approved of. She was very, very funny, easy going, never did a stroke of housework, went dancing almost every night, couldn't cook, didn't shop except to nip across the road to the corner shop to buy whatever they might have for a meal. She had lush, thick, beautiful, dark hair and eyes like my mother and my grandmother: very Gallic looking. Aunty Vi, like her brothers, had thin sandy hair after their father. She worked full time in the Bakelite factory making plugs and casings for radios. By the colour of her skin she looked as though she had worked in the bomb factories too: always sallow, yellowish, jaundiced looking. She smelled slightly of Bakelite.

Unlike our mother who'd cloaked herself in widowhood, Aunty Ella intended to live, have fun. She didn't wear black, and many accused her of not caring about her husband. Both sisters were disgusted by her attitude and tried to persuade her into a more becoming public widowhood: they failed. Before Uncle Bob was cold in his grave she and her neighbour Maud, also a recent widow, booked a holiday in Blackpool, while Aunty Vi and my mother grumbled endlessly about her unbecoming, unseemly behaviour: she was wanton, they said.

Unfortunately during this holiday Ella and Maud were knocked down on a zebra crossing by a hit and run driver. Both were critically injured with very different though life-threatening injuries. Aunty Ella's beautiful legs were shattered: she had a broken hip and crush injuries to her major organs, especially her kidneys. She had serious head injuries. Maud had serious head, chest and leg injuries. My mother and Aunty Vi sat by Ella's bed only just controlling their '*I told you so, this is your punishment for being wanton,*' dialogue. Yet they were unable to hide their disapproval; it was etched in their faces and I'm sure they shared these thoughts with each other. Aunty Ella was unconscious for some weeks in intensive care having had immediate life-saving surgery which included a brain operation and a metal plate implanted into her skull. There was much more to come.

Once Ella was off the critical list she had more metal plates inserted into her hip and legs and still required kidney surgery. So we recommenced our Saturday and Sunday visiting routine, at a different hospital on the other side of the river: the Queen Elizabeth Hospital in Gateshead. We'd take two buses, one into Newcastle and then one over the Redheugh Bridge into Gateshead. We played cards, did jigsaws and got bored.

When Aunty Ella was discharged, with a serious ongoing police investigation and court case to face, she needed lots of help and support, and I started to see her alone. Ella injured was just as much fun as her uninjured self, despite her horribly disfigured legs and feet – she had to have specially built-up shoes, two walking sticks and a wig. She wore a wig for a long time and it always had a green tinge to it. When her hair did eventually grow back, much thinner too, there was much discussion between the sisters about whether she dyed it or not. She denied it, they said she was telling lies: she'd always told lies. Their other moan was that if she didn't lie, she romanced: Ella was a romancer! In other words she gilded the lily a bit: so no one ever knew what the real truth was. She died aged 81, and her hair was still dark and not dyed. My mother duly ate her words. Despite her injuries and disfigurement Ella was determined to get the best out of life. She did daft things and was always laughing. Uncle George had a similar temperament. Ella made us laugh from her hospital bed, always sending herself up. Her friend Maud was not so resilient, and the accident shortened her life.

Four years on they won their court case. It had taken the police a very long time to track down the hit and run driver, and both women won substantial compensation. She didn't tell anyone how much and the family speculated wildly: in today's money it was likely to have been in the region of £100,000, maybe more. Then, to the absolute shock and horror of her twin sisters of mercy, Aunty Ella announced that she was going to use the money to go and see her daughter Sheila and her family and son Brian in Australia: not by a direct route but via a world cruise, one way around the world and the other way coming back. She would have her kidney surgery in Australia privately: one kidney, by this time, had already been removed. She told her sisters her plan while they were visiting her together in hospital, just before she was to be discharged.

No words are adequate to describe the two sisters' reaction: only a camera could have managed that. They screamed at Ella in high-pitched voices. She was irresponsible; this was a waste of money and stupid. I am sure my mother was jealous – jealous even though Ella had lost her looks and her ability to walk unaided. Aunty Vi was shocked and said Ella had always put herself first. What they didn't know at the time was that Ella needed life-saving kidney surgery and had taken her daughter's advice to have it done in Australia. I think, too, that they were not sure she would come through and she wanted to see her family and grandchildren before she died. All the sisters could say to this was, '*Well don't expect us to keep you when you have spent all your money.*'

The family thought Ella was selfish, profligate; a spendthrift. They believed she should have invested her money and stayed at home grieving. To their credit though, the sisters' relationship stayed intact and they could always say what they felt because Aunty Ella didn't ever fall out with anyone: the bonds held strong. Emily and Vi thought her slightly mad; she certainly was eccentric.

Ella was no housewife either. The family labelled her slovenly, not in her person, just her home. She had a mongrel dog called Gip and two cats. The dog was snappy and bad tempered; the cats violent. They had no garden, only a yard which was so full of animal faeces it was a health risk. I hated going into the yard but I had to as Ella had an outside toilet. We had to play a very weird game of faeces hop-scotch to get from the back door to the loo: not a game I would recommend to anyone. I would stand on the back doorstep trying to pluck up the courage to begin the game, then I would make a dash, jumping from one clean spot to another: it was a precarious outing. There was worse to come though. Aunty Ella's outside toilet was not a place to linger in long. It was neglected and filthy. She never cleaned it and the only paper was newspaper. There was a heavy wooden seat which I wouldn't sit on for love nor money, though this wasn't the worst thing about it. Her toilet was home to myriad beetles and enormous spiders. I would stand perched over this dirty bowl with my eyes darting hither and thither watching for spiders, and daddy long-legs – which for years I thought were Danny long-legs – horrible black beetles which just might crawl into my secret cavities. I shook all the time, terrified of every inch of that toilet: I became arachnophobic. Usually I had to take my mother with me to keep watch; one pair of eyes just wasn't good enough. If it was dark it took little imagination to scare myself silly, and the increased danger of standing in dog muck was just too stressful for me so I would hang on until we made the long journey home. Years later, and after her Antipodean and American dream holiday, Ella had her dining room made into a toilet and bathroom: it wasn't much cleaner but was safer. She was most unlike her sisters.

Her kitchen was awful too: large, damp and green with washing hanging from the ceiling, a filthy cooker and absolutely no luxury at all. It didn't matter to her as she never really cooked. We had the same meal at Aunty Ella's every time we visited. She would give me the money to go to the corner shop for sausages and a tin of baked beans. She cooked the sausages till they were black and crispy and I loved them: it is the only way I can eat sausages even now. I don't like them much, I never did, and I like them even less if they are pink and floppy, running with fat.

To get to her dining room, where Aunty always set the table for our scorched meal, we had to go down very steep steps from the scruffy lounge and kitchen to the 'arctic'. The flat was always very cold, even with the gas fire on, but the dining room beggared belief. It was the most miserable room I ever entered as a child and there we would sit at her large table as though we were in an expensive restaurant: an incongruous experience. Everything was oversized and pretentious even though dirty and shabby.

The best room was her bedroom, which was indeed a boudoir with nice 1920s-style cream furniture, silk curtains and bedspreads, all pink and silky, definitely a place of seduction. She had make-up and perfume too. We were rarely allowed to go into her bedroom but caught glimpses through the half-open door in the hallway: I knew it was a room of secrets, very personal.

When she married Uncle Bob she became stepmother to his three children. She must have been a good and loving stepmother as she had very close bonds and relationships with them and her grandchildren until she died. She lost three babies of her own: two died in-utero and she had one miscarriage. Her life had not been easy but you would never have known: she laughed, joked and danced her way through life, hiding her deeper feelings perhaps. Amazingly she didn't give a damn what anyone thought, dismissing her sisters' criticisms as water off a duck's back. She was free, and irritatingly so to her sisters.

After she had banked her compensation she sailed away for over two years, sending us postcards from all over the world and her destinations. I remember being seduced by her postcard of the Sydney Bridge and by the idea that someone could have such an adventure. This made a great impression on me. I made up my mind then that I would go to Australia too. Some of our classmates, Aunty Ella's daughter too, had taken advantage of emigrating using the £50 assisted passage so I understood the pull of Australia. Ella had her kidney operation, the doctors saved her kidney, and she had a wonderful time cruising, returning happy and satisfied via the United States. Postcards came from Hawaii and New York, where she went to dinner with extremely up-market people – I have her formal invitation and the menu. I was mesmerised by her adventures and she talked about them long afterwards, giving me the travel bug.

She remains for me one of the kindest and most comical women I have ever known. She and Uncle George, as well as my mother when she was well, were the funniest people: our sides would be splitting with laughter. When my mother was well she too had us doubled up in laughter; she was very witty, could make anyone laugh, but it waxed and waned with her moods. She shared Ella's eccentricity but it manifested itself in a different way, mostly in her quirky thinking rather than in her behaviour. Aunty Vi on the other hand had a dry ironical/sardonic humour, equally as funny, and all done with a very straight face. Others didn't think she was funny and this always surprised me: I have a memory bank full of sardonic comments made by Aunty Vi in all seriousness. If you appreciated her humour she would giggle at herself, such an endearing aspect of her otherwise suppressed personality. She could send herself up and liked doing so. According to the neighbours in Melkridge their father, my grandfather, had a very wicked sense of humour but no one in the family confirms this, seeing him as strict and bad tempered. This is how many saw Aunty Vi too. Perhaps their humour was too subtle for their contemporaries, or their more serious demeanour meant others couldn't see beyond it.

By September 1963 I had won my place in the GCE class, along with three other girls and two boys. We joined the class at Walbottle East School the following September. We were thrilled and so was my mother, she was very proud. We were a very mixed bunch but as a class we got on remarkably well: there were many characters in our class. Two of my closest friends stayed with me and we remained friends throughout our school days as well as making new friends. I was not as mature and fashionable as some of our new classmates, and during the fourth year I flirted with some of the more racy girls but couldn't really join them as they lived further away which involved public transport. Besides I didn't have the money. My paper round bought me the basics but not a night life. I remained on the fringes of the group but didn't socialise with them.

Remarkably, my mother managed to take us on holiday: she was very canny with money and saved so we could go to a boarding house in Scarborough each year. We travelled by coach, which was very exciting. We also had trips by coach to Uncle

George and Aunty Jenny's to see our cousin Colin in Morecambe.
We saw them one bank holiday a year. We'd catch the coach in
Newcastle to go to Penrith and then drop down to Kirkby Stephen
where we'd stop for coffee. Our mother always took a picnic and
flask of coffee just as she'd always done when Dad was alive. The
scenery on this journey was spectacular, and on a recent trip north
I drove my own sentimental journey across the moors to Penrith
then Alston and down to Newcastle. We loved our time with
Uncle George and family: they were fun and our mother was
always happy in the company of her elder brother to whom she
was close all her life. He and Aunty Jenny were happy-go-lucky
and they made her laugh again. She enjoyed her walks along the
prom in Morecambe eating ice cream. She loved her evening drink
from their posh cocktail cabinet in the corner of their lounge.
They didn't know how she was when we were alone as a family,
and I didn't tell them.

When we holidayed in Scarborough our mother was never
happy with the boarding house (bed and breakfast). She chose
these hotels from the *Evening Chronicle* but when we arrived they
were never quite as good as she'd imagined. She fantasised about
how good they would be and was disappointed when they were
not as she thought, or the food was poor. The first two days she
would have a silent huff, her anger and frustration obvious. I
think now that this was less likely to be about the B&B and
more about finding herself the only single parent and woman
alone in the dining room: her grief was always near the surface
and watching other happy couples could not have been easy. Once
she'd accepted and got over whatever upset her she relaxed and
we had wonderful holidays. We'd spend the day on the beach,
we have always been beach lovers, walk the prom in the evening,
spending time listening to the brass bands. One year she booked
tickets for the Concert in the Park in the evening: Der Rosenkavalier.
I was lost in wonder in the scenery, drifting in clouds of happiness
in the music as I snuggled under our blanket. The sun went
down and the sky darkened. I was dumbstruck with happiness

and this remains my introduction not only to operetta and opera but also to a life-long love of open-air concerts.

Our mother had a beautiful soprano voice and sang with a local choir: her rendering of 'All in an April Evening' remains imprinted on my mind and my senses. I can turn the switch in my mind and hear her today, any day. I would sometimes play the piano and she would sing. David inherited her pure tones and could sing as a boy: he says he can't now. I sang with the school choir and we sang one Christmas Eve on BBC television from Hexham Abbey: that was a highlight of my sixth form years. I sing with the Salisbury Community Choir now, after almost forty years of not singing anywhere except alone in my own house. It has taken over a year for me to feel my vocal cords are beginning to get over the shock and find their notes again. I do love singing and have always sung around the house while doing the cleaning or when I'm listening to music. It has been, until now, an intensely private experience. I am enjoying singing again.

I was very happy at school and loved learning, trips away and walking with the church youth club: running the infant Sunday school, and playing the piano for their singing. I was in the Brownies and then the Girl Guides. My Aunty Marie was Brown Owl but didn't favour her children or me: we had to do exactly as we were told. We loved our camping holidays with the Guides. David was in the Air Cadets; he didn't take to Cubs or any structured activity really. He suffered frequent absences from school as he picked up every infectious disease going. He had his tonsils out when he was five and must have felt quite abandoned on his own in hospital. How lonely he must have been, as well as frightened. During the fun times we could relax: there was equilibrium. We knew how to have fun and we enjoyed ourselves; our mother too.

I was successful in my GCEs and able to transfer to the grammar school sixth form. We had to have seven passes above grade C level so we could transfer. I loved revising in the garden in the sun: my summer memories of no school, just revision and planning my day as I wanted are bliss. When we collected our results the headmaster at our school said he'd changed his mind; he wanted us to stay and start a sixth form in his school. Two of us, a boy and myself, decided we didn't want to fulfil his ambitions but our own, and said no. We discussed with the others trying to raise a mini rebellion really, trying to persuade them to come with us. They decided to stay, and he and I walked over the grass to the grammar school and registered there. The secondary school sixth form didn't work and the others joined us after half term in October.

I loved it and studied extra GCEs as well as my three A levels. We had brilliant teachers and the most influential headmaster: Mr Bosomworth, who has remained my role model throughout my life. My tutor on my MA course many years later, George Campbell, had been teacher-trained by Mr B and shared my views of his abilities and skills: both were my role models.

During this time my social life was busy and I had a boyfriend who was also in the choir and the same church. I was able to integrate with his friends and he with mine. I made new friends as the year went on. I could not have been happier. He was also in the school orchestra and played the clarinet. He had a very good tenor/bass voice. Life was very good indeed. Miss Evans, the deputy head, was our choir mistress, a tiny vibrant woman whose bark was worse than her bite. I was frequently out socialising though I worked steadily, never brilliantly in term time, but always pulling the stops out for exams: I'm the same now. I coast but when necessary pull the stops out.

During our first year sixth we had our own sixth form centre and we could do pretty much as we wished. We socialised at break times and lunch times along with our record player, coffee and tea. We were given immense freedom, which I have always appreciated. I was able to renew my friendship with the boy whom I'd sat next to during my last year in junior school – the one I'd been moved from because we talked too much and had too much fun. We were all shocked to the core one Friday morning break-time to learn that he had been killed in a car accident. He didn't want to continue in the sixth form, so had found a job. He'd accepted a lift, only days after leaving school, and had been killed outside our doctor's surgery in Newburn. He was an only child. I was heartbroken: he was a lovely guy, beautiful in fact, and it broke my heart. I think of him often even now: a life snuffed out in seconds. These experiences make you appreciate life and all one has. I have never forgotten him. We'd been unusually shy meeting again as teenagers and I wish we had had more time. His death above all others; and the near death of my friend who'd been knocked down by a car on her way to school when we were in our third year, taught me how fragile life is; can be. I'd witnessed four sudden deaths in six years: there one minute and gone the next. It seemed to me death stalked me and I was frightened, anxious.

19

1965–67

During my sixth form years Mam found a boyfriend. It wasn't exactly a romantic meeting, you could say it was more a practical and opportunistic one. We had just returned from our holiday in Scarborough. While we were there I met a very nice guy, partly through my brother who'd befriended this guy's family. Mam was furious when she saw me walking along the prom with him, his brother and my brother. She went berserk, said I was wanton, that people would think I was cheap and we had the most terrible row in the bed and breakfast hotel. Aunty Vi was with us and had already mediated Mam's three-day huff and silence when the B&B was not as she'd expected. Surprisingly, as she was known to be very strict, Vi mediated on my behalf telling Mam he was a nice guy and that she should give me some freedom. Mam reluctantly did as she was told, as she always did with Aunty Vi. I had some lovely times with my new man, David was always with us and it was very good for him to have male company. We swam and walked, played rounders on the beach and even went to cafés.

He came to stay with me in the October, having written frequently in between. Weeks later a man from around the corner, whose wife had run off with another man, stopped at our gate to talk to Mam. He was a tall, well-built, quiet man; we didn't really know him but saw him each morning and evening coming back from his mother's at the Leazes, past our front door. It wasn't many months before he and she were exchanging pleasantries. He eventually asked her out for a drink. She led the courting game by giving me his supper to take around to his flat! I argued about this, I didn't want to do it, but she was adamant: I had to take his supper as it would be unseemly if she did it herself. She obviously worked on the principle that the fastest way to a man's heart is through his stomach, especially as she had not had this pleasure with Dad's troublesome coffee-cup-sized stomach. I really did not want to do this chore, in fact I was embarrassed beyond words entering a strange man's flat with his supper on a tray and then having to go back and get the dirty dishes. I was mute, the only time in my life I have been without words or conversation. Gradually, Bob crept into our lives. From very gingerly sitting on the edge of our settee, perched stiffly on its edge, he gained Mam's confidence. I'm sure this peacock show wasn't intended or deliberate: it was a nervous position he took up knowing the situation was very difficult. He'd come in for a coffee after their first date, a drink on a Sunday evening. He had a car so they'd go into the country and Mam thought she'd become a queen. Bob was very shy, inept with women, children and teenagers, and when he was nervous he stuttered. As a child he'd had a terrible stutter. I felt sorry for him and his unease, but right from these early meetings I didn't take to him. I tried hard for Mam's sake but I just couldn't like him and neither did David. I knew intuitively he wasn't the man for Mam. That sounds arrogant. I was inexperienced and didn't even know why I thought this, but there was just something wrong. Gradually he became part of our life and we too ended up going out with the new couple.

I think we succeeded in liking him but it became a very different story when they decided to get married, rather quickly really. Our first joint holiday was to Devon and Cornwall. We drove overnight via Bath to Cornwall for a camping holiday. Mam wanted to see Royal Crescent and the Roman Baths. We slept in the car in a car park on the wrong side of Bath so never did find either the next morning. Bob experienced Mam's first huff. She was so disappointed by what she saw she insisted on leaving, suggesting that pictures she had seen in magazines were lying about Bath as a beautiful city – she could see nothing beautiful about it. So we journeyed in silence to Devon where we pitched the tent; no one had any idea how to erect this enormous tent. It was pouring with rain and the camping site was a sea of mud. We were not happy. Mam blamed God for not seeing we were special and needed very hot weather and a dry field! She and I slept in one part of the tent and David, Bob and my boyfriend (I was back with the previous one having been scared off my holiday boyfriend who was five years older than me and rather forward) sleeping in the other half of the tent. It was a dreadful holiday, wet, muddy, cold and damp. The weather mirrored our mood.

We were all at sixes and sevens, not knowing how to behave, how to be, or how to have our holiday as we always had had our holidays: we were all restricted. Bob had no idea, poor man, and it wasn't his fault really, he just didn't know how to handle his new girlfriend or her children. David was very quiet and I was horrible. I was argumentative, selfish and angry. It was madness, we had never lived with this man, she hadn't lived with him, and yet there we were trying to be a family.

Mam stuck strictly to the rules even as a middle-aged woman: no sex before marriage, yet here we were squashed into a small space in a muddy field; squashed in a car sightseeing. It was nothing short of a nightmare. There were rows between my mother and me, between my boyfriend and me; and between David and Bob. Our mother had the idea that it was good for David to have a man around, it would help him and her to ensure that David didn't get into any trouble or go astray which in Geordie speak meant he would avoid becoming a delinquent. So Bob was the big man showing David the ropes: how to be a man! Bob had had a very poverty-stricken and authoritarian childhood: he'd trained as a coffin maker and then a joiner. He'd served in the Second World War. He'd come home alive when few of his colleagues had, a nervous wreck. He had had a frightening and dangerous war and never ever talked about it: he was an old man before we knew these facts. His father was very skilled with the leather belt. Bob doted on his mother and sister. What none of them knew, and we were slowly learning, was that Bob, quiet and dignified, always smartly dressed, was a tyrant when crossed. He had a wicked temper and it was easily roused. We first saw him lose his temper on this holiday. We thought it was a blip in an otherwise quiet man.

After our holiday Mam told us she was getting married, as Bob's divorce had been announced. The wedding was to be in October. I was just going into the upper sixth, travelling to interviews for teacher training college, and in the holidays working in Fenwick's French Café on Northumberland Street. I was not pleased when Mam told us. In fact I was deeply shocked and very upset. I pleaded with her, asking her to wait, let us get used to the idea first. She was adamant, '*I've had no happiness. I've had a hard life and you're being selfish, want to prevent me getting married and being happy. You are just selfish, selfish. You always think of yourself.*' I was mortified. It was true she'd had a very hard and sad life but I didn't know what that had to do with marrying Bob. We were just learning to be happy again, happy together, the three of us. We'd hardly started that process never mind achieved it. That night I ran away. I ran to some church friends in West Denton and they took me in. I was distraught and at first could not tell them what was the matter. To their eternal credit they put me to bed and didn't ask any questions. Their parents were out and when they returned they too just accepted the situation and the father drove to tell my mother where I was. She and Bob came to get me the next day: she was ready to kill me. She ranted and raved as he stood on the sidelines. Her rant was on the same theme: I was selfish. I gave up and gave in, defeated by her anger and accepting I was selfish. I have been afraid of being seen as selfish ever since, to my great cost. I was very religious at this point. I was studying A level Religious Knowledge and was just beginning to query some of my beliefs.

We had excellent forward-thinking teachers who challenged us to re-think history and religion in a very positive way. They were both religious themselves, one a Methodist lay preacher and the other a Baptist Minister, but extraordinarily open and honest. My views about the Bible, God and Jesus were constantly being challenged: I was especially dumbfounded when the nativity story was challenged and we were told that it was perfectly possible that Mary was pregnant before marriage and that the escape to Bethlehem was not only about taxes but to avoid her being stoned to death, the customary sentence for wayward women.

I crumpled under Mam's accusations and I learned to cry. I had hardly ever cried, now I wept buckets of tears, alone in bed at night. I came to the conclusion that I would go a long way away to college. When I first applied I believed Mam needed me, so I had decided that I would go to a local college to be near her and David. Now I decided that I could be free and go where I liked.

My mother didn't expect the ructions her marriage was about to cause: Aunty Vi was most unhappy about it. She had taken against (as we say in the north east) Bob. She did not like him and I was comforted by her thoughts and feelings. I had had no idea she shared my view. Poor David, it was to be five years before anyone knew his views too. He was only just twelve when Mam and Bob married. He kept his own counsel as he always did. We never did know what David thought. Mam and Aunty Vi had their first row: the first I had been conscious of. It was heart rending. Aunty Vi tried to counsel Mam, as she always had, but her arguments were easily defeated as her brothers and sisters contributed to the view that she was straightlaced and therefore against this marriage because it was unseemly for middle-aged people to be acting like a pair of teenagers; and of course because Bob was divorced. Divorcees could not marry in church and so she would not be able to recognise the marriage. No one else shared her views or if they did they were not prepared to say so. I think we all, including me, knew our mother needed some chance of happiness but there was something about this relationship that even in those early days was less than happy: I think guilt lurked in the background. Mam and Aunty Vi did not speak to each other for two years and were not to know what tragic events would bring them together again.

Aunty Vi went on seeing David and me, and she never mentioned the wedding plans nor distorted our view in any way: she was absolutely honourable. Even if I tried to get her to talk to me about how I felt she would not engage in that discussion, simply saying that sometimes we just had to accept things. Some bitter things had been said during their argument. I know Aunty Vi would have loved to make up but Mam was entrenched in her view that no one wanted her to be happy. The wedding was fixed for half term, because she was still working on school meals so it had to be the holidays. I was to be bridesmaid. Their honeymoon was to be four days in Edinburgh and I was to look after David. This was to be the first time that we had been alone in the house overnight. I had a red wool coat with a grey fur collar and a little red hat as my bridesmaid outfit. David had a brown corduroy jacket and wool trousers. Mam had a turquoise suit, a pencil skirt with a slit up the back and a matching three-quarter jacket with a black velvet collar, and had the most wonderful hat made in the same colour. They were married at Throckley Methodist Church and she didn't attend the Church of England again until she was in her early seventies. They wouldn't marry her so she ditched them. I also left and began to attend the Methodist Church because she was unhappy with the Church of England: she expected them to change the law to marry her. She didn't know that she would be long dead before the process of changing the church marriage laws was in process. In this our mother was ahead of her time because she couldn't have her own way. The wedding breakfast was in our front room and the neighbours were our waitresses.

David and I were like beached whales over the four days we were alone. The neighbours kept an eye on us but we had never been alone in the house. We were entering a new life and we had no idea how it would work out. I had a lot to think about, especially what they were up to on their honeymoon. I still knew very little about sex but had begun to have some uneasy feelings when I was kissed or cuddled by my boyfriend, I had no idea what they meant. I did know that people made love but had little idea exactly what this entailed. I presumed that it involved kissing and cuddling but couldn't be sure what came next. My imagination was exercised trying to work out what would be going on 'at night' between Mam and Bob. I didn't like the fact that whatever it was he would be doing to her, it was that way around, he would be active and she would be passive, it replaced what she had had with my Dad. I sought out my cousin and she furnished me with the facts. I learned most of the facts of life from my cousin. We often gathered at my cousins' house on Newburn Road where, in their small lounge, we youngsters would have privacy, while the adults talked in the lounge. She knew everything and completed our education (mine and my friends') over hot chocolate.

I did, though, have other interests to take my mind off the situation. I was busy; I taught in the Sunday school, played the piano and occasionally the organ. I worked on Saturdays and during school holidays. I sang in the school choir, did voluntary work, was still helping with guides while studying hard for my A level mock examinations. I hadn't much time for grousing and was enamoured at this time with Billy Graham's religious views which didn't allow me to brood: Billy and God didn't like brooders. There was too much of God's work to be done. So we fell into a very uneasy alliance in our home life with peace only being punctured by rows between Bob and Mam, usually over David. She desperately believed this was what David needed, but Bob had learned authoritarian ways from his father: he was also a very strict union man and so learned more authoritarian ways from his work as a union leader. There was no grey in any argument, only black and white. It didn't matter what side you were on, black or white, his side was right and there was no way anyone could win except Bob. So my mother was always trapped between her new husband and her son. She couldn't cope with, nor solve, this dilemma: these were stormy times and I was glad that I was about to leave the unhappy household.

I treated Bob with respect, but always stood up for myself and David, and I called him Dad to keep the peace (my mother insisted I called him Dad, which I could never understand). Every time I said the word Dad, I felt a traitor. I told myself it was just a word after all, he showed me no affection and I gave none in return. I did try to meet him half way but if he became too much of a bully to any of us, I'd wade in and try to stop him. When he lost his temper he could be violent. His response to any of my reasoning was to tell me I was mad. Eventually my mother would also tell me I was mad. He'd say, '*There's something wrong with you, you're mad, you need to see a doctor.*'

Bob was a very political man and he politicised our mother over the years, but he was an authoritarian socialist, communist some would say. He had been sacked a number of times because he would not back down. He was referred to by his colleagues and other union members as a communist. He had a stormy personality and the only person who didn't see this side of him, and on whom he didn't ever turn was his grand-daughter. She loved him: telling my story is very hard for her. I feel for her.

Our mother tried her best to protect us, but she needed Bob and so she walked a tightrope, loving him and hating him in equal measure: it was a very ambivalent relationship. She often talked to me about their rows as I grew older. When he'd first met Mam he had been very generous with presents and money: he bought her a fur coat, a gold watch. He didn't buy her another thing after they were married; no birthday or Christmas presents. There were no clear boundaries for us children any more and we couldn't win, no matter what we did, because our mother swapped sides depending on the situation. We lived on swings and roundabouts. For the ten months I lived with them there were many storms; gales with some calm spells later. Our home once again mirrored our northern weather, just in a different way from when our father had been ill.

20

Monica

Calm spells in our house were not only peaceful but also happy, always interesting and often exciting. I really enjoyed my two years in the sixth form, in school and socially too. Planning my future was thrilling, as was exercising my independence; this was definitely a very good time for me as I had not expected I would leave home, so the sense of freedom and expectation was tremendous. I'd always expected I would stay close to home to look after my mother and David.

I travelled alone to my interview for college in Staffordshire via that Godforsaken major junction and station: Crewe. I enjoyed the experience, finding my own way there and back as well as staying in the college overnight. Standing on Crewe station I did not have the feeling of excitement or the lure I'd always had at Newcastle Central Station, partly because the steam trains had gone, and I guess I was actually very nervous about my interview.

I liked the college, the setting and the accommodation, so eagerly accepted the place I was offered. I was deeply satisfied and my mother was very proud. I met another interviewee and we got on well during the two days we were in the college, making the transition the following October easier to face and cope with. Before I could have a future I had to pass my A levels if I were to become the first member of my family to go on to higher education.

I was in the middle of my mock A levels, studying hard in January 1967, when I opened the *Newcastle Evening Chronicle* after my tea and couldn't believe what I was reading on the front page. I didn't want to believe my eyes and the connections they were signalling in my brain. I read and re-read what I had just seen over and over again: an account of the brutal murder of my cousin Monica in her own house on an army camp at Herford near Hannover, West Germany.

The report said that Monica, a young wife and mother, had been murdered at 11 a.m. on 17 January 1967 (the previous morning) after taking her five-year-old daughter to school. Her husband had been arrested by the German Civil Police Special Investigation Branch (SIB), assisted by the Royal Military Police. He was being questioned as he had returned to the house to collect his briefcase at around the same time. I read this account over and over again, my heart thumping in my head while simultaneously trying to burst through my chest wall: I will never forget that feeling. I then walked calmly, defying my heart, through the hall into the kitchen where my mother was washing up. I handed her the paper, pointing to the story and said, '*Read that Mam.*'

Irrationally I was still thinking that either my mind was playing tricks with me, or the *Evening Chronicle* reporter had made some terrible mistake. I could not take in the information nor did I really believe that it related to our family: there must be another Monica Fewster. My mother read the piece and stood there shaking, washing-up suds dripping from her hands. Then she shouted for Bob. The urgency in her voice brought him from the bathroom. There was no screaming or shouting, no anger; just utter disbelief. '*It's a mistake, I'll ring the Chronicle,*' he said confidently.

He was half dressed but rushed out of the back door, along the street to the telephone box. It was just before 5 o'clock and he managed to get through to the editor who confirmed the details of the story, the address in Germany and Monica's mother's address – my Aunty Vi. Somehow, without knowing how, we made the decision to go to Aunty Vi's. We moved like ghosts through our house, put on coats, walked down our steps and into the car: not a word was spoken.

My mother and her sister had not spoken to each other for eighteen months, they'd not healed their rift over my mother's marriage to Bob, so we didn't know how my aunt would receive us or react when we arrived. We didn't discuss this, but it hung like a banner from the car roof as we drove the twenty-minute journey to Ryton: we all knew she might not let us in. We didn't have a telephone and neither did Aunty or her younger daughter Pam. We had no way of letting them know we were on the way. Not only that, we were on our way but still believed that there had been a terrible mistake and that we'd find Aunty happily knitting in her chair as we always would in the evening.

I can't remember who opened the door to us but we were allowed in to find Aunty in her usual chair (the one I still have in my lounge) now seeming smaller, frailer. My cousin Pam looked on like an eerie ghost, her husband standing behind her towering over the rest of us. Aunty remained seated; we stood around. Aunty gave us the few details she had; they amounted to less than those in the newspaper. To our horror we found the story was true, and to make things worse we understood that the army had released the story to the press before they had let the family know that Monica was dead, never mind explaining just how she had died. The army had sent two telegrams: one to Aunty Vi and one to Monica's husband's family. Neither had arrived before the story was released to the press. Bob's relative, who'd received her telegram first, came to call on Pam, who opened the door, full of fun and smiling as she always did. '*Oh my God, she doesn't know.*'

'*Know what?*' said Pam.

The cousin then told her that Monica was dead. The official telegram said Monica had 'passed away'. I've always thought this a funny phrase, 'passed away'. Passed where, when, to whom, why, how? We were used to passing things to one another, passing the parcel at birthday parties, passing out parades, passing out, that is, fainting, but death as passing away has always seemed to me a strange way of putting it. 'Passing over' I have always understood; passing from one life to another, to eternal life, to heaven, but passing away seemed to mean floating away physically, of one's own volition, out of sight, out of mind, something you choose to do; 'to pass away'. Rarely was the word 'death', or 'died' or 'dead', ever used in the area where we lived: euphemisms always replaced truth in our childhood, gentler terms to reduce the shock and grief. For the childish mind these triggered all sorts of weird imaginings. In Monica's case there had been nothing gentle about her passing away: it was cruelly violent.

Monica had taken her daughter Lesley, aged five, to school as usual that morning. She then returned to get on with the chores of the day. Her husband Bob came home for his briefcase and had a cup of coffee with her before returning to work. Shortly afterwards someone knocked at the door; it was someone she knew because she let them in. There was no forced entry. Within minutes Monica was fighting for her life. The killer was badly scratched because she had his skin under fingernails. She'd put up a terrific fight before she was knocked down, hitting her head against the fireplace. She was knocked unconscious and died from head wounds by the fireside in her lounge. The fight left a trail of destruction from the kitchen to the lounge. What is even more surprising was that their house was directly opposite the NAAFI but not a single person heard anything, saw anything. From these limited facts the army decided, as did the German police, that this was 'a domestic'. Their conclusion was cut and dry: Bob was responsible for his wife's murder because he had popped home. They'd had a row and it had got out of hand was the explanation we were given then – and for almost forty years.

It is a dreadful numbing experience to be told that your daughter (or any relative) is dead, but to be told they have been murdered, that she might have survived had she been found earlier, that she'd bled to death, and that her husband probably killed her, is beyond any immediate comprehension. Aunty Vi steadily, quietly, uttered these facts from her ashen, shrunken face: her eyes remained dry, as did ours. According to grief theorists the first stage of grief is numbness. Well, we were well and truly numbed. None of us could take in what had been said, or happened; we were disbelieving. We were all, except my stepfather Bob, 'acquainted with grief' as Handel so eloquently puts it in The Messiah, but this grief was not only one too many, it was beyond grief as we'd known it hitherto. At this point my stepfather had his parents and sister, nieces and nephews alive, and so did Pam's husband. This death had happened overseas; we were not there; it came suddenly, violently out of the blue; it was not because of illness, nor accident, there appeared to be no reason for it; she was young, only 37 years old, healthy, happy; it all seemed so very murky and complicated. Someone, perhaps her husband, had taken her life, Monica's life, and there seemed no reason why anyone should do that. It suggested home was not such a safe place after all, as we'd been led to believe.

In 1967 murder was not talked about as much or as frequently as it seems to be now: the word was not common parlance and was certainly not uttered in front of children. Neither was violence or sex. If it was talked about, it was in rather reverential terms as it was the 'crime beyond crimes' for which the penalty was death. To take another's life was a sin. 'Thou shalt not kill,' had been drummed into us in church, Sunday school and school, and was part of our ethical and moral code. I didn't believe in the death penalty then and never have as an adult either. I was in favour of abolition and I would find it very difficult indeed if the death penalty was ever restored.

My parents (my own father) had been abolitionists, but my stepfather was not and had never been such. Under his more authoritarian and communistic tendencies (and regime in our house) my mother reverted to wanting the death penalty retained, rescinding everything we'd been brought up to believe, and I found this very hard indeed. My stepfather had a powerful 'rant' when it came to anything where intellect as well as emotion was involved. His arguments were always wanting, and rarely had any logic whatsoever to a developing eighteen-year-old. He always knew best, and if I tried to argue with him my mother became upset, cried, and he would tell me I was quite mad. I knew nothing; I hadn't been in the war as he had, so I knew nothing. It was pointless arguing with him but I would keep trying! I'd fight my corner for what I considered to be liberal justice.

I'd always thought hard about justice, probably because of my father's ability for debate and love of politics, the important thing being in the case of a crime, the legal process for establishing guilt, punishment and seeing justice to be done fairly as well as humanely. I hope too that I have also been able to forgive. My stepfather couldn't and he was influencing my mother, who'd always made up her own mind, as had her mother. My stepfather was a solid Labour man through and through but he had some very non-socialist ideas when it came to justice and forgiveness. I was upset and confused, but understood that everyone around me was very angry, full of vengeful anger, and it was distressing. I was angry but could not for the life of me see how lynching someone else would help at all: all I wanted was for life to go back to the way it was and if it couldn't then let the police find the perpetrator and bring him to justice. I was convinced it was a 'he' as was everyone else.

One of the major problems with the police investigation became clear early on: the army was not keen on having the German police (it was their jurisdiction) roaming all over its property and asking questions, especially of its soldiers and families. The relationship between the British Army and the German Police was fraught with tension and we believed this was one of the reasons the case was not solved.

Aunty Vi told us that they were waiting for the army to give them permission to travel to Germany. Monica's husband Bob was arrested almost immediately, and as a suspect he had to undergo a battery of humiliating searches and tests. He was subject to inspection, and samples were taken from his skin, nails, hair, pubic hair, clothes, saliva: anything and everything that might shed light on 'the killer' and bring him to justice. Bob had no choice and defence against the law. How he felt having found his dead wife, suddenly being a widower as well as a suspect, I cannot imagine: it is beyond imagination. My heart bled for him. He had to ask his friends to pick Lesley up from school, neither he nor she was allowed into the now taped-up and guarded house. Lesley could not go in to get her favourite toys for comfort, clothes, not even a toothbrush; she never went home again. Aunty Vi and Pam were anxious to get to Lesley as quickly as possible to bring her back to England, as at that point she had neither mother or father.

A few days after our visit they left for Germany and eventually Monica's funeral: she was buried in the British Military Cemetery just outside Hannover. They returned with Lesley who was to live with Aunty Vi for the foreseeable future. The good news was, if it was possible for anything about this to be considered good, that Bob had been released from custody for the funeral and that there was no evidence that he was now a suspect. He resigned from the army immediately but it was a long while before he could leave Germany. With his release more facts were available: he found Monica's body when he returned home for his lunch and immediately called in the military police. One clue to the murderer was the fact that a food mixer they'd bought on their tour of Tripoli was out of its box on the kitchen table (they'd gone from Edinburgh to Tripoli to Germany in the first ten years of their marriage). This mixer was large, clumsy and heavily old-fashioned. They'd decided to advertise it for sale in the NAAFI. The killer used the sale of the mixer to get into the house. He stole a few pounds and a radio too. So Monica had recognised her killer as someone on the camp she knew and trusted, and so let him in. What we didn't know until later was that Bob had sold a car via the NAAFI noticeboard the day before, and the killer probably thought here was a lot of money in the house. Monica had not been raped, one of my aunt's biggest fears – although I knew nothing of this at the time as no one would have mentioned rape to a young woman then: it would have been talked about in whispers so I didn't hear. What the killer had not expected was Monica's feisty defence of herself. She was tall, willowy, slender, so the killer would not have expected that: he was badly scratched, the police said. Monica was gentle, dignified, and fighting back must have taken her killer by surprise. Aunty Vi always said that had Monica been murdered in Tripoli she would not have been surprised – she'd been to see them twice so knew the city – but the fact that it was in Germany shocked her to the core. She had travelled to spend time with them wherever they were posted.

Still numb, with my stepfather raging at home about going out to Germany himself to find the killer and kill him, hang him or chop him to pieces, and my mother agreeing with these sentiments, my thoughts were for Lesley. I knew how I felt after my father's death and I knew that was coming, so I could put myself to some extent in her five-year-old shoes. She'd gone to school with Mummy in the morning, then her daddy disappeared for days without any explanation and she was not allowed into her house ever again. I wasn't Lesley so I couldn't know how she felt: I could just try to understand. What sense could any child make of such circumstances? She was not told that her mother had been killed, murdered; just that Mummy had gone to heaven with the angels, like going on a day out and not coming back! She had multiple losses in a few hours in one horrible day in her life. She had one life when she said goodbye to her mummy at the school gates and another very different life by lunchtime when Mummy should have been at the school gates to collect her. I argued vehemently with my mother and Bob, and their constant talk of 'an eye for an eye and a tooth for a tooth'. Neither would listen to a silly eighteen-year-old and I couldn't cope with their contradictory behaviour – especially my mother's. I repeatedly told them so too. We were at loggerheads, with our angry grief spilling over into our newly formed reconstructed family: Bob had not even met Monica, and Aunty Vi had never spoken to him: he was reacting to my mother's intense grief; my mother was distraught.

Our extended family was traumatised by these events and could not make sense of them. Monica's husband Bob had been the major suspect and no other suspect was interviewed for over twenty years. We could never put the case to bed as no one had been charged or convicted of her murder and the suspicion loaded on Bob was terrible: it never actually went away. This hurt me so much and I still cannot fathom how any of the family could have believed this, including my mother. Bob had always been kind to us; he'd been particularly good to David when we stayed with them after our father's death. I'd been their bridesmaid and remembered their tremendous joy when Monica became pregnant: they'd married later than most, when she was 28 and Bob 29. They waited five years before conceiving Lesley. I remember when they were on leave from Tripoli, Monica standing in Aunty Vi's kitchen doorway and glowing with her intimate knowledge of her pregnancy. I hadn't been told but I knew. Monica was very slim and I could see the outline of her new bump. Their relationship was close and loving: he seemed gentle and when we stayed with them they seemed to be very happy. They had a bubble car in which they drove around Edinburgh and before that a motorbike and side-car. He was tolerant of Aunty Vi; called her 'Ma'.

The suspicion never really left Bob: he was forever in the frame and he became quiet and kept his distance from the family. He found work, which was mostly night shift so he could be with Lesley for longer periods of time. When he was at work she stayed with Aunty Vi who'd retired from her job at the mental hospital laundry where she'd worked for years, to be able to look after her. Bob then bought my cousin's house just up the road so they could share care. Pam and Alan were moving south for his job so once again Aunty Vi put her own feelings aside to care for her grand-daughter, using the same strategies she'd used with her own father-less daughters. She also had the courage and grace to let her other daughter go south without resentment or a scene. I felt for her as she struggled with her own sadness and provided structure, attachment and love for Lesley. She was only in her mid-fifties; she'd had such a hard and brutal life and yet she made the most of it without histrionics. She was a tough old bird but I am sure she wasn't as tough in private.

I think, until Monica's murder, I had coped with my losses, not well, but I'd adjusted, although I'd not stopped missing my father. I adored Monica and couldn't make sense of her murder or her death at such a young age: the violence and senselessness was beyond me and my empathy was with Bob, Lesley, Aunty Vi, Pam and her husband Alan. I was simply devastated and it affected me badly.

I had slept fitfully and very badly since my father's death; I was bedevilled by anxiety especially at night. My mother had a habit of locking all our doors then pulling the mallet and the washing machine from the wash house to the back door every evening, in case someone broke in. She herself slept little; was forever wandering the house at night, scared stiff someone would get in. No security there! My role model was not the best when it came to security. I was also worrying and constantly checking myself for signs of illness, especially cancer. Not that I would have known what to look for, yet I was convinced that I'd die young too. I got the panic attacks under control by sheer will-power. My mother didn't know anything about my feelings or fears.

Now I was terrified in my own house: I lay awake at night too frightened to go to sleep. If I did fall asleep I'd wake with a start, sitting bolt upright in bed, sweating, my heart pounding, simply terrified. I had bad dreams about attacks and murder, and what I imagined had happened. I also dreamt of snakes curling themselves around me and strangling me. I was always running, trying to beat invisible terrors, fighting back. The most frightening was the tsunami: I was always running away from a tidal wave. At first I did not make it and drowned, then over the years there was a bridge that saved me, the tide pulled back, or I ran faster and got away. In stressful times, even now, I have my tsunami dreams. During the night I'd get up and check all the doors, ensuring they were locked properly – a habit I still have to fight.

The least unusual noise or light and I'm awake, up checking, peering down the stairs to ensure no one has broken in. Sleeping soundly is an experience I have not had much of. More now as I have got these anxieties under control, though not totally. I still wake from sleep with a sense of 'being on guard', of vigilance. I don't have nightmares now, but I used to have terrible nightmares. I became terrified of men and anxious about being in the house alone during the day as well as night. I'd check doors and windows, the locks, time after time. During the day I wanted the doors locked, and my anxiety about intruders has lasted all my life. I have an exaggerated sense of 'man danger' and my own vulnerability, especially with strange men. Consequently I have found it hard to make relationships with men unless I have known them for a long time, or through work or hobbies. Logically I know this makes little difference in reality: you can know someone and yet not know them too. This has had consequences for my romantic life and my choices of men in my life. Going home with a strange male after a party or dance was never a choice for me: it still isn't. I have missed out on a lot of fun as a result. At the time I didn't cry, but I was angry, argumentative and moody. I became much more aggressive. It has affected my marriages too: I mistook security and protection, peace of mind, for love.

I tried to help Aunty Vi with Lesley as much as I could. On Saturdays or in school holidays I'd read bedtime stories and take her to the cinema with her younger cousin. I often put Lesley to bed. One night after our story she told me that her mummy had been killed by a man. I was dumbfounded, as no one in the family had told her what had happened. She said the children at school had told her that her mummy was not with the angels, she had been killed by a nasty man. I didn't know what to answer and went to get Aunty Vi. She came upstairs to Lesley and settled her, controlling her anger until she was back downstairs. She was very cross about parents who tell tales to children! I dread to think how muddled Lesley was about her mother's death. This was 1968 and parents didn't tell children very much. They didn't explain as we try to now: nothing had changed since my father's death.

Having been told of Monica's death I went to school as usual the following morning: though in a kind of trance. We were beginning our mock A levels that morning. I went into registration and joined my four friends sitting on the biology benches: yet nothing in my life was normal any more. One friend asked me if I was all right and I told her what had happened. She looked at me as though I'd dropped in from a planet in outer space. They were, I think, without words, though at the time I felt they had just ignored what I said. Now I know they didn't know what to say – who would know what to say? What I'd told them was beyond their experience, unreal, unimaginable: there was nothing they could say. We heard about prostitutes being beaten and murdered: and were often told such women deserved it! That was the extent of our knowledge about violent men. Violent men who beat their wives and children were just left to get on with it and their wives didn't talk about it because of the shame. We said no more about it, ever. It was so awful it had to be ignored or somehow the world we inhabited might never be the same. It was as incomprehensible to them as it was to me. I got on with my mock examinations and my life, sleep deprived but coping.

During the following weeks I cannot remember crying, and never saw Aunty Vi or Pam cry. I immersed myself in my revision and my mock examinations and that's what I've done most of my life: immerse myself in work and family. I have always been able to immerse myself in books, studying, achieving: the great 'Ros protection racket' when things go wrong. I love reading and study but I think I have sometimes used it to bury my head in the sand and consequently missed out on fun, especially when I was younger. I created a myth: if I was doing something sensible and useful, I would be safe. I'd had a great sense of fun, sometimes risqué even, but I became very serious indeed and a somewhat intense individual after my father died and more so after Monica's death.

My mother became demented and very aggressively angry. Her tears would issue forth at the drop of a hat, especially after we argued: she and Bob needed to find Monica's killer and wreak their revenge. She'd go from anger to convulsive tears, desperate angry tears, unlike the sad tears of New Year's Eve. These were fighting, murdering tears and if she got her hands on the murderer she would tear him limb from limb. She'd put his head on a pole for all to see. My mother was broken and was never to be mended again. She'd had many 'mendings' and 'fixings' like a loved broken toy, but this time she didn't mend and I don't think she wanted to either. There comes a point when the 'mending' becomes almost impossible, the toy can hardly be glued together again and it is put in a chest or drawer because it is loved, but is now only a memory, beyond saving. The child doesn't love it less but is able to move on to something new, begin again, love a new toy; this doesn't exactly replace the old but is an extension of it somehow.

My mother was unable to 'move on' as they say. She was immersed in her anger, regret, grief, hate – becoming almost insane, more than slightly mad. She was never quite the same again. She'd had a hard recovery after that New Year's Eve followed by many breakdowns, yet she fought back, regained her sense of fun and her sense of the ridiculous, her ability to work hard. Now the fun seemed to be gone for good. There were glimpses now and then but the dominant mood was sadness and paranoia: she had a stridency she hadn't had before. Considering she'd only been married for four months she should have been blissfully happy, having fun. Bob's attitude at home caused her worry. She found it hard to stand up to him and I think she was disappointed with her new life and love, but at that stage could not have admitted it. She did later when she left him, though she went back. She was struggling with her marriage and her guilt for having replaced our father. Grieving again, trying to support her sister, she lost her way completely.

We had a memorial service for Monica at Greenside Church,

the very last time Aunty Vi attended church. She'd been in the choir and a regular all her life; now she didn't believe in God; any god. She'd raised her children in the same way; she vowed, after Monica's death, she'd never go again and she didn't, except for weddings and funerals. This was her revenge: she'd done all God expected of her, not only in the family but in the community too, and as far as she was concerned he had deserted her and she rejected him. Her anger was directed at God. I didn't cry during the service, which my boyfriend attended with me, but when we returned to his house for supper I was sitting on the sofa and tears poured down my cheeks: I was convulsed with tears, they just wouldn't stop. My future mother-in-law – I didn't know it then, but that's what she was to become many years later – looked at me and said, '*Eeh, hinny, tears are no good, you just have to put these things behind you and forget about them. Put it behind you now. Pull yourself together now.*'

This was said from the safe distance of her chair: everyone in the house at that point gave me a wide berth: no cuddle or arm around the shoulder, no sympathy, though there was empathy in a funny sort of way. This mirrored everyone's reaction to Monica's death: it felt like a stigma, no one dared touch us in case our ill luck or curse was passed to them by mistake. This was not true of course: they just didn't know what to say, didn't have the words. It literally was beyond comprehension, and besides, worse had happened to them in two world wars. That too was the truth: it had. This was nothing compared to war and I understood that. I think people felt because Monica had lived away for so long and we'd only seen her intermittently, our grief should be directly proportional to such absence. It wasn't. It seemed hard for them to understand that absence, distance, and the fact that the murder had taken place in another country, did not loosen the bond; nor reduce affection, moderate love or loss, or make grief bearable.

What hurt us most, though, was the oft-made comment that suggested we didn't know Monica very well. This was never said directly but the meaning was always clear: for Monica to have 'got herself murdered' she must have been having an affair! This made me mad. Even if she had been, is that justification for murder? I found these comments hard to forgive. I still do when I hear it said now: it is also said of rape victims. Unreasonable behaviour becomes an excuse for violence. There is no excuse for taking another life no matter how unreasonable the behaviour. The almost criminalisation of victims turns murder inside out and back to front: as it does with rape victims too. It exacerbates grief and slows down recovery.

I was talking to a priest some years ago and he said, *'But she was only your cousin not a primary relative.'* I was shocked at such a perception: is there a hierarchy of appropriate grief, I asked? Is there some form of 'quality control for grief' which helps us to fit the perceptions expressed around us; some kind of checklist for how grief should be? If you don't meet the criteria, then there is something wrong with you?

As my mother and her sisters were widows, all young widows as it happened, we were closer to them and our cousins than we might have been. We supported and cared for each other and had very strong attachments. Monica and my mother were very close and our aunts and uncles, cousins, were our refuge after my father died. Grief reactions are inextricably linked with the strength of the attachment and relationship, past and present experiences, age, developmental stage of life and what is currently going on around you. I had only just begun to recover from my father's and others' deaths when Monica died. Her death was so sudden and so unexpected it was hard to know what I felt.

I doubt too that anyone really recovers after murder, or any brutal sudden violent death such as those in Iraq and Afghanistan and now Libya, or some terrible accidents. Too many questions remain unanswered. There are no goodbyes or time for understanding the situation or illness, or to come to terms with these deaths. Your life is one way one minute and a totally different way the next. Violent crime, accidents, sudden death changes your life forever: the world does not seem a safe place any more, and violent crime damages one's spirit: the 'joie de vivre' is destroyed and has to be rebuilt brick by brick. Murder damages one's soul, the deepest part of our being, as it feels as though it kills our belief in the goodness of our fellow human beings. It is necessary for us to reach out to others, and it was for me then: to keep my friends close, my family close, God close. My mother stopped believing in God, I didn't. I needed Him then, more than ever. I didn't question Him as the rest of the family did.

I threw myself into my exams and hoped for the best. Histrionics and misery were not an option for me: there was Lesley to see to, Aunty Vi and my mother to support. There was a free summer coming up after exams were over. I had to work and there was also much fun too, before everyone departed for university or college: many had to go straight to work. My heart was heavy but I tried to get on with my life and managed to do so until the end of my third year in college. No one really knew then what was going on in my heart or head. The false self is a slow developmental process and only partly, if ever, conscious. It is like squeezing yourself into a dress that is one or maybe two sizes too small. I was too small for my grief. With effort I instructed myself to breathe in tightly, pull in those muscles, pull all the flabby bits, the hanging-out flesh, into my dress. Those frightening emotions in my mind and body had to be controlled. Just like loose flesh in a too-tight dress, they were unsightly and might cause mayhem.

If a dress was too tight I'd look in the mirror and know it looked tight, but talk myself into believing it would be all right as long as I walked tall and kept breathing in! What an effort it all is; the relief when you get home and take the dress off. You can breathe freely again, be yourself. We've all done this, I'm sure, squeezed into a size too small, kidding ourselves it will be OK. I did the same thing with my emotions: squeezed them into a small space somewhere in my brain where they wouldn't bother me. I didn't realise they, like the spare flesh in the too-small dress, would spoil my look, leak out everywhere when least expected. So unwittingly I repeated this behaviour over and over again, day in and day out, for years.

You see, it is possible to convince yourself, even though at a subconscious level you know it is absolutely stupid and untrue, that it will be fine – until you forget to breathe in and the zip bursts, the buttons pop, the cuddling breasts, too close to each other for comfort, pop out over the dress and you become cross and upset. To prevent such a horrible accident with my emotions I'd just try to breathe in even more deeply: I'd keep pulling at the imaginary dress to make it more comfortable, push the escaping flesh back in, and so the dress and my overflowing flesh didn't win, didn't burst at the seams, to my and others' embarrassment.

This analogy mirrors how tightly I first restricted and then held onto my emotions. How many times have we all done this with a dress and how long does it take us to learn to buy the right size for our body and shape, to learn how much more elegant the dress then looks? We are prepared, when immature, to kid ourselves, be uncomfortable and look ridiculous, to deceive ourselves. Others almost expect it. It is the same with emotions; it is expected that we will control them and not embarrass others or ourselves.

We make excuses when challenged, defend ourselves, kid ourselves: we thought the dress fitted, looked nice, or it will look better when we diet, lose weight. We say we don't care what the fashionistas say, we'll be who we are, dress how we like. Self-deception is beguiling: we really come to believe in our false sense of self. The effort required to keep our determined flesh under control takes a lot of energy and it is exhausting and debilitating. We know we do not look or feel good.

Such is the false self: it takes up too much of our energy to keep our emotions under control in public and private. It took up far too much of mine. It takes up too much of our energy to keep everything locked up inside so the world does not see our distress, fear, weakness; and it changes our mode of communication and relating to others. We are ready with the defensive comment, reaction, up for the fight, trapped in a permanent round of 'fight or flight'. Like my flesh being strapped in too tightly to make me look thinner, more attractive, if I made a great effort I could strap down my emotions too: fasten them down. Yet, like my escaping flesh, my emotions leaked out all over the place, threatening my perception of myself; others' perception of me. The resulting disarray was there for all to see, especially in my final year in college. Not all the time of course, though it was easily triggered by difficult emotional events and in work situations more often than I'd have liked or wanted: I'd give myself away, especially if I was very stressed and pressured.

Despite this analogy my false self protected me too. I did as well as I could in my mock A level examinations and life went on as normal as far as possible. No one knew my inner turmoil, my fear and grief, nor my hypervigilance at night. In the end it was this that wore me out: over a lifetime the cumulative lack of stage-four sleep ground me down. This ongoing, ever-present lack of sleep feels to me something like a rough sea, always running over the same pebble gradually changing its shape, wearing it smooth 'til it is without its characteristic markings, uniqueness, personality and its power to resist. When you don't sleep regular hours, spending half the night awake in a state of panic and fear, you cannot give of your best no matter how important it might be to do so. It is not long before that proverbial sea runs dry. Rest is not easy to find when there is a career at stake, a living to be earned, chores to do and most important of all, children to be looked after: it all becomes a vicious circle. My mother knew this too; her patterns were the same. The less you sleep, the more you need to sleep: and sleep never comes easily in desperation or when other duties call.

And so I left for college a clone of my mother: a sleepless young woman in a green wool worsted suit more suitable for a fifty-year-old than an eighteen-year-old. My mother had saved her money to send me to college with a beautiful vanity case, a present for passing my exams, dressed as she thought I should be dressed for such a career move. I appreciated her sacrifice even though I knew it wasn't appropriate. To my peers I looked a proper old-fashioned fool. Neither my mother, nor I, knew what students wore, as we'd had no students in the family. I am reminded of Alan Bennett's mother buying him the most beautiful leather suitcases to go to Oxford University and his horror when he saw the travelling attire of his peers: it does nothing for one's street cred.

I felt similarly in my suit, newly permed hair and stiletto heels. My mother would not allow me to wear flat shoes because I was too small, nor would she let me have my hair straight – it needed height, she always said, to make me look taller. I wanted to die when I saw how my fellow students were dressed: their freedom was in their style. It was some time before I could join the student ranks proper but I eventually did by making some new clothes myself. I kept one set of 'mummy' clothes to go home in.

Re-making my emotional self was not so easily solved: there were no patterns, sewing machines or tools, for me to be able to re-construct and re-design my mind – not then.

21

Addendum

Thirty years later, my life is still very busy. There have been surprises and interesting detours, as well as times when I needed to chart extremely difficult waters. On balance I've had a varied and exciting life and career. In 1991 I was approached by Wiltshire Victim Support Service – this is a voluntary organisation that specialises in helping victims and their families after a crime by giving advice including legal advice, support and counselling, with a referral to specialist services if necessary. They also help victims or their families to apply for compensation from the Criminal Injuries Compensation Board especially in the case of serious crimes – rape, murder, serious injuries, assault, serious accidents – where it is deemed there is criminal intent. They wanted me to become their training coordinator, a voluntary post. They believed I had the skills for this work, as I had been recommended to them by another voluntary organisation. I have always tried to do voluntary work and have helped a number of organisations with training their management team, staff or volunteers.

The chief executive explained the role they wanted me to play, which was to train their volunteers in basic counselling skills: volunteers were allocated to a case after a request for help by the victim or the families of victims who needed support (families could not request help for the victim, only for themselves). At this time Victim Support was a relatively new organisation and developing fast. My work would include training the more experienced volunteers to support victims of more serious crimes including murder and eventually rape. Victim Support worked in partnership with the police who refer victims to the service (if they wish to access the service) as part of the investigation into the crime. The police coordinating officer took part in all training as well as being a member of the management committee. The Deputy Chief Constable was also a member of the management committee.

I sat quietly for a long time after this was explained to me, thinking about the invitation. I needed to think about the implications of this work, ethically, practically and emotionally. Eventually I said I would like to accept, but that the organisation needed to be aware that I had experienced the murder of my cousin, and a serious hit and run accident that had involved my aunt and resulted in a criminal case and compensation. I felt they needed to be clear about my experiences before I was ethically able to train others. The coordinator felt that such experience was 'to the good' rather than problematic, but understood my need to be careful and ethical. After much thought and discussion with the committee I agreed to take on the role. I spent some years as their trainer, then as a management committee member and finally chairperson of the organisation, work I enjoyed and feel privileged to have been asked to do. When I took on this work, in addition to my professional employment, I knew I hadn't completely come to terms with Monica's murder and I was honest about this: my grieving might have run its course but I had not come to terms with the fact that the army and the German police had not arrested anyone for the murder. It was not a closed case: it was neither solved, nor finished.

About ten years after I began this work I retired from my profession and from my role with Victim Support. I now had time to find out the true facts of Monica's case: I knew I had to visit Monica's grave, to find out the facts about her death, how the case was managed, the mistakes that had been made in the investigation and why after thirty-five years no one had been charged with her murder. Twelve years previously, in 1988, the family was told that a woman had walked into a police station in Leeds to say that her husband had murdered Monica. He had been a NAAFI employee and had run away the day after the murder. He had lived two doors away from Monica and her husband Bob. Bob (who was then living in Australia, as was his daughter) had been asked if he wanted the police to investigate this further. He said no, he emphatically did not want it all raked up again. The family respected his decision, but I felt that my cousin, brother and myself, as well as the rest of the family, had a right to information and to bring this long saga to a close. It had had far-reaching effects for us all. Aunty Vi, my mother and my stepfather died without peace of mind, with no answers either. I was also determined to get an apology from the army regarding their handling of the case and especially for refusing to fly Monica's body home for her funeral and burial, which is what Aunty Vi, her sister and the family wanted. We had no funeral to attend. We couldn't say goodbye, and for me this was the third time this had happened. My mother, stepfather, my brother and Aunty Vi had travelled to Germany in the summer of 1967 to visit the grave and have a holiday, but I had to work to save money for college and couldn't go with them. David says it was the most miserable holiday he has ever had. Under the circumstances this is understandable.

While I was working with Victim Support I happened to send Pam (Monica's sister) a programme for a Victim Support event that I was chairing on the effects of murder on extended families, just for information. We talked, and she said that throughout these thirty-five years she felt that we had all forgotten not only Monica but also the tragic circumstances of her death, that no one cared, the family had just forgotten. This was far from the truth – when a case is not closed and there has been little resolution, no funeral, it is not easy to forget. The tragic circumstances of this case meant it was actually unforgettable, no matter how many times people suggested it would be better if we all forgot about it and got on with our lives. You have to get on with your life but that doesn't mean you can erase events from your heart or your mind.

I was touched by Pam's response and understood how lonely her grief had been. I was so saddened by her comments that it served to drive me on with my plans to try to find some resolution, and this was made easier by Pam's support and agreement to do so. In 1967 and for the years immediately afterward we were all victims of the lack of knowledge and understanding of not only grief and grieving, but also of the effects of long-term complicated grief that arises from such serious crimes, especially those that are not resolved. From Kubler-Ross,[1] one of the first to research grieving, we learned how profoundly unresolved grief can affect physical and mental health.[2]

Freud had written about the relationship between grief and melancholy but this had not been explored through systematic research until Kubler-Ross began her work with dying patients and their families. In our family's case we were also at the mercy of military secrecy and protocol: the military closed shop. The victims of the bombings of 7 July 2005 also found it hard to understand the delay, the lack of commitment to justice and paying of compensation in their recovery and rehabilitation. We hear of victim's families in murder cases having to drive their own quest for due process and justice, as well as compensation, themselves: the Stephen Lawrence case is one in point. Yet we are also learning how sensitive and difficult such cases are for the victims' families, the police and other services, for extended families and friends as well as sometimes for communities.

In our case we had the army to contend with, and for me this was the second brush with the closed ranks of the armed services and their secrecy. But I was more skilled and confident than my mother had been and I was determined I was going to find out the facts, and do something positive in partnership with the army in memory of Monica. So I went to the top: to the General Chief of Staff of the Army. I wrote to General Sir Michael Walker in 2002.

I found we had a whole jumble of erroneous facts that were

obviously passed from relative to relative and changed or embroidered in the process. Or, more likely, we were never treated with the respect necessary as secondary relatives and so by the time we did hear what was happening we were given re-arranged facts. Accurate facts are crucial for families and friends as part of the recovery process. This was my first big step in understanding the murder and the investigation especially the late stage investigation in 1981.

I duly met with Colonel (Retd) A. F. Carter MBE, the Regimental Secretary, Royal Signals, at Blandford Camp. This was a coincidence in itself as I lived in Salisbury a short drive from Blandford Camp, the headquarters of the Royal Signals, Bob's regiment. Col. Carter was brief and efficient on the phone, saying he didn't like wasting time so could we meet and get it sorted as soon as possible. I answered in the affirmative, after thirty-five years the sooner the better as far as I was concerned. On the day we were to meet I jokingly said to my husband that I had better dress in bright colours rather than my favourite black in case the colonel thought I'd been in mourning for over thirty-five years. And I don't dress in black because I'm melancholy, I just like it; it suits me. So I did, and wore red as well as black. The colonel was cautious when we met, no doubt wondering if I was going to cry, whinge or criticise, perhaps become angry and histrionic. When I repeated the comment I'd made about my dress he roared with laughter and the atmosphere was immediately lighter.

He took me through the possibilities for a memorial. The prize I'd suggested, for the soldier who excelled in communication each year, after all this was the Royal Signals, was not a possibility but he had other suggestions. We settled on votive candles and matching altar candles for the garrison church at Blandford. They had just had a frieze made using peat wood, beautifully carved, for the backdrop to the altar, and he suggested that the same designer could carve the candlesticks. After walking around the gardens and the museum, where he suggested other possibilities for a memorial. I agreed the candles were the most appropriate. As we walked back to his office he said he would introduce me to his deputy, a retired major, in case I needed any further advice or help while he was on holiday. The major was nervous, red-faced, sweating profusely and hopping from foot to foot and so I thought he was either in a hurry, about to have a heart attack, or indeed puffed out from rushing around: he appeared to be very agitated. The colonel introduced us and introduced me to the staff and explained why I was there and what we had agreed.

The former adjutant then engaged me in conversation about the memorial while still hopping from foot to foot. And then to my surprise confessed why he was so agitated. He had been the adjutant on the camp on the morning of Monica's death and was the coordinator for the investigation. I couldn't believe what I was hearing. After I had chatted to him and tried to put him at his ease, he said, *'You know that their house was opposite the NAAFI, don't you? No one saw anything; surprising wasn't it? Well, because no one saw anything or heard anything we treated it as a domestic. We believed that was the explanation.'*

I looked him straight in the eye and said, *'But it wasn't was it? It wasn't a domestic. Monica was murdered and you made a mistake. Thank you for being so honest.'*

I didn't make it easy for him, let him off the hook so to speak, but I accepted what he said and I think he was glad to have it off his chest. I didn't feel angry or upset by this news, after all we had always known that this was the case and now we had the truth it was easy to see why the investigation was not as effective as it might have been. We had always blamed the army for preventing a thorough investigation by the German police and the army blamed the German police for tardiness and confusion. Now it was easy to see the difficult relationship for both investigative teams in the highly charged atmosphere following Monica's murder. The army must have found it very difficult indeed to have the German Civil police crawling over their camp and their paper work. The interesting thing is that even if it had been 'a domestic' it was still murder, and there was a need for an objective commitment to a full investigation.

I think the frustrations of both investigation teams and the tension between them meant that both were hindered in their investigation. This does not let the army off the hook, they must have known that they were a man short in the NAAFI following the murder: this should have raised suspicions even while they were holding Monica's husband in custody. Why didn't they follow this lead more closely? It was a major error and the ex-adjutant was trying to acknowledge this fact and say sorry. I am very glad he did, as it was out in the open for the first time.

This was a major breakthrough for the family as we had been thought to be anti-army, neurotic, not able to let it go, bothersome and critical. Perhaps we were all of these but it got us nowhere in those early days of 1967: our intuition had been accurate and mistakes had been made. The army had protected itself or at least tried to without too much thought for the relatives. The colonel, the former adjutant and I parted amicably and I was taken to be introduced to the army chaplain who would handle the memorial development. We had such a good chat, including how relatives would cope with soldiers (their sons and daughters) being killed when on peace-time duties in trouble spots over the world. Little did we know then how many soldiers and civilians were to be killed in Iraq and Afghanistan. We discussed at length how this might be handled by the army in future.

I came away with a rough idea of how the project was to develop. I also had an appointment to talk to the designer. I paid many visits during this process to approve the beautiful Celtic design; Pam, David and I put half the money in for the memorial and the army paid the other half, a very real achievement for all of us.

The votive candle stand bears the notation, '*In Memory of Monica Fewster tragically killed on 17th January 1967 in her home at Herford Camp, West Germany.*' It stands to one side of the altar, complemented by a candle at each end of the altar. The bishop blessed these one Sunday morning and my friend and I then joined the dignitaries for lunch. It was a very moving occasion and I felt we had achieved a long-lasting memorial to Monica, as well as having closed the case by understanding and knowing the facts. I was able to pass these on to Lesley too as she had not known the circumstances of her mother's death. The secrecy had held through nearly forty years.

As the General Chief of Staff says in his letter, the suspect was interrogated by the German police in 1981 on suspicion of Monica's murder but insufficient evidence was found, although he admitted stealing money from the NAAFI. He was in prison at that time for unrelated crimes, but we understand these are related to serious assaults on women: he had also assaulted his wife before a separation and after reconciliation. No other suspect has ever been found, interviewed or charged with Monica's murder.

Monica remains one of only two army wives to have been murdered in their own homes while on tour with their husband while living in army property. The other was a casualty of an IRA bomb targeted at an army camp in Northern Ireland: an innocent victim. Both women were innocent victims.

Following the memorial blessing by the bishop I set off for Germany to see Monica's grave for myself. I sat quietly by her gravestone and felt a weight lift from me. She is buried surrounded by children's graves: children of army personnel. I then saw what looked to be half of a bridge just to my left. I walked over to the structure and the groundsman was nearby. I asked him what this was and he directed me to the inscription. It was an underground prison where Jewish children had been murdered during the war. I was deeply moved – Monica was surrounded by other victims. Somehow it seemed fitting and I felt sad, very sad, for the children and their families. The cemetery was beautifully kept and looked beautiful.

I was able to come away at peace with myself.

---

[1] Weston, R. Martin, T., & Anderson, Y. (1998). *Loss and Bereavement: Managing Change*. Blackwell Science. Oxford, UK.

[2] Kubler-Ross, E. (1969), *On Dead & Dying*, Springer, NY.
Kubler-Ross, E. (1973), *On Dead & Dying*, Social Science Paperback.
Freud, S. (1917), *Mourning and Melancholia*, SE, Vol. XIV, W.W. Norton, NY.

Afterword

I hope you enjoyed reading my story: perhaps you are wondering where I am and what I am doing now. Am I flat on the floor, sad and depressed? The answer is no. I am very much alive and leading a full and happy, busy life, although of course I have had sad and difficult times too: as we all do.

Salisbury is a very beautiful and happy place to live. It is always full of music, theatre and friends. This year I have been the mayor's escort: one of the greatest privileges of my life. It has been wonderful to visit so many organisations and groups working hard to improve the lives of our citizens. It has been an even greater privilege to spend time with our armed services and their families, who face such difficult situations in Afghanistan and Iraq, as well as those who have been seriously injured as a result. I have been truly amazed at their courage and humanity and that of their families waiting at home.

To tell you the truth, until ten years ago, I had not thought much about my past life: I'd worked full time, completed both a master's degree and a PhD on top of a full-time job; at the same time as being very much a family person. My daughter and I had a very good relationship and spent school holidays in Worthing and in Newcastle keeping close to friends and family. We can look back on many very happy times: she also often travelled to her Granma's by herself or with a friend during the summer holidays. They travelled to spend holidays with us too.

I was privileged to have the opportunity to work all over

Europe, something I really enjoyed and appreciated. I was lucky enough to have three research scholarships abroad: to the USA, Australia and The Netherlands. I grew and learned from all these experiences. I've always been resourceful and never frightened of travelling alone: I found I loved travelling with my work and look back on many very happy experiences. I was busy but also enjoyed my free time and holidays, was involved in community work, especially with Victim Support, and regularly visited the north east to see my family. I knew though that my second marriage to someone much older than myself was in very real trouble, though we have survived and found a way of living that suits us both.

I now have a beautiful grandson who has brought so much joy and happiness into our family: it is always good to witness a child finding his feet in the world and developing as a personality. To spend time with a child discovering the world as he sees it opens one's eyes to new perspectives on old experiences and out-of-date knowledge. He keeps me on my toes and is a pleasure to be with. I have to run to keep up but we love our cycle rides, writing stories and swimming. He is learning to love the theatre too and has taken his first steps onto the stage at school and here in Salisbury at the Playhouse: he has inherited his mother's ability to act and write, and her love of books, and his father's considerable artistic and musical talent as well as an astute ability for systematic thinking and computer technology. His whacky sense of humour is like a mixed bag of sweets from a jumble of eccentric characters in both extended families. His cultural heritage is multi-grained, like a delicious loaf of very tasty granary bread!

He loves his Granpa too, and he has taught me to see things I have taken for granted in his Granpa: so I too see Granpa with new eyes. That is the benefit of a long marital relationship despite its many frustrations, ups and downs, separations. I cannot ignore the fact that my husband's peacefulness and contentment with life, his political perspective, his ability for the long view, has given me stability for the first time in my life. I would be unfairly mean if I didn't acknowledge that. Instability can become an easy habit if it is all one has known: the danger of repeating the familiar patterns is always lurking. You can develop a habit of needing a problem to accompany you wherever you go; like lugging that suitcase around yet again.

Of course one is marked by experience; though I do believe that mine has helped me to be more understanding of others and empathetic to those in difficulty, struggling with life, long-term illness and problems. I do not think I do the work I do by accident, though I have come to it as a career late in life and with a more clinical eye following an academic teaching and research career.

Although it has taken a long time I have been able to integrate my experiences. They are, and will remain, an integral part of me. I have learned from them as well as being able to use my experience throughout my life to support others in positive ways.

Above all, even in those early days with my mother, our Geordie black humour, our native cultural ability to make on the spot, off the cuff humorous remarks, enables me to see the funny side of most situations, to send myself up; it has saved me time and again. Laughter saved me. This above all else saved my sanity; it still does. As have friends and family who have supported me over the years, as well as my love of the arts, theatre, music, opera, reading, yoga and travel. These opened my mind and educated me in ways I could never have imagined. All life and learning are laid bare in the novel: lessons for survival are taught through stories and music, the arts, as well as through counselling and therapy. My father gave me my enquiring mind and our then free education and effectively funded university education system gave me opportunity. My mother gave me my feminist beliefs, unwittingly helping me to understand that women do need education and skills to be able to look after themselves if need be. I hope I have used both well and will continue to do so. I have been very privileged indeed.

Acknowledgements

Thank you to my family, friends and colleagues who travelled with me and supported me on my writing journey. It is impossible to name you all, though I appreciate and love all of you.

To my husband Brian, my daughter Louise and her husband Larry, my brother David and his partner Caroline: you have given me love and support and challenged me positively throughout the development of this book.

To all my cousins and to my one surviving aunt, Maria: thank you for agreeing to the publication of my story and giving me much love and acceptance.

My understanding of my story grew with the gift Roger and Maggie Stansfield gave me when I worked in their school: Faversham School, Newcastle upon Tyne, jointly funded by MIND and Newcastle Education Authority as it was then. All that you taught me by example I have continued to use in my work and life. Working with such amazing people, teaching and care staff, including David Allnut the deputy head, first showed me what unconditional acceptance really meant: your philosophy for healing hurt and abandoned children changed my life and my understanding of child development. Your willingness to fund my advanced diploma set me on a career path I would not otherwise have been able to take and could never have imagined. I will be forever in your debt.

My understanding continued to grow in my work with Peter Kelly: you gave me the confidence to write my story down so others may learn. Your patience and clear boundaries gave me a safe place to explore my legends and myths, bringing the sparkle back to my eyes: and into my life.

I am grateful to my university tutor George and his wife Meg who have given me so much encouragement and love. To my very dear friends Jackie, Liz, Trish, Sue, Veronica and Dennis: you encouraged me on my journey and your love has been invaluable and will remain so. To all those who read the draft version and gave support and encouragement, offered advice and recommended changes: Sandra and Philip, Veronica and Dennis and their friend David, Liz and Peter, Jackie, Libby, June and her daughter Amy, my cousins Pam and Alan, Anne, Pat, Carole, Brian and Joan, Colin and Brenda, Caroline and Mary in Throckley: your love and interest has spurred me on. To my colleague and friend, Terry Martin: you always understood and I valued your perspective.

To my cousin Sheila and her husband Raymond, who reached out and broke the long silence about my father's family and my early childhood: this was the most precious healing gift. Sheila died a few years ago but she gave me my own story to replace my myths and legends: she returned the glitter to my eyes and my life. Sheila also put me in touch with my Australian relative who had completed a family tree of the Morgan family: this too was invaluable as was my distant relative in Durham who shared her family history research with me. Both helped to fill in the gaps especially in my Nana's family. Thank you.

To Gwyn Davies who instinctively understood at the point when I needed space and time. This turned out to be the most wonderful gift anyone could have given me.

More thanks: to Lesley Waller, professional photographer who took the picture for the book-cover: I really find it hard to have my picture taken so it was no easy task for her. To those who have offered to review the book: Professor Luisa Stopa, Professor of Psychology at the University of Southampton, Helena McKeown, Lesley Waller, Mary Grant and Ellie Lloyd Jones. To the Mayor of Salisbury, Mr Brian Dalton, who asked me to be his escort for the year: what an amazing year it has been. To Will, my precious grandson: Treasure history, reading and writing and you will always know who you are.

Thank you to everyone in Haltwhistle, without whose help I could not possibly have put my family story together: I am deeply grateful to you all for giving me so much time, making me so welcome and filling out my story. Special thanks to *The Haltwhistle Times* owner and reporter who was so willing to place my advertisement asking those in the area who might have known my mother and her family to contact me. The following neighbours, friends and acquaintances replied:

Jean, from Moor View Haltwhistle, who wrote to me about living in Moor View where my maternal family lived. Jean introduced me to her neighbour Doreen who owned and lived in my grandmother's house. Doreen allowed me to walk around in my grandmother's house: the scar of the range was still there in the wall and I was able to run my hand up and down the scar. I saw the step from the parlour to the shop, and later to my grandfathers' bedroom: the room where he died. I touched it, stepped on it: my memories made real, tangible. Doreen and Jean also sent me the following:

- The front page of Holy Cross Church magazine dated November 1946.
- The baptism notice for my cousin Carole.
- Photographs of my grandmother's back lane – just as I'd remembered it.
- An article on Melkridge dated 1996. '*There are 18 houses making up the terrace, they are made of stone (as well as brick around the back)* [and] *were built in 1902.*'
- They said that grandma had her shop at number 10 and the Herdmans had their shop at number 9. According to an 1804 map of Northumberland I have on my kitchen wall the spelling was then 'Milcridge'.

Vera O Hagan who wrote to tell me she '... *had a visitor this morning, Mrs Crow whose grandmother Mrs Turnbull who is 90 and still going strong, lives in Haydon Bridge, knew your family well* [she'd lived in the big house opposite my grandmother's house]. *She is very keen to have a chat with you. There is also a letter for you so I will forward it to you. It's all very exciting!'*

I telephoned Mrs Turnbull and she invited me for coffee: we chatted for almost two hours and she never flagged. She knew my grandparents and was able to tell me what a wonderful person my grandmother was: hardworking, capable, intelligent and loving. When the twins were born, her mother sent her to my grandmother's with pink nightdresses for the babies – all she could give during the war. She said, '*They always had an open house. They'd help anyone who needed it.'*

Mrs Turnbull was around when my mother was courting my father, and for their wedding. She told me about my grandfather's, her brother's and a neighbour's return to the village, having been demobbed. She recalled them walking into the village: '*They were filthy, absolutely filthy, ragged, very thin, and flea ridden. All had had mustard gas poisoning but survived.'* She recalled how her mother had been disgusted with their state, and how she stripped the uniform from her son's back and got him into the tin bath, deflea-ing by scrubbing him almost raw.

She described my grandfather as a very happy man, always cracking jokes, playing games, easy going and leaning out of the window conversing with passers-by. Of course, she said, it wasn't like that on their/his return. '*They were quiet, worn, and not the same men.'*

I also received an email from Robbie, the grandson of my mother's friend Peggy. I spent an afternoon with Peggy who regaled me with stories about my mother's school days, their teenage years, going to dances in Barden Mill where there were often soldiers flirting. She said, '*Your Aunty Ella* [my mother's elder sister] *loved the men and was the best dancer in the area: she had such smashing legs.'* I remember my mother's joy each Christmas when Peggy's Christmas card arrived. How wonderful to put a face to the name I'd read each childhood Christmas.

A letter arrived from one of my mother's school friends, Elsie Steel:

Dear Doctor Weston

Reading your letter in this week's Haltwhistle Times I found very interesting, for I knew your mother Emily. I'm 75 years old and lived at number 8 Moor View until I married and moved in 1949.

I remember your Grandma, Mrs Lambert, having the little sweetie shop in her front room. When my brother and me were young, on a Friday night we had a treat, a whole half penny to spend on sweets.

During War-time when for various reasons we had to leave home I just lost all trace of Emily.

Many years later my husband and I were on holiday at Scarborough. We'd been to a show, called at a tea shop and there was Emily with her husband. What a lovely surprise! It was as though we'd seen each other only a few days previously.

Moor View hasn't changed much, the new bungalow and the public House (The Three Horseshoes) are now private houses. Melkridge too, you will easily remember: one new home and both the chapel and the church now private houses. However Melkridge and Moor View now 'nearly joined' with new houses.

The small grocery shop has been a private house for many years. I worked there for a while after leaving school at fourteen. We sold everything for the household including paraffin for the oil lamps. No electricity till many years later.

The school on the hilltop is also a private house.

A few of us young girls including Emily frequented dances at Bardon Mill in what was called the 'Tin Hall' which today is still there. One big interest for us girls then was the visiting soldiers who were stationed at Ridley Hall! This was the beginning of the war. I was then working in the forestry but can't remember what Emily was doing.

I do hope some of this has been interesting and not too boring. I hope you enjoy your days here in Haltwhistle. You are welcome to call anytime. Of course I am wondering if Emily is still around.

Yours faithfully
Elsie Steel (Mrs)

PS I was a Ferguson when Emily was around.
I've just remembered the 'Bastle' which was near the village green was removed in the early fifties. We called it the 'Reading Room' where billiards was also a pastime for the men. It was from there we were supplied with our gas masks. Today no one would have dared suggesting removing it!

I also had a letter from a man in Nottingham who still took *The Haltwhistle Times* even though he'd lived in the Midlands for many years. He knew my mother and her brothers and also mentioned their open house and general affability, and my grandfather's jokes. I am indebted to these kind neighbours and friends who were able to tell me so much about my mother and her family when I visited them.

I spent a week, and then a second week, at The Centre of Britain Hotel on the main street. Opposite the hotel is a plaque stating that Haltwhistle is the 'Centre of Britain'. During these weeks not only was I in the centre of Britain, I had at last found the centre of not just my birth but also much of my childhood: the centre of my mother's childhood and adolescent years. What a privilege for me. I'm grateful to the then manager of the hotel and his staff, who looked after me, made enquiries for me and generally helped me to understand Haltwhistle and Melkridge as they are now and as they were when my mother was at school.

Thank you to the owners of the School House, who were happy to show me around and share the old pictures of the school my mother attended. To the owners of the house that was the old church, a really beautiful and tasteful conversion, thank you for spending time with me and showing me the records.

The landlord (retired) of the Three Horse Shoes told me my mother was a laughing, happy teenager who was very, very attractive, and confirmed that my grandfather did indeed like his pint.

To all those who welcomed me to Sunday Service at Haltwhistle Church, a beautiful friendly service where the hymn that morning was *Love Divine all Loves Excelling* – my parents' wedding hymn: I was deeply moved and shed some very tender tears, my imagination running riot as I pictured Mam and Dad walking down the aisle on their wedding day. I stood where they had stood for their first wedding pictures, their photograph in my hand to guide me to each picture location.

Grateful thanks to Father Vincent McLean, the Roman Catholic priest who so caringly and carefully looked after my father in hospital, visited us regularly and gave my mother and us much love and comfort.

I hope I have not omitted anyone, but if I have forgotten to name you, I am sorry: your contribution to my story mattered to me very much indeed – thank you.